IMAGES
of America

Around Scottdale and Everson

On the Cover: Members of Boy Scout Troop 4 pose with their musical instruments in 1928. The organization was sponsored by a group of Everson citizens and was noted for its 23-piece drum-and-bugle corps. The troop was one of seven units in the Scottdale District Council under the leadership of Thomas Rutherford. Leo "Rusty" Ziemanski, second from left in the first row, was the first Eagle Scout from Troop 4. (Authors' collection.)

IMAGES
of America

AROUND SCOTTDALE AND EVERSON

Paul E. Eckman and Tom Zwierzelewski
with the Scottdale Historical Society

ARCADIA
PUBLISHING

ISBN 978-0-7385-9259-6

Published by Arcadia Publishing
Charleston, South Carolina

Printed in the United States of America

Library of Congress Control Number: 2011945636

For all general information, please contact Arcadia Publishing:
Telephone 843-853-2070
Fax 843-853-0044
E-mail sales@arcadiapublishing.com
For customer service and orders:
Toll-Free 1-888-313-2665

Visit us on the Internet at www.arcadiapublishing.com

To Bobbi, Ruth, and Uncle Joe, and in memory of Alice, Eddie, and Lorraine.

Contents

ACKNOWLEDGMENTS

We are deeply grateful to the following individuals for assistance, information, and photographs: Susan Ansell, Arlene Bair, Sam and Martha Bair, Michael Banaszak, Jessica Barclay, Dennis Beran, James Brilhart, Georgia Brown, Elizabeth Carter, Daniel Clara, Mona Coffman, Kenneth Colbert, Edward Cope, Dora Curry, Elaine DeFrank, Barbara Dzambo, Joseph Eckman, Marjorie Eckman, Jerry Eicher, Elsie Ellis, Thelma Evans, Joseph Fagan, Jacob Farrah, Dr. Peggy Farrah, Robert Ferguson, Kimberly and Jonathan Fox, Denny Gaal, Marilyn Gaut, Dina Harshman, Robert Harshman, Joseph Hawk, Lisa Hays, Jonathan Hrovath, Van Hughes, Glenn and Carole Johnson, Stanley Kamenda, Frank Kapr, Dirk and Mary Kaufman, Chuck King, Sharyn Kmieciak, Bobbie Kramer, Kelly Linn, Julie Ludwig, Melvin and Delores Malik, Peter Malik, Matthew and Patricia Miller, Marion Mitrisin, David and Joyce Moore, Michael Mahousky, Tinkey Nist, Donald Orlando, Milford and Winifred Paul, Bob Percy, Angelo Pallone, James Price, Jackie Rabenstein, David and Kathee Ramsey, Eva Reed, George and Jane Salem, Suzanne Sanner, Phyllis Saretta, James Scardina, Hilda Schuster, Marjorie Scott, William Seaman Jr., James Smith, Lisa Snyder, Diane Stefani, Michael Sterrett, Carol Tacconi, Shirley Taft, Cassandra Vivian, Amy Washington, Carol Westerman, James Whetzel, Delores Wislowski, Ian Yuhouse, and Mary Ann Zozula.

We also wish to thank the Crawford, John Farrah, Marion Nowicki, George Santmyer, and Don Zimmerman families for sharing their memories.

Special recognition is extended to the Scottdale Library for hosting our public solicitations during extended hours and to the following organizations that granted us access to their collections: Frick Reference Library, Scottdale Bank and Trust Company, *Scottdale Independent-Observer*, Scottdale Mennonite Church, Westmoreland County Historical Society, and the West Overton Museums. We are also thankful to the Everson Borough, Senior Citizens Club, Veterans of Foreign Wars, and the following Scottdale-based groups that provided assistance: the American Legion, the borough office, fire department, the Scottdale Historical Society, and the post office.

The owners of images used in this book are acknowledged in the courtesy lines; all other photographs are from the private collection of the authors.

Due to publishing guidelines, we could not include all available pictures in this volume; however, they will be used in future projects sponsored by the Scottdale Historical Society.

INTRODUCTION

Scottdale was incorporated in 1874 from East Huntington Township, Westmoreland County. Everson was formally established in 1903 from land in Upper Tyrone Township, Fayette County. In spite of these different beginnings, they share a common history that included the birth of a nation, the settlement of the Trans-Appalachian frontier, and the growth of industrial America.

Before European settlement, the area was home to the Delaware, Wyandot, and Shawnee Nations, all of which were dominated by the Iroquois Confederacy. The stream that separates Everson from Scottdale (Jacobs Creek) was reportedly named for Jacob, a Delaware chieftain who maintained a log cabin near Iron Bridge.

During Colonial times, George Washington explored the territory for the Ohio Company and, in 1755, served as a volunteer aide to British general Edward Braddock on his ill-fated campaign to oust the French from the Forks of the Ohio River. Part of the trail used by Braddock crosses the region approximately one mile east of Everson and continues in a northeast direction to Prittstown.

The first permanent settlers were primarily English and Scotch-Irish who migrated from Virginia and Maryland in the 1760s. Some were veterans and business associates of George Washington, including William and Valentine Crawford and their half-brother, Hugh Stevenson; John Vance; Isaac Meason; James Galloway; and Benjamin Whaley. The Stevenson family settled in the Everson Valley, and Meason held patents for nearly 600 acres in Scottdale.

Between 1790 and 1800, a large number of German Mennonite immigrants came to the area from eastern Pennsylvania. They were prosperous farmers and purchased most of the land from the original settlers. Some of their surnames were Loucks, Stauffer, Ruth, Stoner, Fretts, Sherrick, Overholt, and Funk. In 1790, Abraham Stauffer settled on 279 acres in Tyrone Township. Most of Everson was built on part of the Stauffer property and on land acquired by Jacob Sherrick from the Stevenson family.

In the 1830s, John Stauffer established a gristmill and distillery called Fountain Mills on 30 acres bordering Jacobs Creek. Another distillery at West Overton was operated by Abraham Overholt, who reportedly produced the best rye whiskey in the country. These industries made Scottdale a market center for agricultural products.

Early settlers were attracted to the area by new land and abundant forests; however, another source of wealth was below the surface in a nine-foot seam of bituminous coal approximately 50 miles long and three miles wide along the base of the Chestnut Ridge. In later years, geologists would call this mineral deposit the "Pittsburgh Coal Seam." Coal had been mined in small quantities since Colonial days; however, demand increased during the age of steam, when forests started to be depleted. Coal was also baked in an oven to produce coke, which replaced charcoal as the preferred fuel for smelting iron and making steel. When coal deposits became depleted in Pittsburgh, furnace operators obtained new supplies from mines around Scottdale and Everson in a process that changed the landscape and culture of the region for the next 100 years.

Four other foundational events occurred between 1871 and 1874. Both the Baltimore & Ohio and the Pennsylvania Railroads extended tracks into the region. In 1872, William Everson erected the Charlotte Furnace and an iron rolling mill on the site of Fountain Mills. In 1871, Henry Clay Frick obtained a loan from Judge Thomas Mellon in order to expand his coke works at Broadford, which marked the beginning of Frick's dominance in the industry for the next 70 years. In 1873, two brothers—Jacob and Peter Loucks—sold part of their adjoining farms for housing needed for the mill workers. The town that grew from these transactions was named for Thomas Scott, then president of the Pennsylvania Railroad. The settlement across the creek was named for Barclay Mozart Everson, who managed the furnace for his father, William.

Before 1870, there were 300 beehive coke ovens in the region. A local census of industry revealed that by 1900, there were 25 coke works with 3,400 ovens within a five-mile radius of Scottdale and Everson. Of this number, 66 percent were eventually owned or leased by Frick, whose corporate offices were located in Scottdale. He also erected car shops in Everson for manufacturing and repairing mine equipment.

Access to railroads and the early success of the coke industry attracted other enterprises, including steel rolling mills; foundries; and companies that produced cutlery, flooring, and caskets. The largest enterprise was the United States Cast Iron Pipe and Foundry Company. Together, these industries employed an estimated 3,000 workers. The mines and railroads provided employment for an additional 3,500 residents.

Coal, coke, and related industries made Scottdale the wealthiest community in Westmoreland County. Elegant mansions lined Chestnut Street and Loucks Avenue. The town had four banks, the first McCrorey's five-and-dime store, 7 hotels, 13 churches, 2 newspapers, and nearly 50 other small businesses. The wealth concentrated in the area enabled Scottdale to sponsor a baseball farm team affiliated with the St. Louis Cardinals. From 1925 to 1931, the borough was the smallest town in the country to sponsor a professional baseball farm team.

The industrial scene was not free of conflict, especially in the mining districts. One of the most violent strikes occurred in 1891, when 1,000 workers attempted to shut down the Morewood Mine. During this action, nine miners were killed and 20 were wounded by the authorities. The bodies of seven victims were transported by train to Scottdale for burial in a mass grave at St. John's Cemetery. Over 8,000 mourners met the train, and 4,000 marched in a procession to the internment ceremony. Labor conflict in the mining districts continued until World War II.

Prosperity ended with the collapse of the stock market in 1929. Most industries closed, including the pipe mill. Unemployment reached 90 percent; in subsequent years, the community was able to bring Duraloy Technologies and the R.E. Uptegraff Manufacturing Company to Scottdale, which provided much-needed employment. Because of advances in technology and the rise of other sources of fuel, the mining industry never fully recovered.

In the late 1960s, there was an attempt to redevelop part of the Scottdale business district, but new highways and shopping centers reduced the potential for local investment. Nearby crossroads and surrounding farmland became the preferred location for new business and industry. An automotive assembly plant and a large electrical manufacturing facility provided employment for thousands in the last 40 years, but the plants closed when the market for products changed and production shifted to other locations.

Regardless of economic trends, Scottdale and Everson remain affordable places to live and raise a family. New schools provide instruction using the latest technology. Residents enjoy a civic culture of music, theater, art, and a strong community spirit. Scottdale celebrates its heritage with an annual fall festival. Polish culture is commemorated in Everson by St. Joseph's Roman Catholic Church. Located 30 miles from Pittsburgh and part of the Laurel Highlands, Scottdale and Everson are attracting new settlers who prefer to live near open spaces where no one remains a stranger.

One

Getting Started

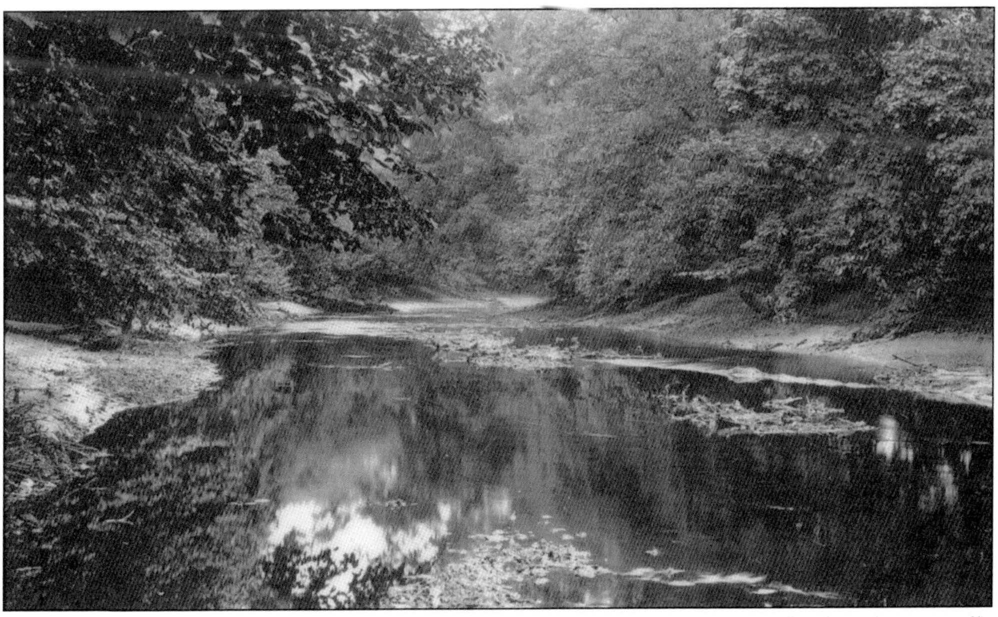

The valley formed by Jacobs Creek was home to Native Americans. Delaware chief Jacob reportedly maintained a cabin near the creek at Iron Bridge. Later, attracted by the fertility of the soil and new land, Scotch-Irish and German Mennonites settled in the valley. (Courtesy Westmoreland County Historical Society.)

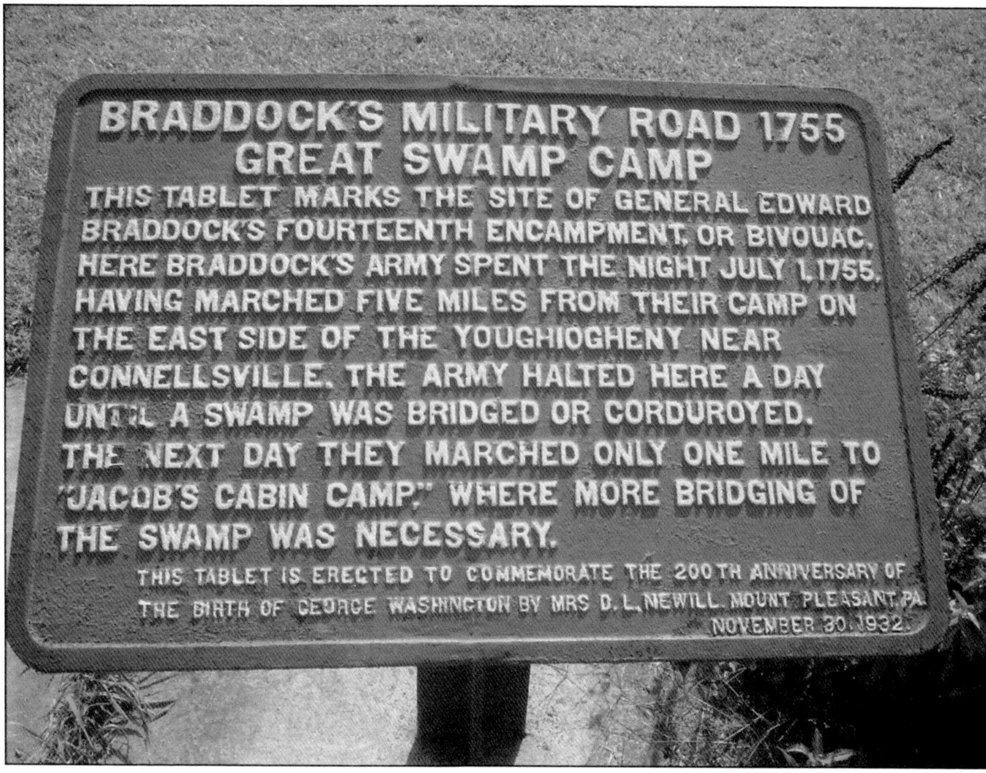

Gen. Edward Braddock spent the night of July 1, 1755, here at the Great Swamp, which is now part of Jacobs Creek Park in Bullskin Township. As noted on the historical marker, it was his 14th encampment after leaving Fort Cumberland.

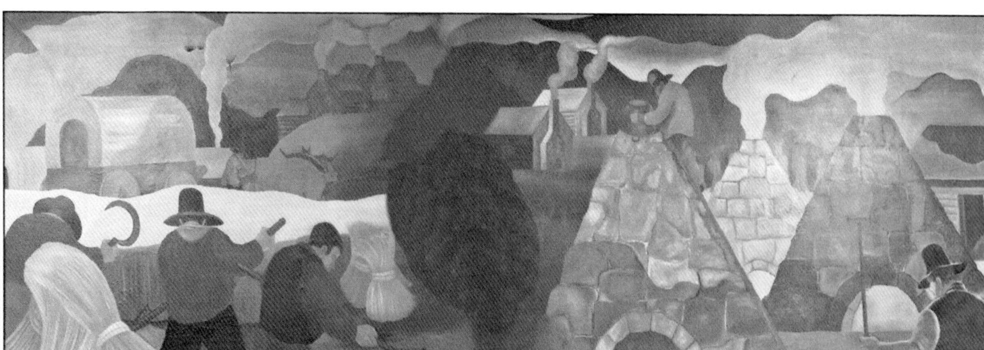

In 1937, Harry Scheuch painted a mural in the Scottdale Post Office depicting the town's early history. Pictured here are sections of the mural celebrating agriculture and the iron industry. Scheuch was one of many artists who painted murals in public buildings for the Works Progress Administration. (Photograph by Jonathan Hrovath.)

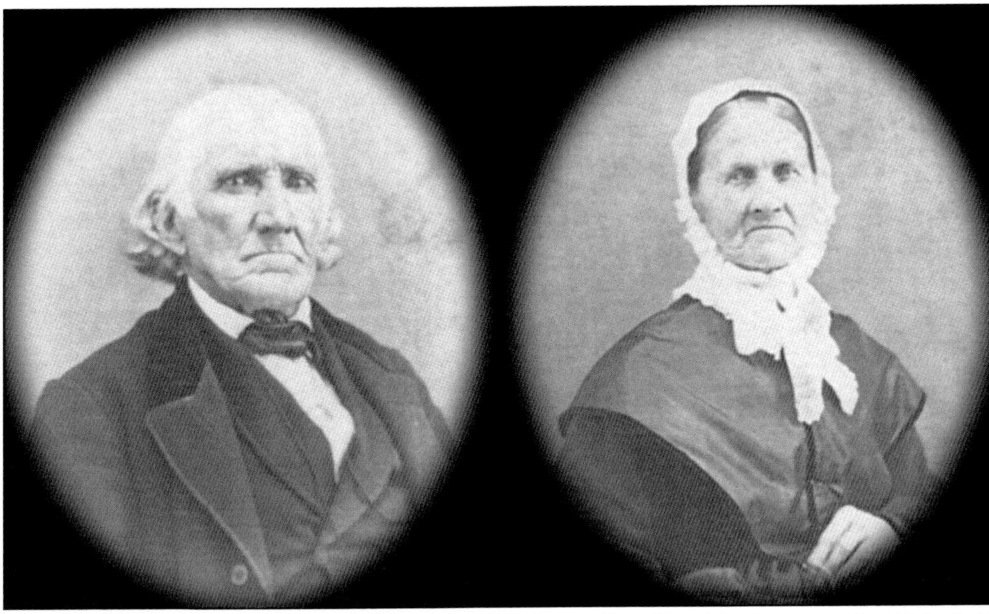

Pictured here are Abraham Overholt and his wife, Marie Stauffer. Abraham was the 10th child of Henry Overholt (Oberholtzer) and Anna Bietler, who migrated in a family caravan in 1800 from Bucks County, Pennsylvania, to East Huntington Township. Abraham became the owner of his father's farm at West Overton. He excelled in business, establishing a flour mill, distilleries, and other enterprises. (Courtesy West Overton Museums.)

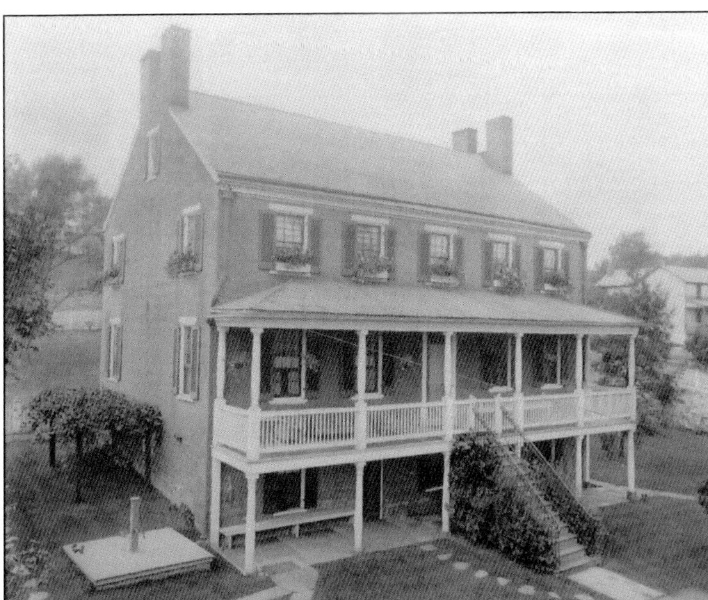

This stately home was built by Abraham Overholt in 1838 and serves as headquarters for the West Overton Museums. Henry Clay Frick was born on this property and referred to Abraham, his grandfather, as the "Squire of Westmoreland County." (Courtesy West Overton Museums.)

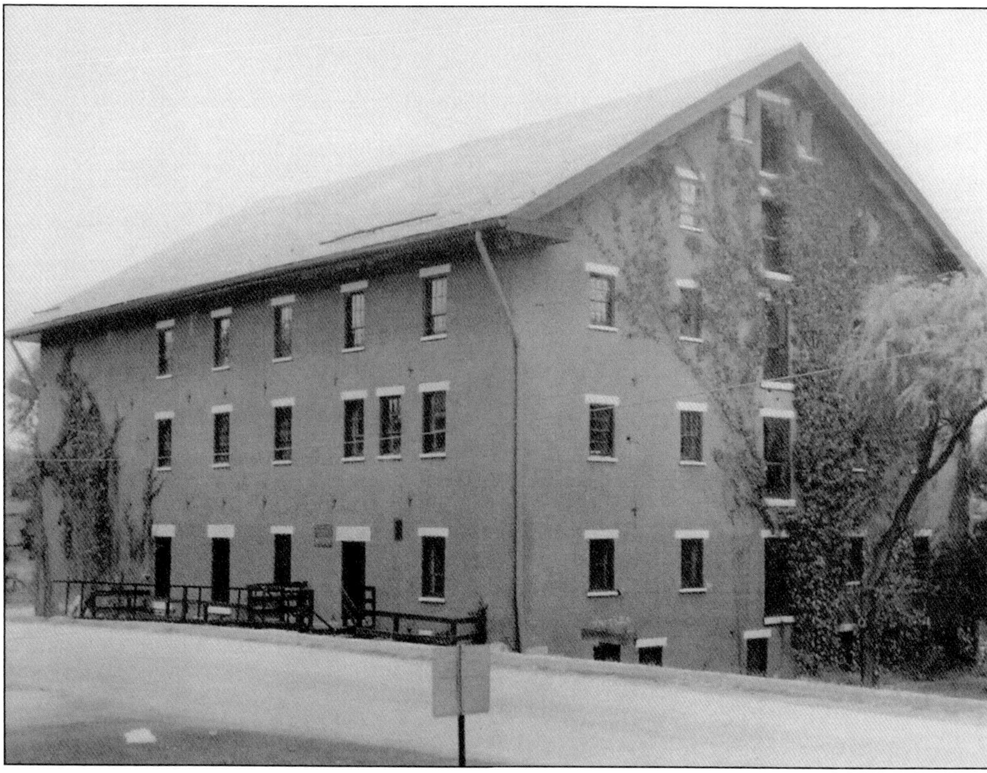

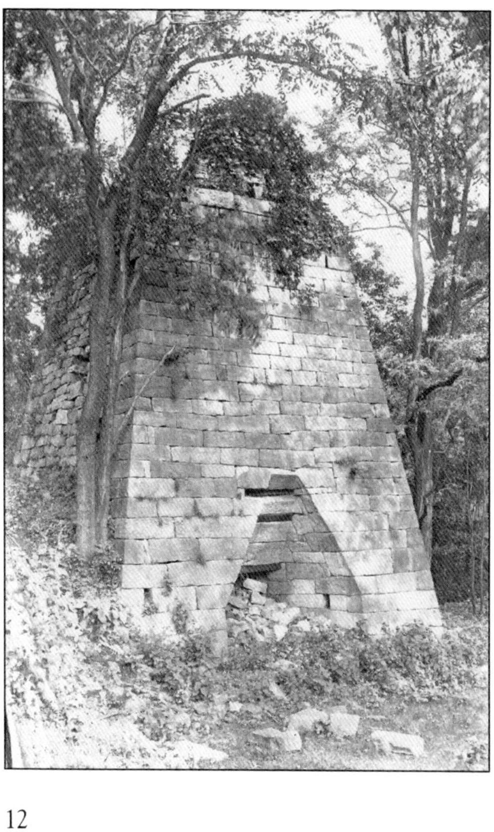

Abraham Overholt constructed this distillery across from his home at West Overton in 1859, producing Old Farm and Old Overholt whiskey, which was famous throughout the country. The distillery was part of a self-sufficient village that employed nearly 200 individuals in the later part of the 19th century. (Courtesy Scottdale Mennonite Church.)

Smelting and casting iron was a major industry between 1790 and the Civil War years. In Westmoreland and Fayette Counties, there were nearly 44 iron furnaces. This furnace at Mount Vernon was built by Isaac Meason in 1806. (Courtesy Joseph Hawk.)

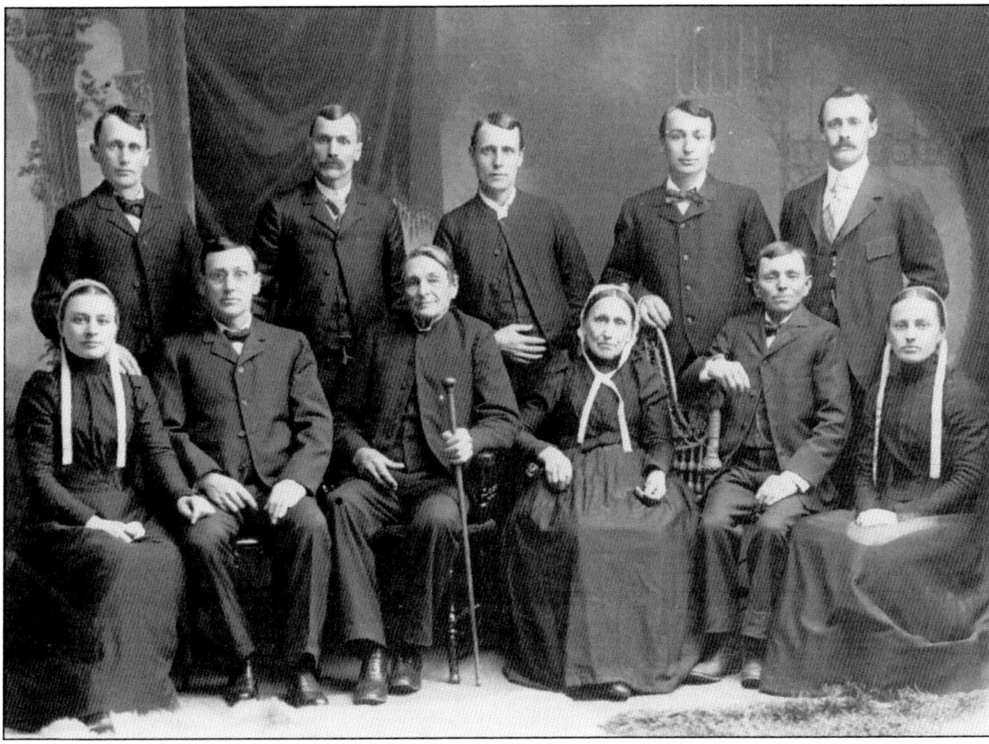

Jacob S. Loucks (Laux) and his wife, Mary Saylor, pose with their sons and daughters in 1903. Pictured here are, from left to right, (first row) Ada, Joseph, Jacob, Mary, Martin and Cora; (second row) David, Abraham, Aaron, John, and George. Their homestead, constructed in 1853, is pictured below as it appeared in 1960. The residence is currently owned by Marlyn Crawford Montgomery. (Both, courtesy Scottdale Mennonite Church.)

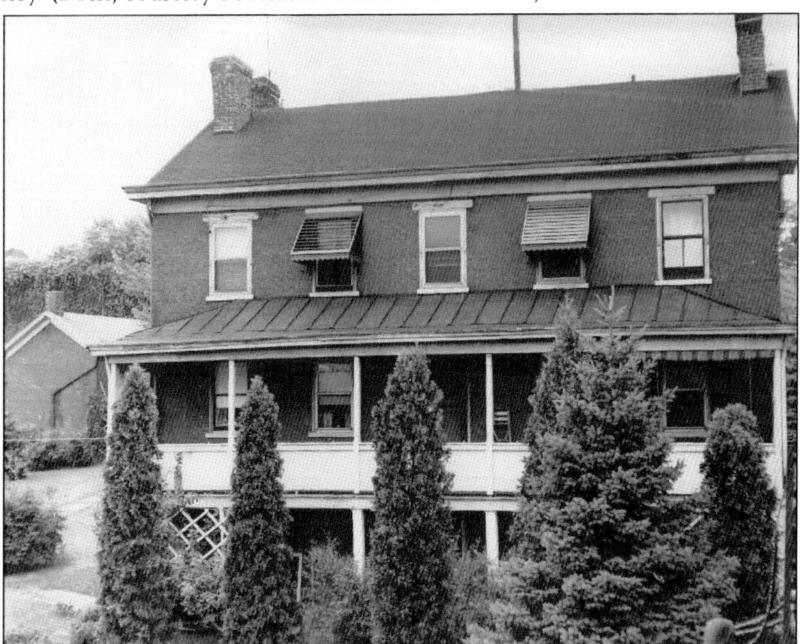

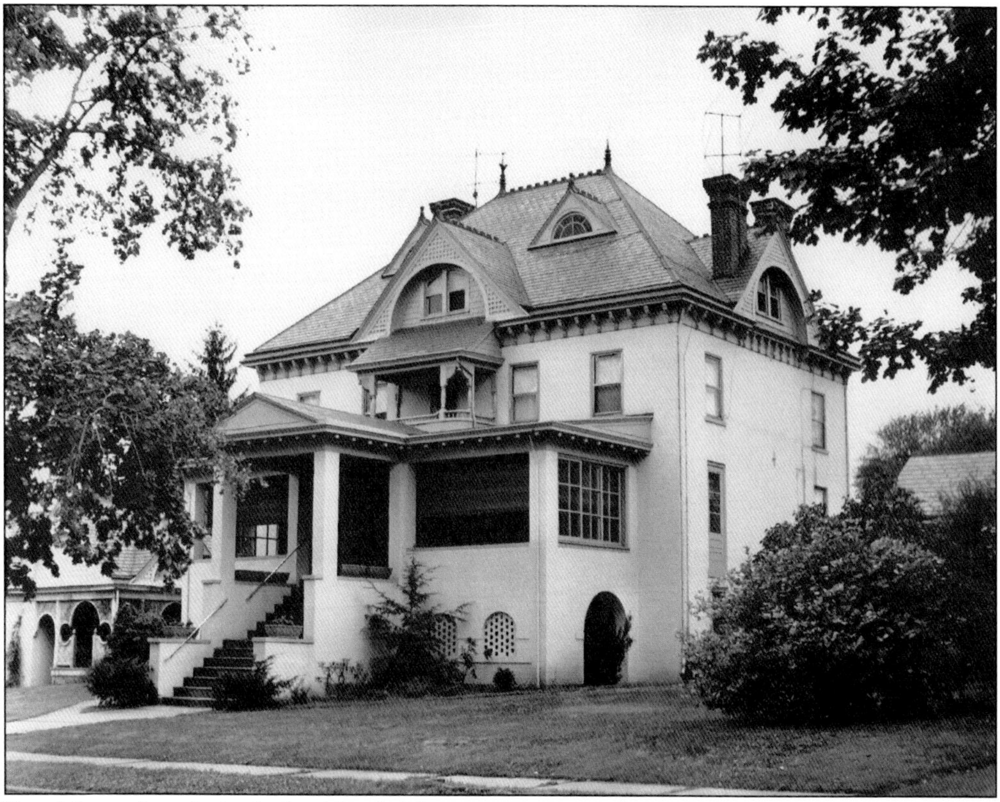

Rev. Martin Loucks built this North Chestnut Street residence in 1835. His son, Peter, added Victorian elements to the original structure in the 1880s. This is now the home of the Scottdale Historical Society. (Courtesy Scottdale Mennonite Church.)

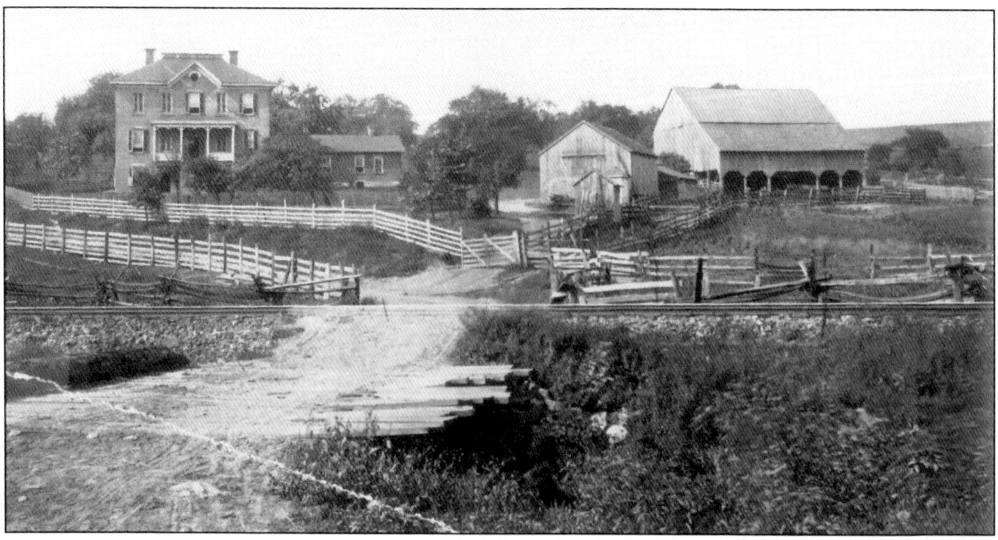

This 1901 farmstead was originally owned by Christian Fretts (Fretz), who migrated to the area with the Overholt Caravan. Fretts's grandson, John F. Stauffer, inherited the property and erected this mansion. The house is now part of the American Legion Home. (Courtesy Scottdale Bank and Trust Company.)

This 1900 photograph, featuring Ada Chamberlin mounted on a horse, depicts a common scene during the haying season around Scottdale. The picture was taken on a farm owned by Abraham S. Loucks in Mount Pleasant Township. Chamberlin, a school teacher, boarded with the Loucks family for several years. The man sitting on top of the wagon was the farm overseer, whose last name was Dollard. (Courtesy Carol Westerman.)

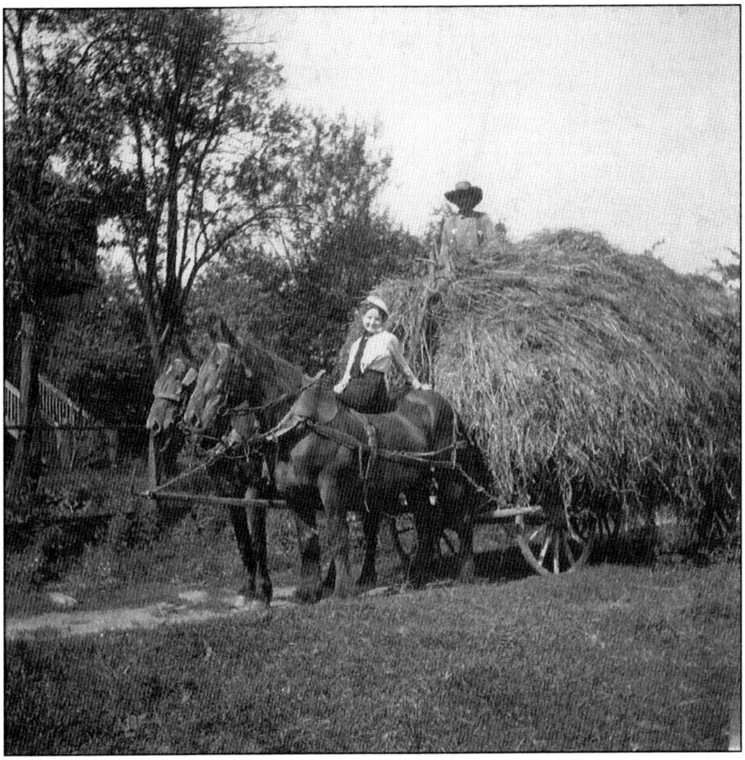

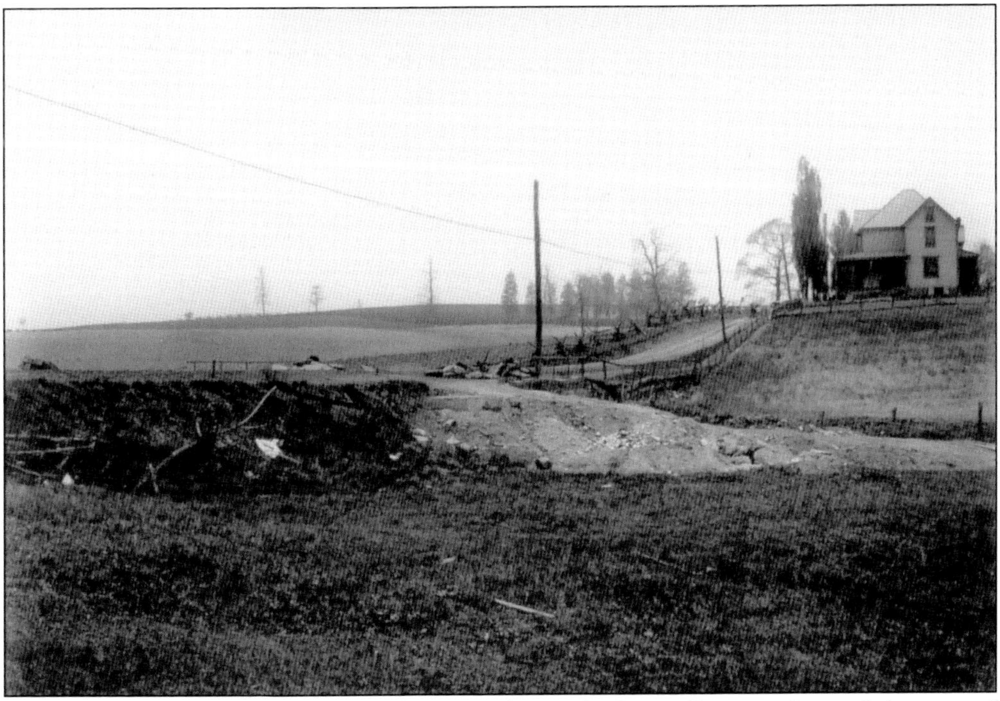

This 1916 view of Pittsburgh Street looking west from Lake Street illustrates the rural character of Scottdale, which endured well into the industrial age. Note the split-rail fence along the road that marks a property line on the Loucks Farm. (Courtesy Scottdale Bank and Trust Company.)

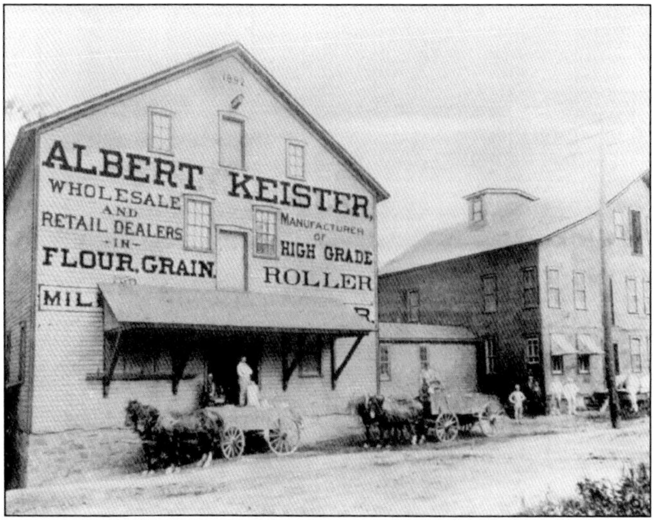

Fountain Mills originated as a place to process grain. Shown here is the feed and flour mill operated by Albert Keister on North Broadway in 1889. The original structure, on the right, was built in 1860. The mill produced 100 barrels of flour on a daily basis and shipped most of its product to Pittsburgh. Albert's father, Solomon, operated a similar establishment beginning in 1842 on the Dawson Road that was known as Keister's Mill. (Courtesy Scottdale Bank and Trust Company.)

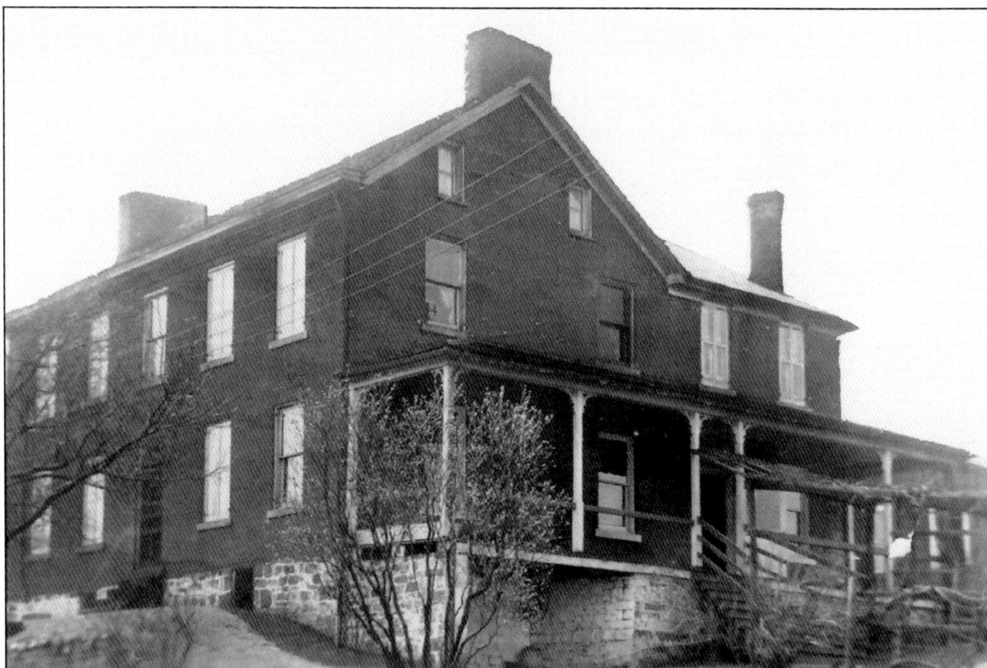

The Mennonites who migrated to southwestern Pennsylvania also settled in Alverton and Pennsville. This house was erected by Henry Shellenberger around 1840. The Shellenberger family came to the area from Lancaster County, Pennsylvania, in 1790. Their land included most of Pennsville in Bullskin Township. The homestead was sold later to Abraham Sherrick, who was an early minister in the Pennsville Mennonite Community. (Courtesy Scottdale Mennonite Church.)

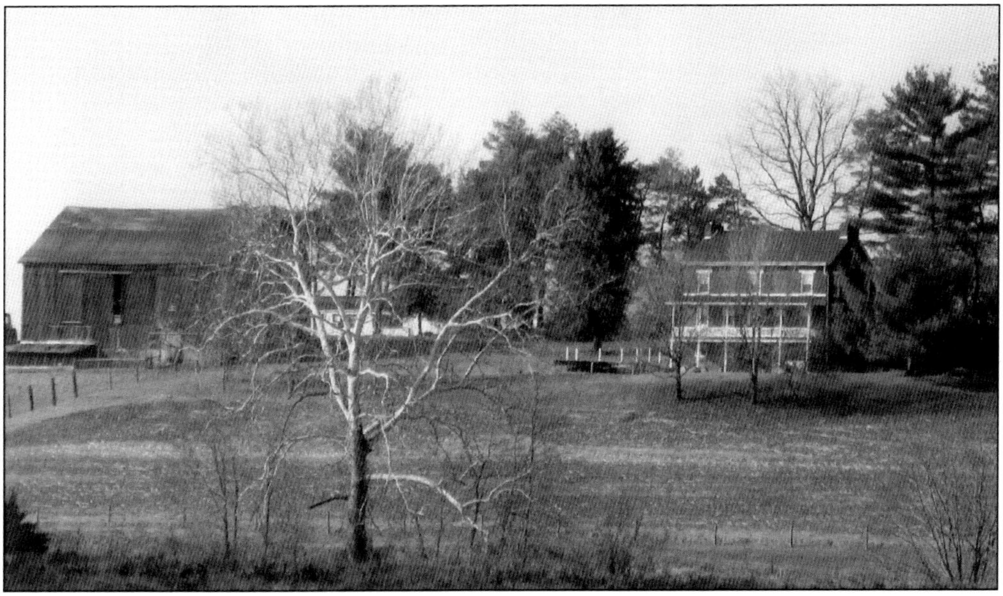

The Sterrett family originated in Northern Ireland and Chester County, Pennsylvania, where some members fought in the Battle of Brandywine Creek during the American Revolution. They migrated to East Huntington Township in 1786 and purchased 325 acres from Isaac Meason. John Sterrett, a grandson of Moses Sterrett, who migrated with his father, built the house on the far right around 1856. The property was also known as the Kelly Farm and is currently owned by Glenn Schwartz.

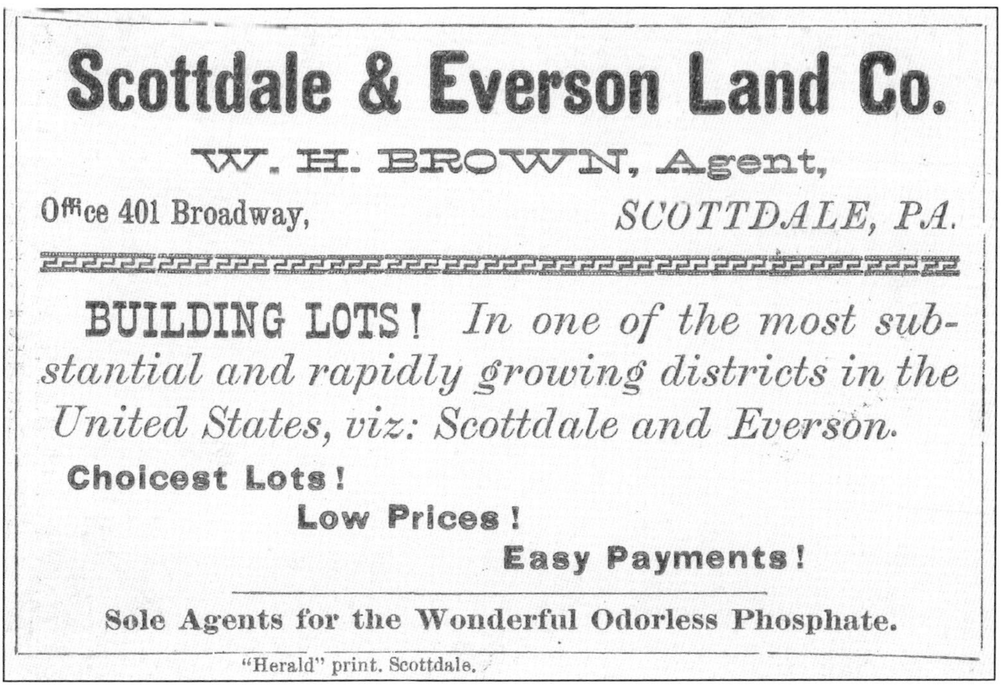

As noted on this business card, the development of Scottdale and Everson was promoted as one of the "most substantial and rapidly growing districts in the United States." (Courtesy Sharyn Kmieciak.)

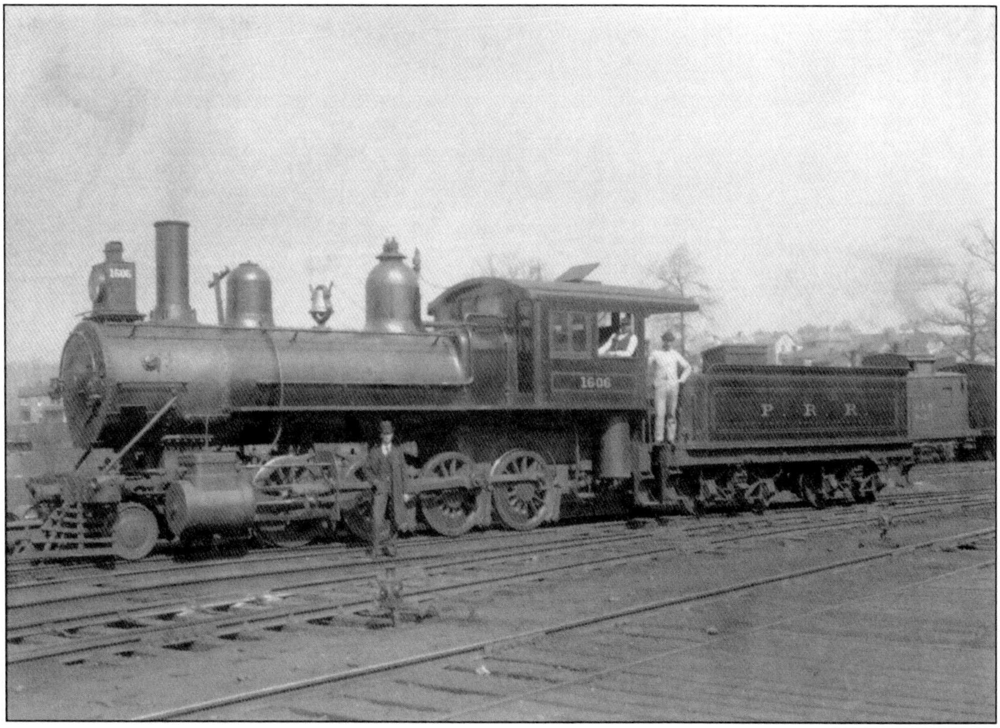

The Pennsylvania Railroad (from Greensburg) and the Baltimore & Ohio Railroad (from Broadford) facilitated industrial growth and provided ready access to national markets. Above is a Pennsylvania Railroad engine parked on a siding in Everson; below is a ticket to and from Everson on the Baltimore & Ohio (B&O) Railroad. (Above, courtesy Denny Gaal; below, courtesy Jonathan Fox.)

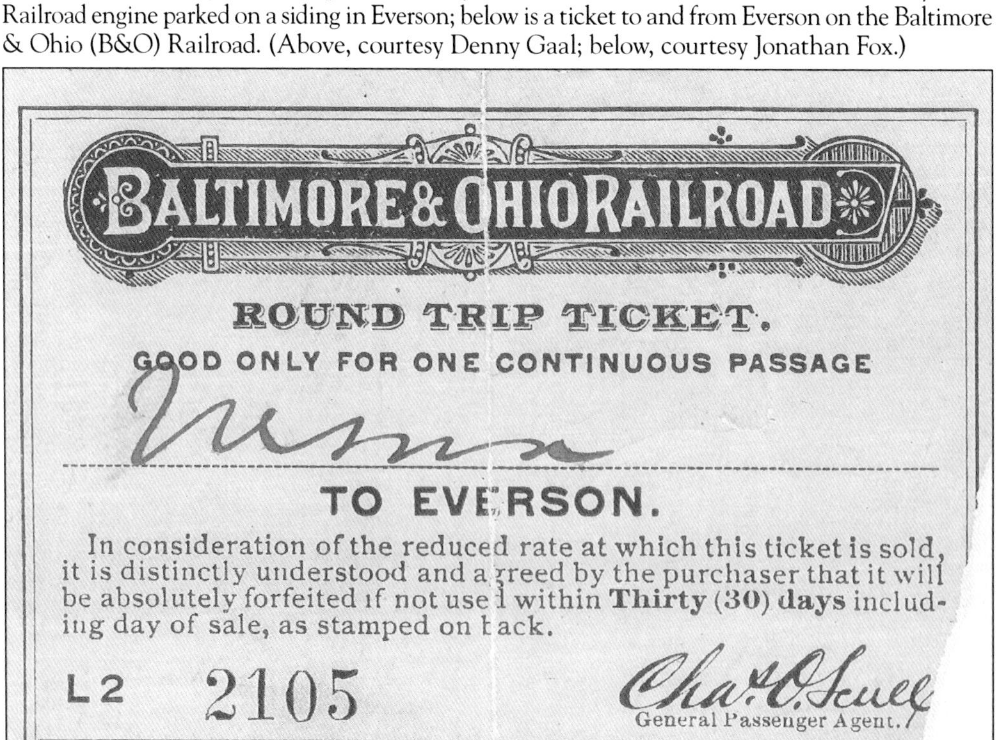

BALTIMORE & OHIO RAILROAD

ROUND TRIP TICKET.

GOOD ONLY FOR ONE CONTINUOUS PASSAGE

TO EVERSON.

In consideration of the reduced rate at which this ticket is sold, it is distinctly understood and agreed by the purchaser that it will be absolutely forfeited if not used within **Thirty (30) days** including day of sale, as stamped on back.

L2 2105

Chas. O. Scull
General Passenger Agent.

A miner inspects a coal face in the famous Pittsburgh Seam, which averaged nine feet in thickness beneath the surface of Westmoreland and Fayette Counties. In the late 1800s, geologists called this coal bed the most valuable mineral deposit in the world. (Courtesy Marjorie Scott.)

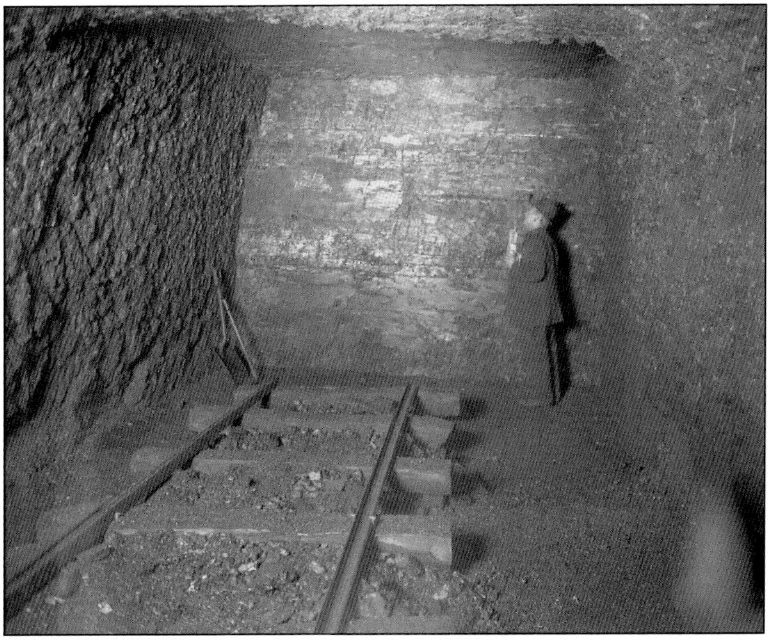

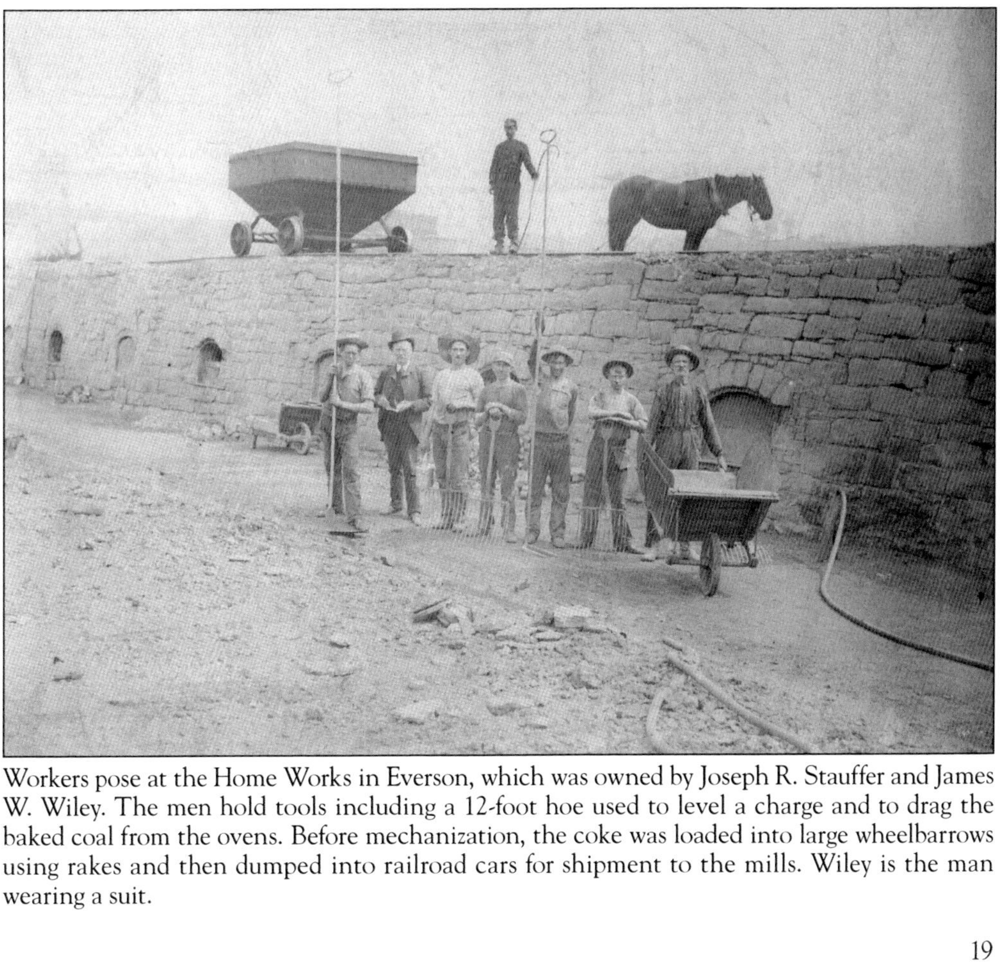

Workers pose at the Home Works in Everson, which was owned by Joseph R. Stauffer and James W. Wiley. The men hold tools including a 12-foot hoe used to level a charge and to drag the baked coal from the ovens. Before mechanization, the coke was loaded into large wheelbarrows using rakes and then dumped into railroad cars for shipment to the mills. Wiley is the man wearing a suit.

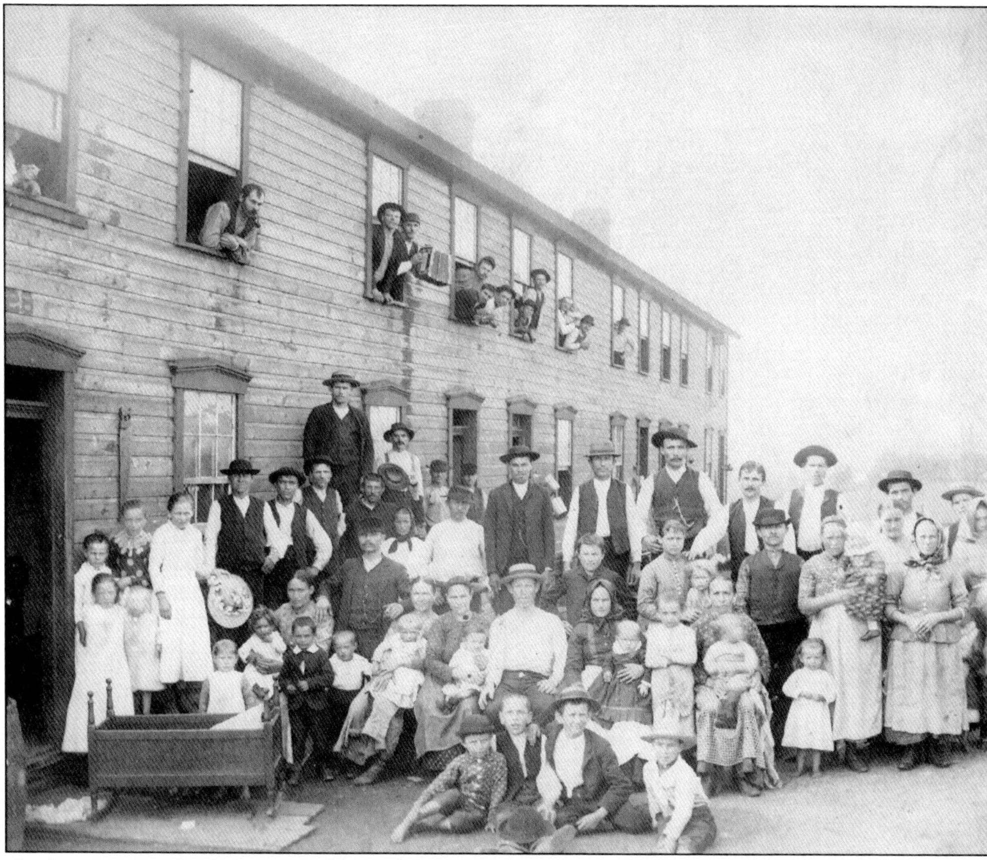

Coal companies built housing for workers and their families. This is the tenement constructed by the H.C. Frick Coke Company at the Valley Works in Upper Tyrone Township, which housed 32 families. The variety of clothing worn by these residents around 1890 illustrates the ethnic diversity of miners and coke yard workers.

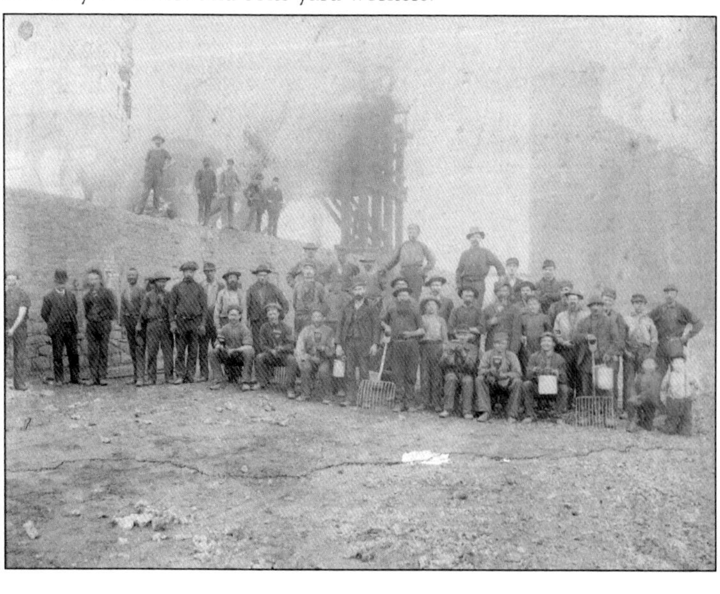

In this c. 1880 image, employees pose for a picture in front of some ovens and the tipple at the Valley Works. Note the two young men kneeling on the far right; boys as young as 10 years old worked for 50¢ a day and did jobs like spraying lubricant on coal cars, operating track switches, and opening and closing ventilation doors. The Valley Works mine was acquired by the H.C. Frick Coke Company in 1882.

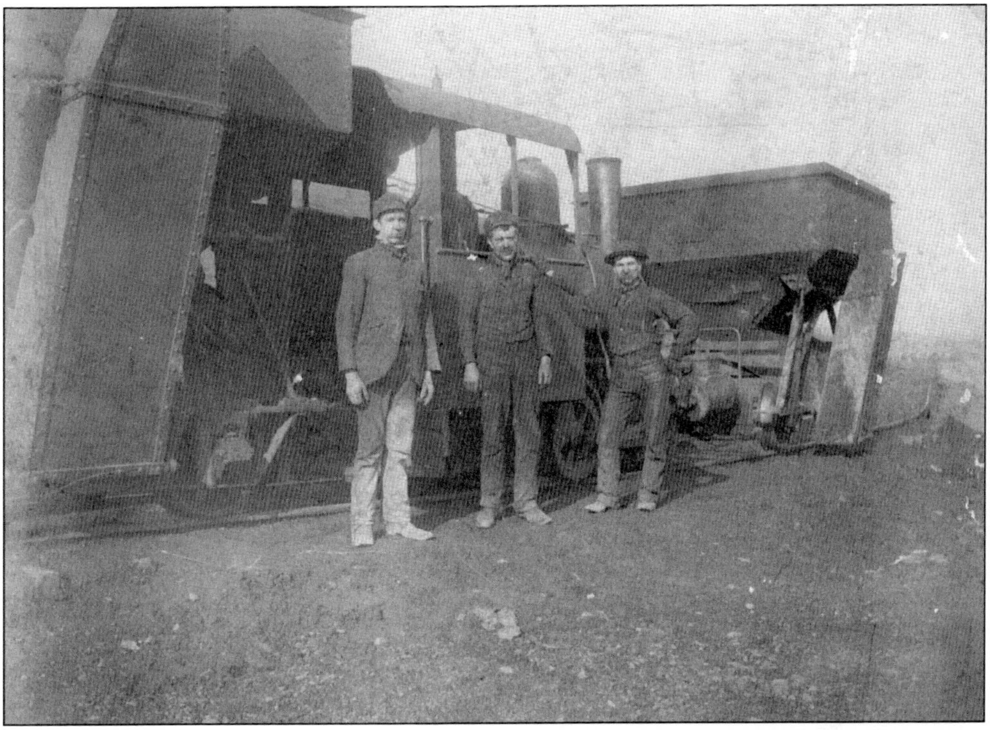

By the close of the 19th century, most large coal companies replaced draft animals with machinery. Pictured here at the Valley Works is a small steam engine called a "dinky" and a lorry used for charging the ovens with coal from the mine.

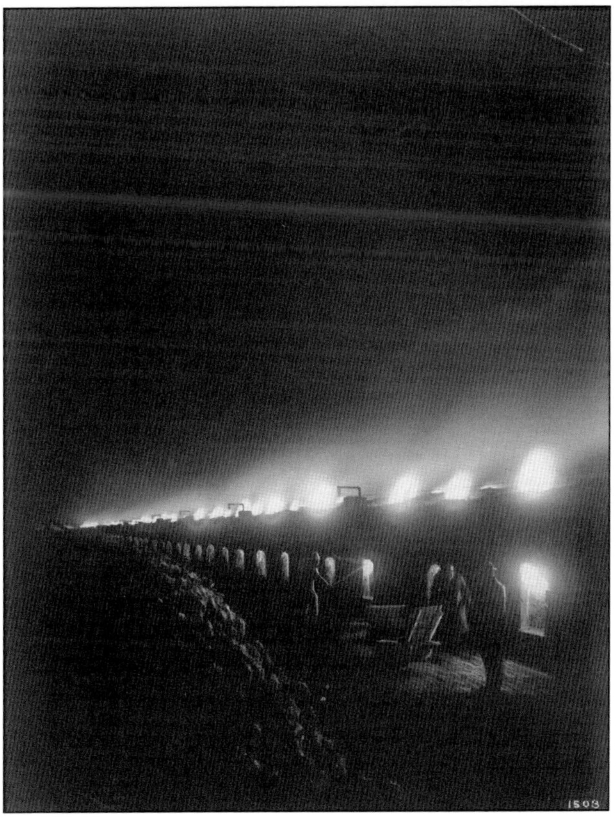

Everson and Scottdale were surrounded by beehive coke ovens that burned 24 hours a day, seven days a week. It was said that a person could walk along the B&O railroad tracks from Broadford to Scottdale at night with no need for other illumination. (Courtesy Marjorie Scott.)

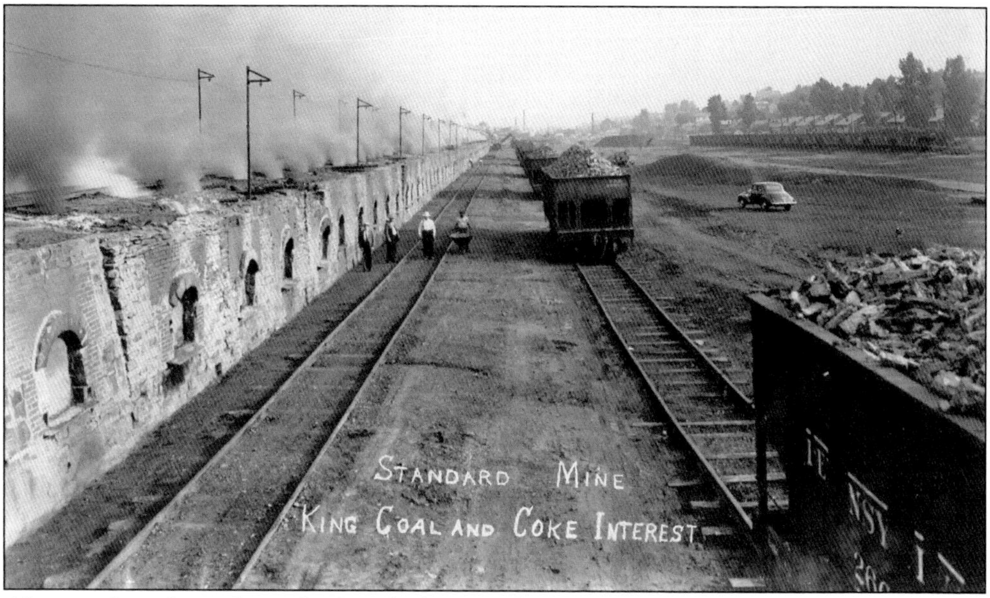

Above is the coke works at the Standard Mine when it was leased by the King Coal and Coke Company from the H.C. Frick Coke Company in the 1930s. The image below is another view of the beehive coke ovens; the machine in the center of the image replaced the manual drawing and loading of coke. In the background is the shaft and slag heap at Standard No. 2, which was the largest shaft mine in the world, extending approximately four miles underground from Standard to the village of Hecla.

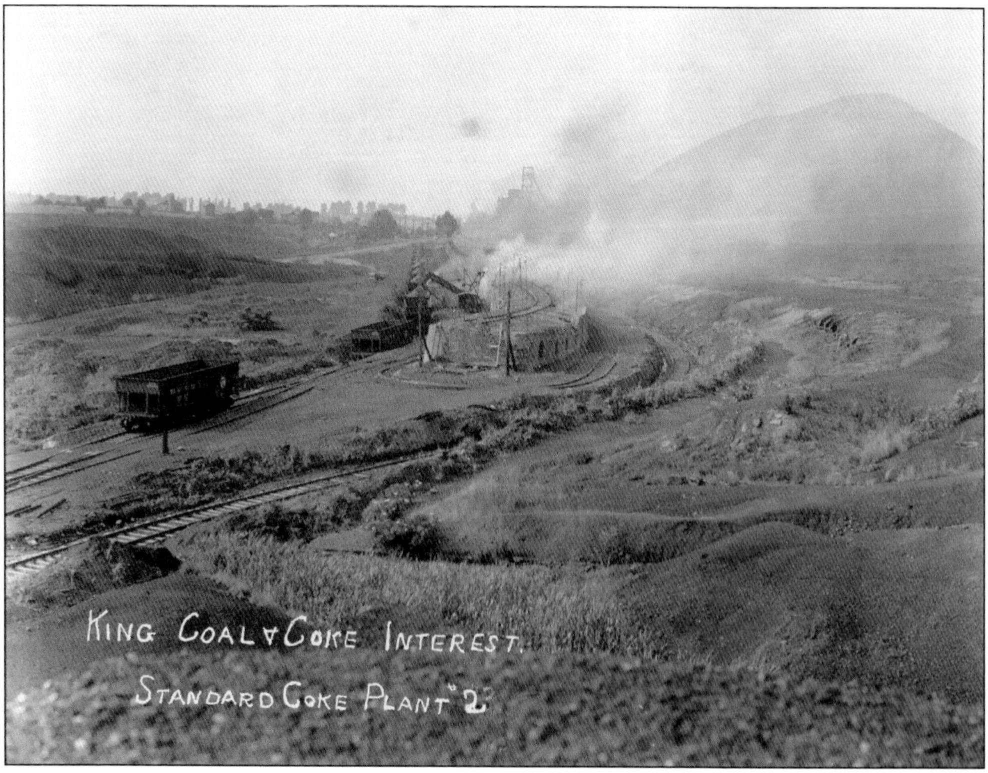

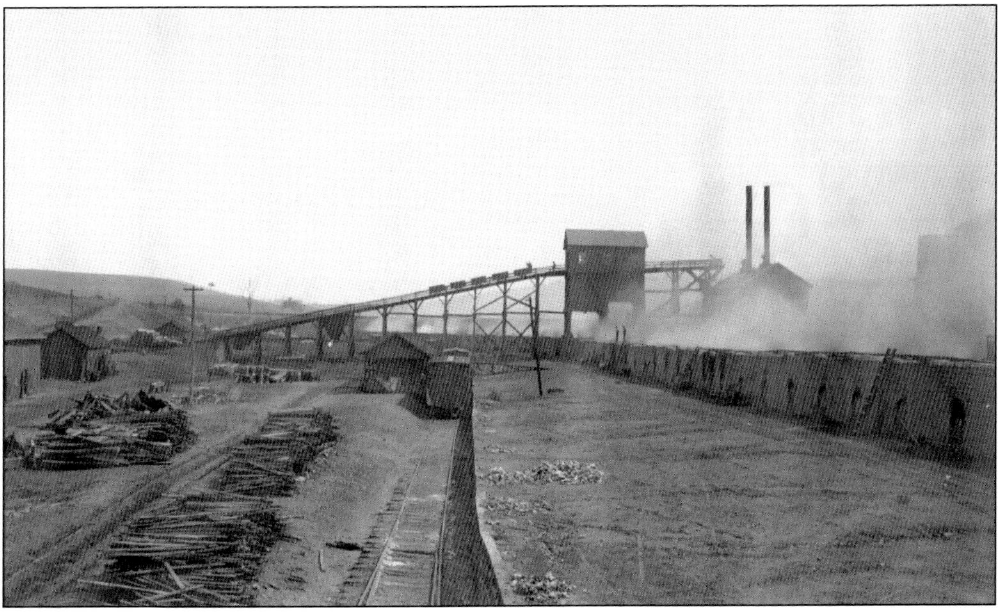

This is one of several mines and coke works near Alverton in 1901. It was owned by the Southwest Connellsville Coal and Coke Company, H.C. Frick's major competitor in the region until he acquired the company, including this operation, in 1903. (Courtesy West Overton Museums.)

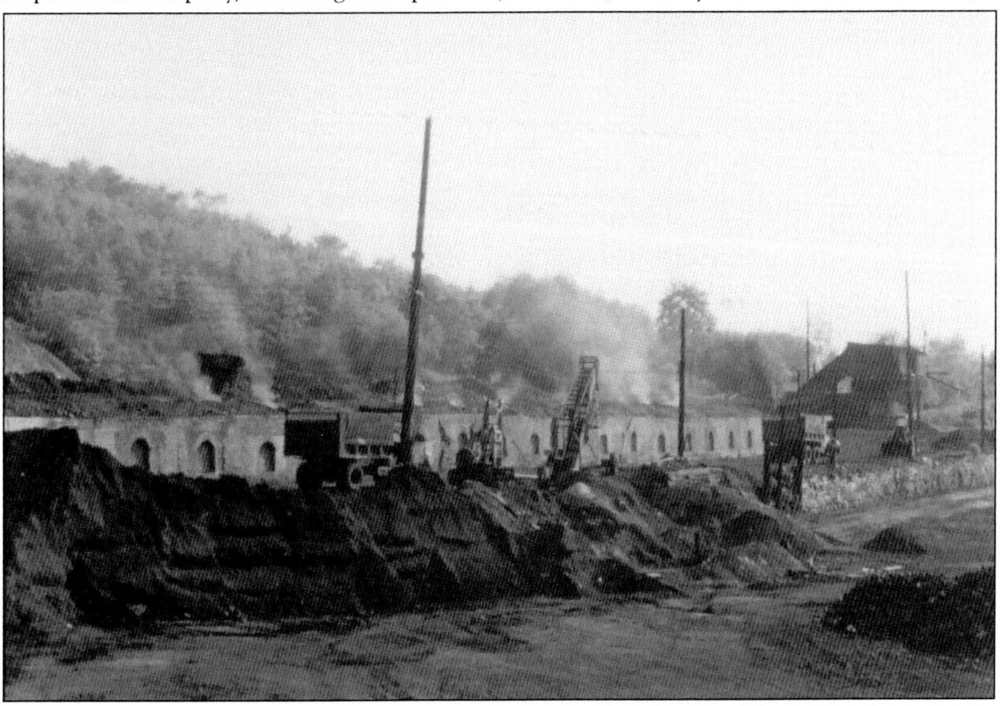

These ovens were located to the left of the Southmoreland High School football stadium. At the time this 1968 photograph was taken, they were operated by Oliver Painter from Mount Pleasant. They were closed a few years later by the Pennsylvania Department of Environmental Protection. This site and the works at Shoef, located southwest of Uniontown, were the last beehive ovens operated in the United States.

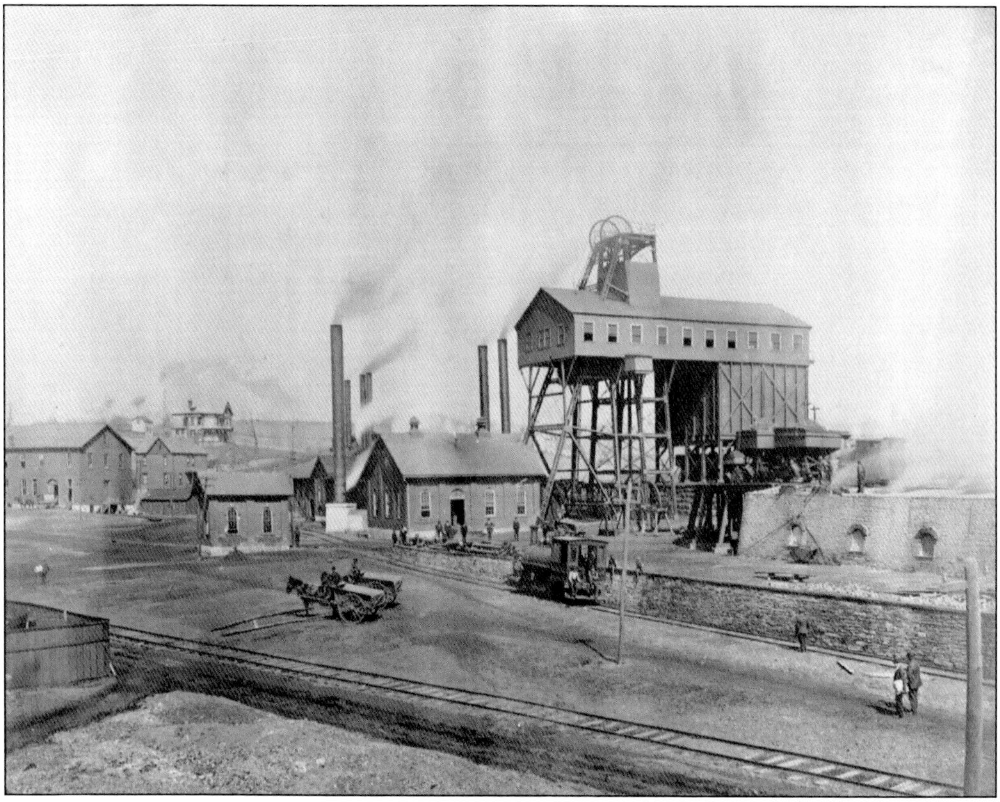

This is the B Shaft and the powerhouse at Morewood as it appeared in 1901. The company store is at far left. The name of the mine was changed to Southwest No. 1 when ownership was transferred from the Southwest Connellsville Coal and Coke Company to H.C. Frick in 1903. (Courtesy West Overton Museums.)

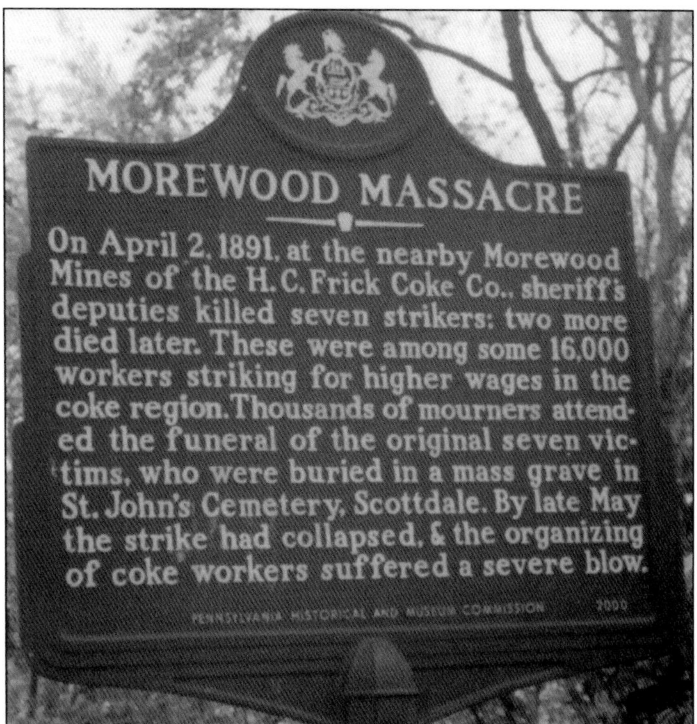

Today, there is no evidence of Morewood except this historical marker near the end of a street in Mount Pleasant that commemorates the violent deaths of nine miners during the 1891 strike in the Connellsville Coke Region.

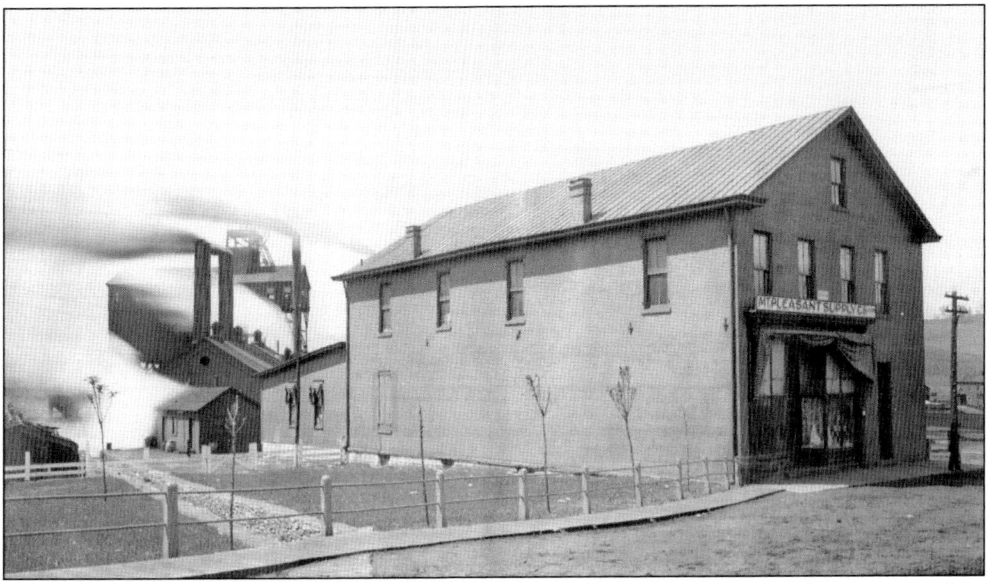

When the above picture was taken in the early 1900s, the store at Morewood was operated by the Mount Pleasant Supply Company. Initially, company stores were needed because mines were located in remote areas and there was no public transportation. Most stores issued scrip, which could be used to purchase food and other merchandise. At the end of a pay period, the purchases were deducted from an employee's wages; sometimes the value of the "check off" was greater than the earnings. The interior of the store is pictured below. (Both, courtesy West Overton Museums.)

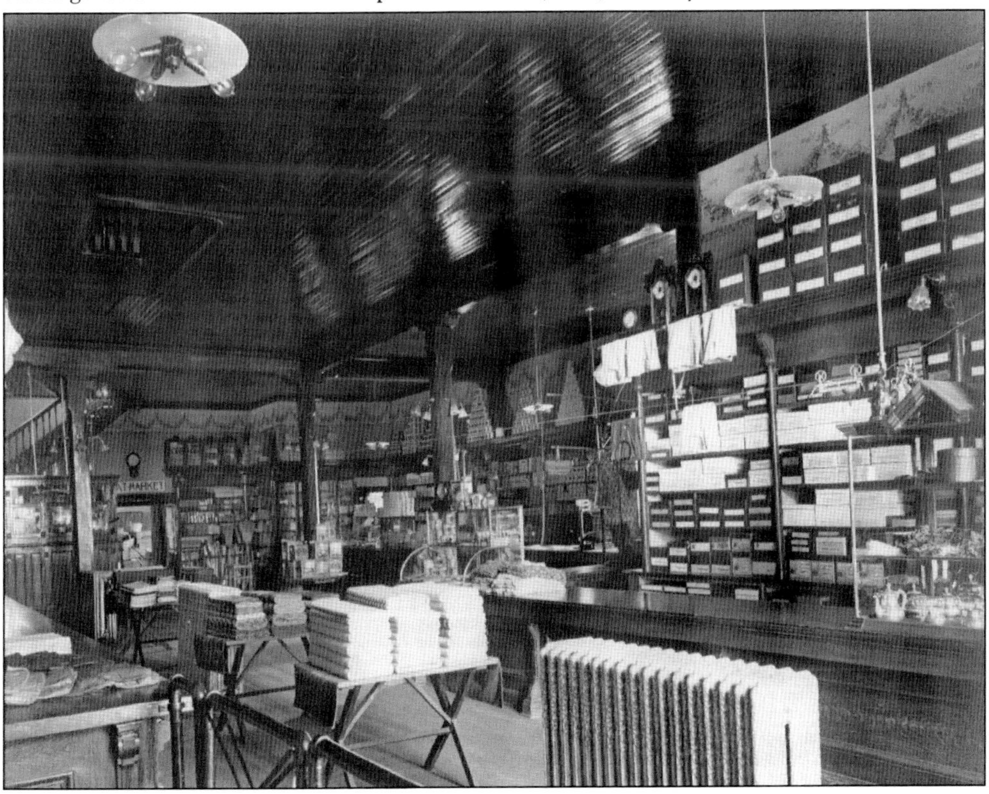

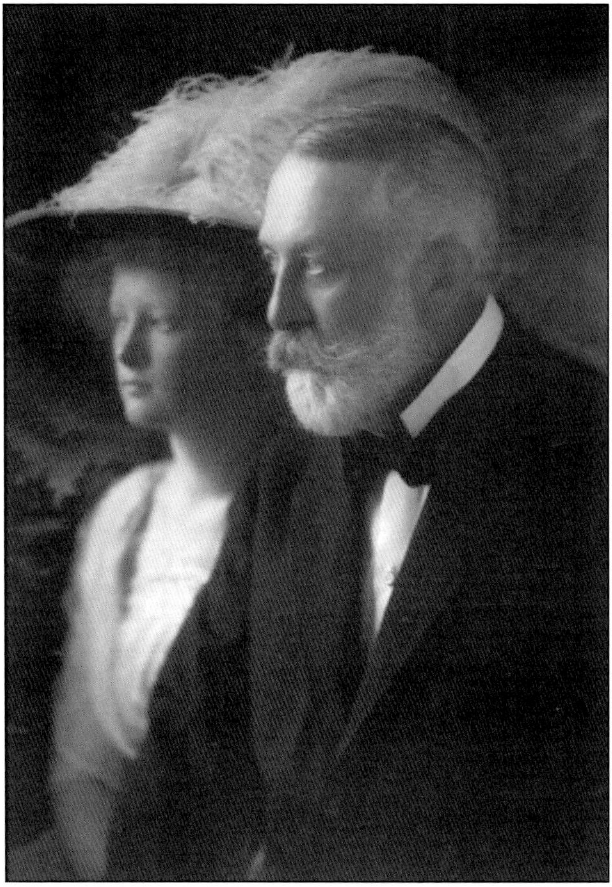

Henry Clay Frick, the son of John Frick and Elizabeth Overholt, was born at West Overton in 1849. In addition to his extensive holdings in coal and coke, Frick served as chairman of Carnegie Steel and as a director of life insurance companies, railroads, national banks, utilities, and Western mining interests. In spite of his business acumen and philanthropy, he is, unfortunately, also locally remembered for his ruthless suppression of unions through the use of force, intimidation, and strikebreakers. Frick's daughter Helen is next to her father in the image at left. Below are the office buildings of the H.C. Frick Coal and Coke Company, located on the corner of South Broadway and Walnut Street. The structure at right dates from 1880; the building at left was added in 1904, shortly after the company became a subsidiary of United States Steel Corporation (US Steel). (Left, courtesy West Overton Museums.)

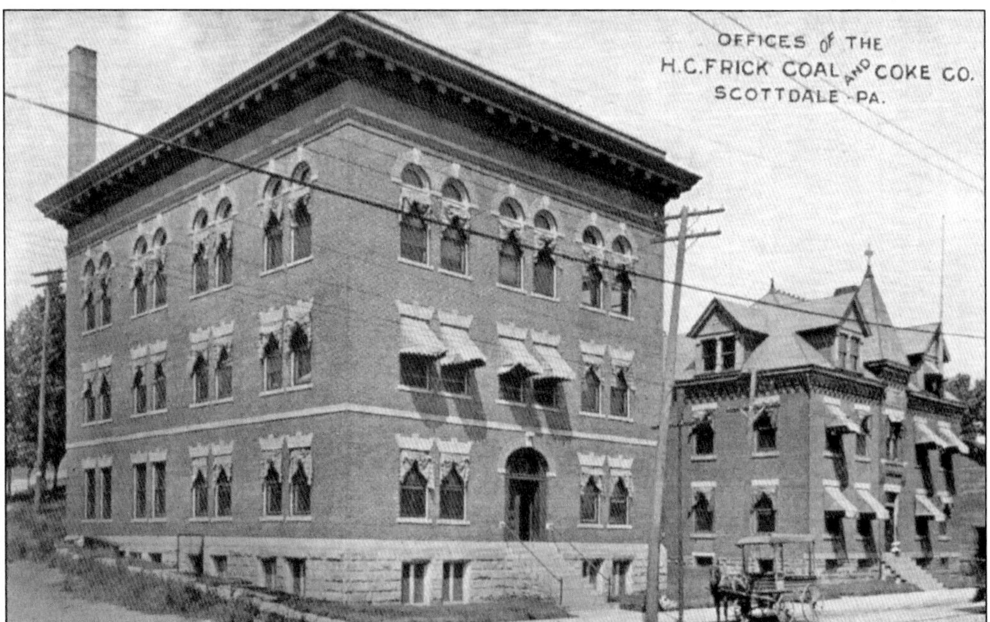

Watson Kmieciak, second from the left, and his unidentified friends show their support for the United Mine Workers (U.M.W.) in South Everson around 1938. Before the U.M.W., miners in Western Pennsylvania were represented by the Knights of Labor and the Miners' and Laborers' Amalgamated Association. (Courtesy Sharyn Kmieciak.)

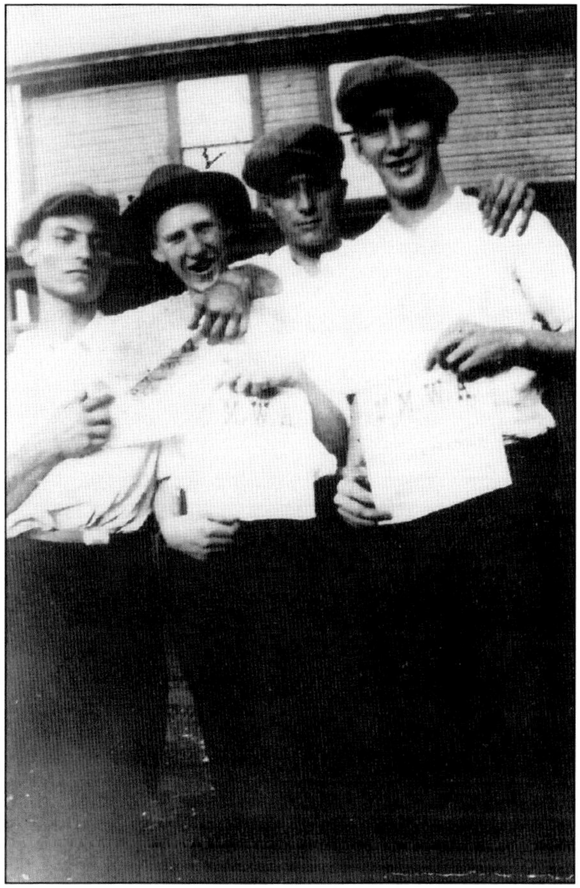

This is the shaft and powerhouse at Leisenring No. 1 after it was purchased by H.C. Frick from John Leisenring, a Philadelphia coal magnate, in 1890. (Courtesy Denny Gaal.)

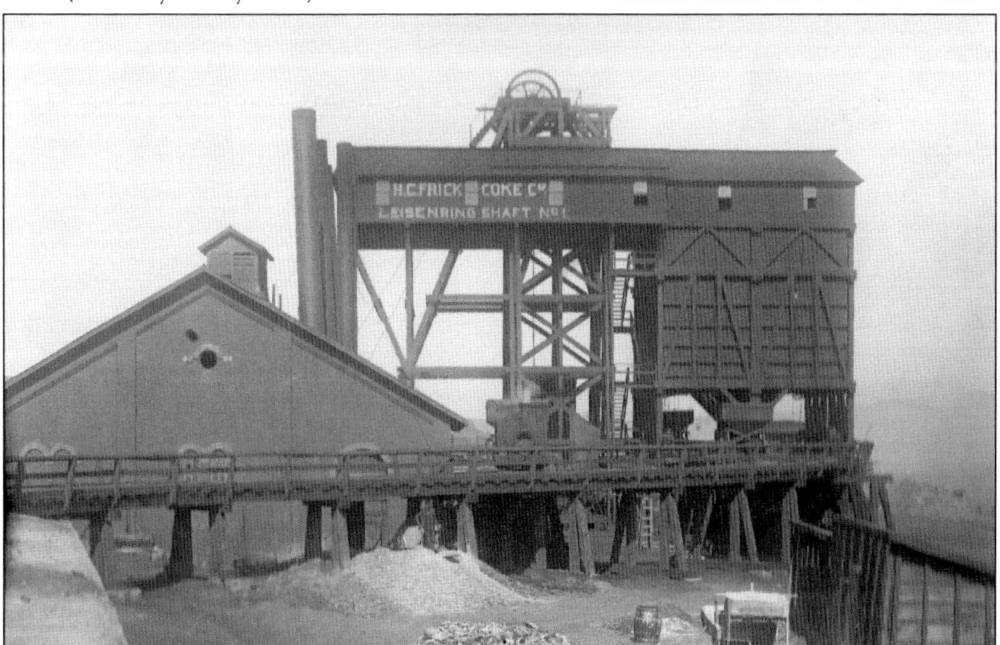

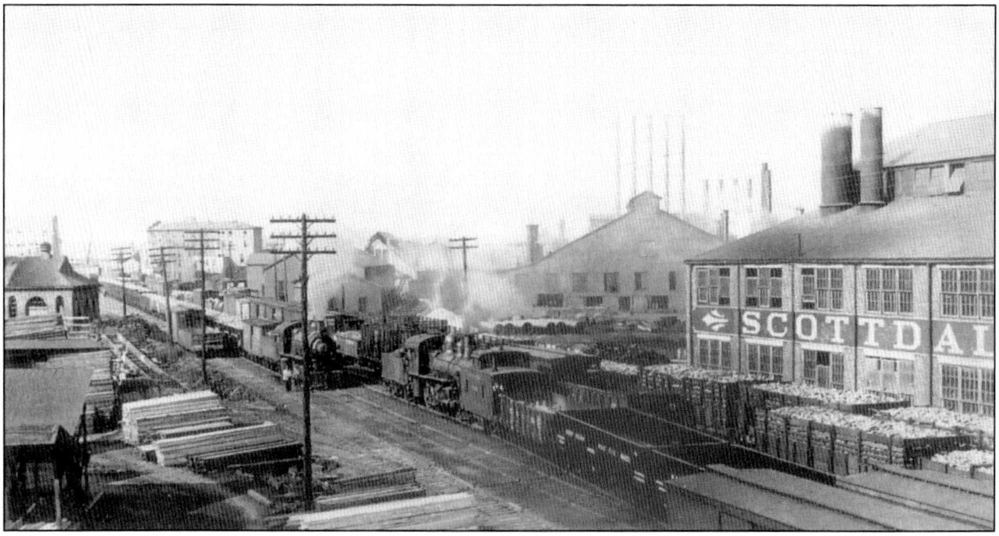

A c. 1920 view from the bridge between Scottdale and Everson shows coke trains (and others with mixed freight) on the Pennsylvania Railroad. Before the Great Depression, the Pennsylvania, the Baltimore & Ohio, the Pittsburgh & Lake Erie, and the Pittsburgh, McKeesport & Youghiogheny Railroads employed nearly 500 workers from the Scottdale area.

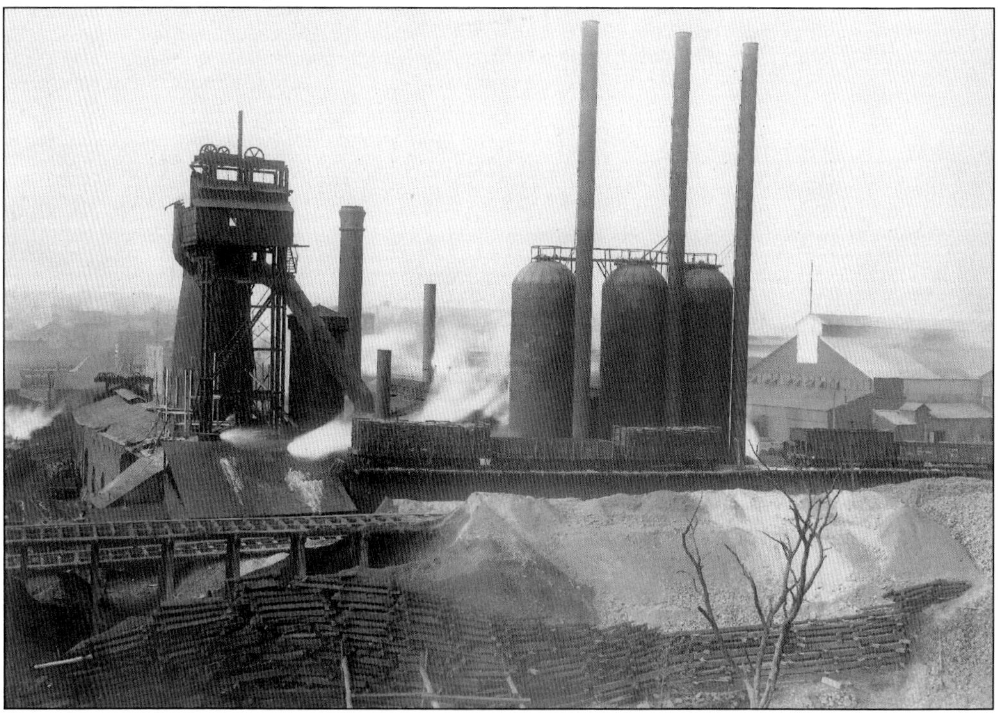

The Charlotte Furnace was erected on the former site of Fountain Mills. Iron ore was mined on the Chestnut Ridge near Mount Vernon and shipped to Scottdale on a narrow-gauge railroad to the Baltimore & Ohio in Mount Pleasant. Coal and coke were produced on Pigeon Hill and sent to the furnace on bridges across Jacobs Creek. In 1886, the operation was purchased by the National Foundry and Pipe Works, which was subsequently acquired by the United States Cast Iron Pipe and Foundry Company. (Courtesy Marjorie Scott.)

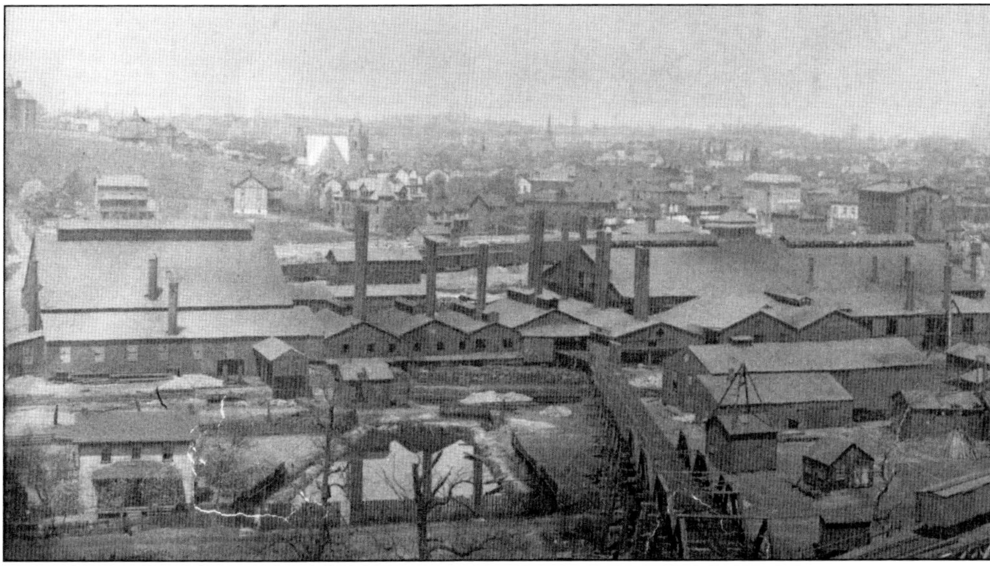

Initially, the Scottdale Rolling Mill was part of the Charlotte Furnace, employing 250 men who annually produced 3,000 tons of finished sheet iron. In 1887, it was reorganized by a group of local citizens as the Scottdale Iron and Steel Company. One of the bridges over Jacobs Creek is in the foreground. The Jacob S. Loucks farmstead is pictured at left directly above this 1905 view of the mill. (Courtesy Denny Gaal.)

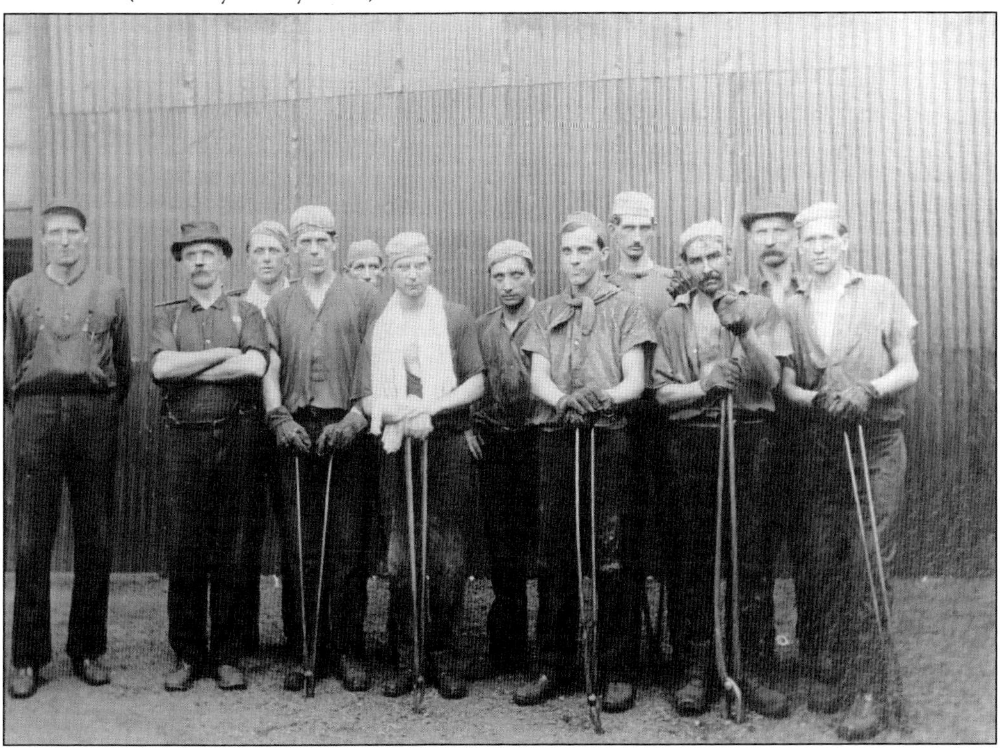

Edward Percy (in the center, with a towel around his neck) and the unidentified members of his crew are pictured at the Scottdale Rolling Mill. The tongs held by some of the men were used for reheating and turning the steel. (Courtesy Bob Percy.)

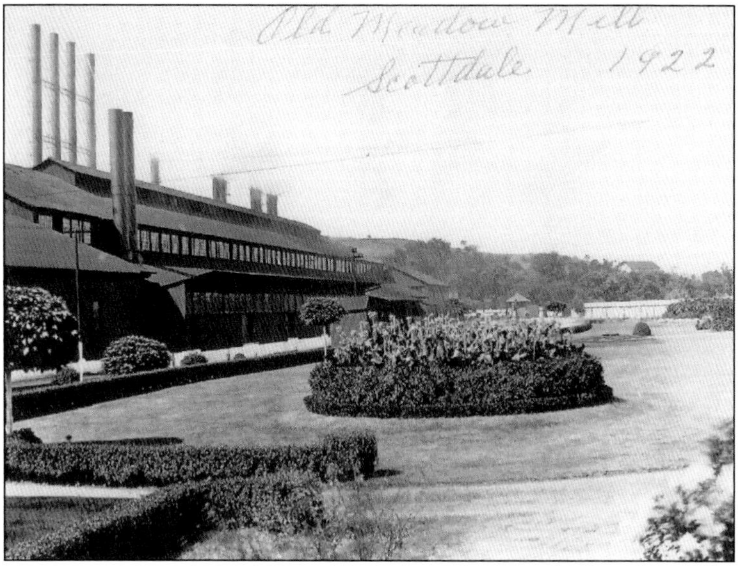

The Old Meadow Rolling Mill, which provided employment for 400 people, was financed by local residents and built on part of the Keister farm near Dawson Road. It commenced operation in 1898 and was later purchased by the American Sheet Steel division of US Steel. (Courtesy *Scottdale Independent-Observer.*)

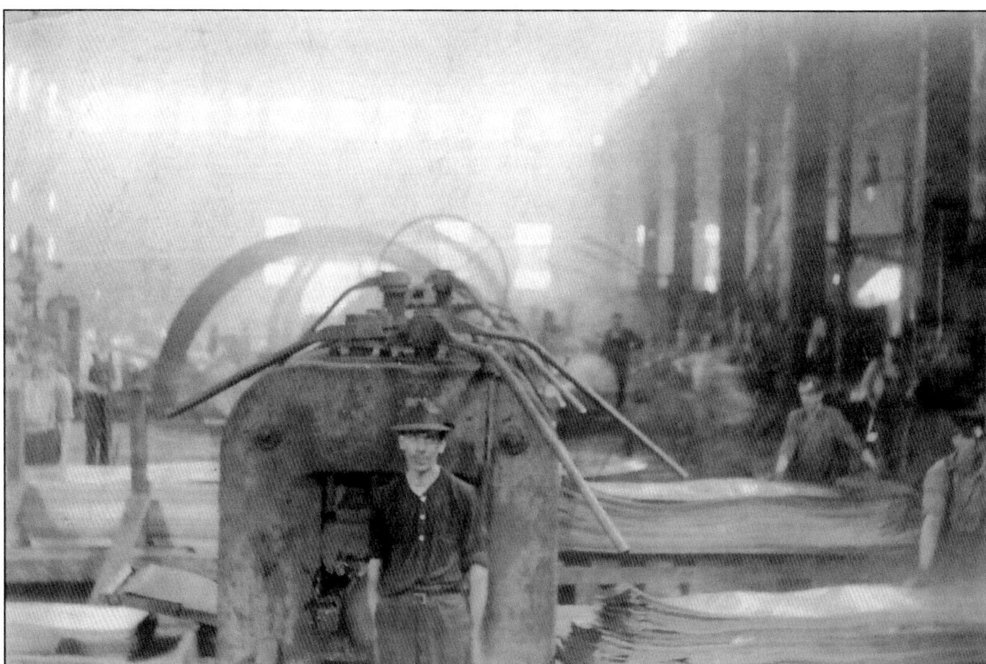

An unidentified worker poses in front of a rolling machine at the Old Meadow Mill. The levers were used to control the thickness of the steel. Operating the machine required high levels of skill and experience.

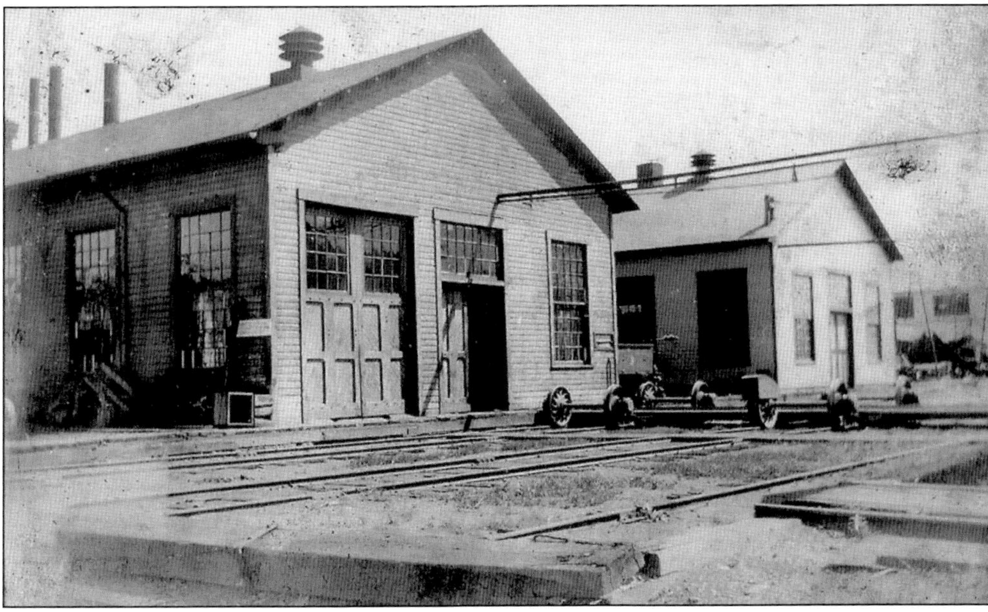

Henry Clay Frick consolidated his manufacturing and repair facilities in Everson, where he employed 100 men and women. Above are the machine and blacksmith shops, with tracks in the foreground that were used to move railroad cars into the buildings. The shops were constructed in 1895 by Walter Clingerman, an engineer who was given a leave of absence from the Pennsylvania Railroad. Clingerman subsequently became president of the H.C. Frick Coke Company. The 1909 image below shows tin shop workers. Andrew Malik is leaning against the left frame of the open door in the back row. His father, Emmanuel Malik, with a mustache and wearing a wide brimmed hat, is in the second row, seventh from the right. Andrew's brother, Emmanuel Malik Jr., is also wearing a wide brimmed hat. He is fifth from left in the back row. The other workers are unidentified. (Above, courtesy Marjorie Scott; below, courtesy Dora Curry.)

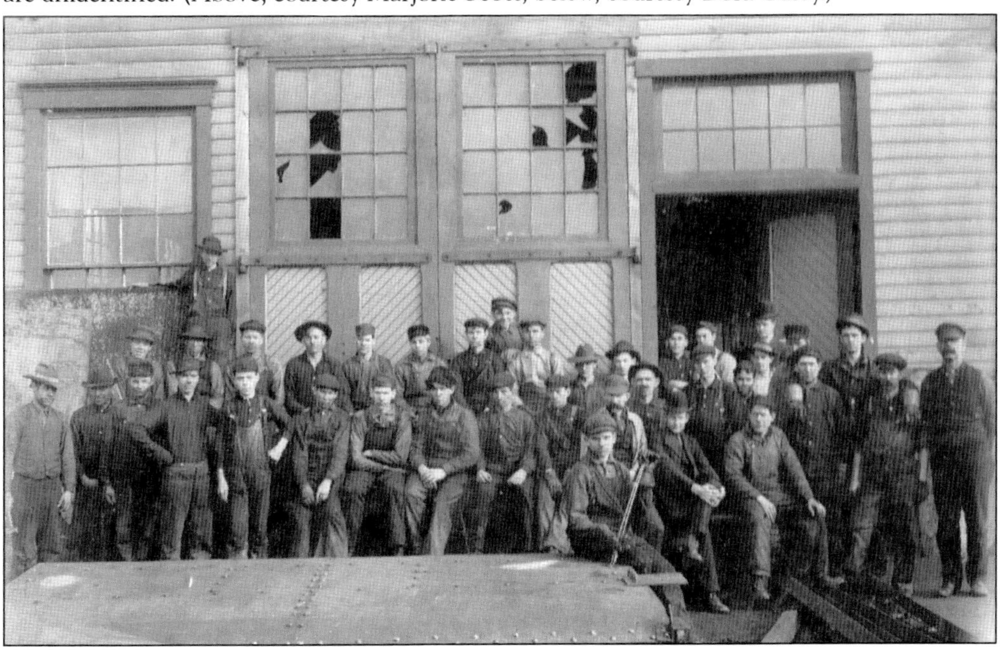

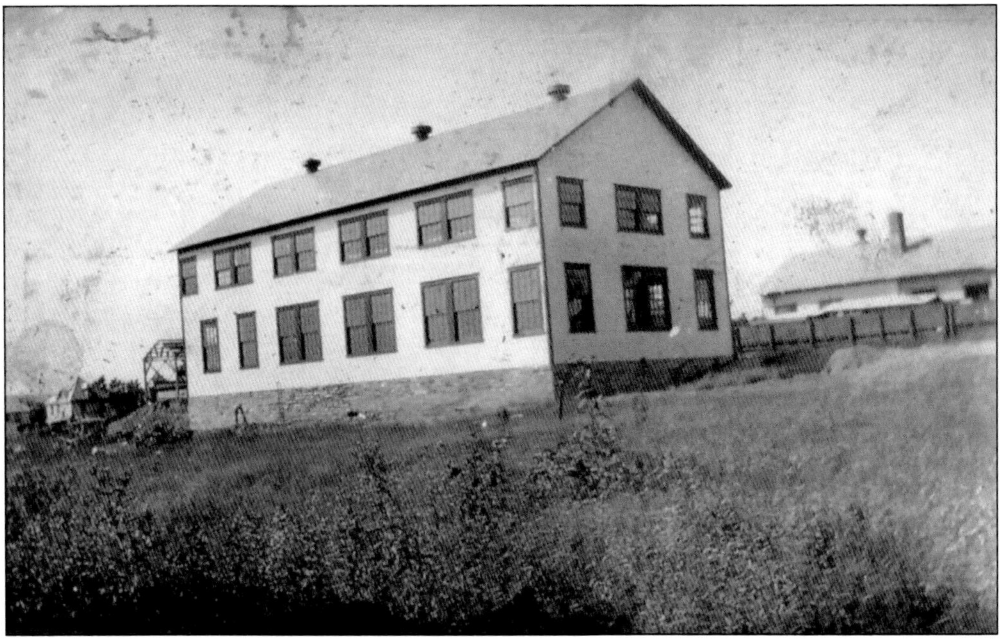

The car shops contained facilities to repair electrical motors used in mine equipment. The repair shop is pictured above; employees who worked in the building appear in the 1917 image below. Although most of the shops closed in 1931, the electrical repair facility continued to operate until the 1950s. (Both, courtesy Marjorie Scott.)

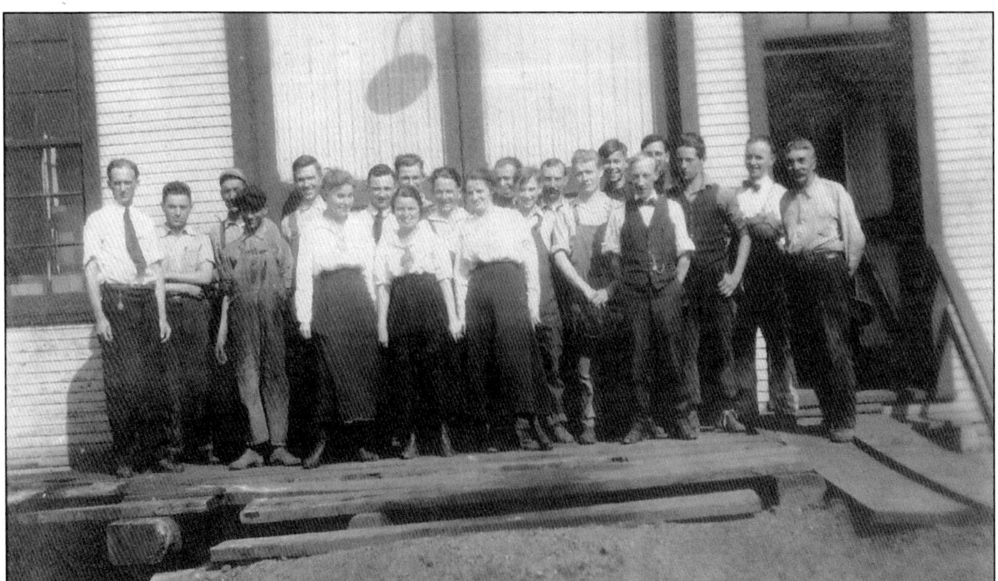

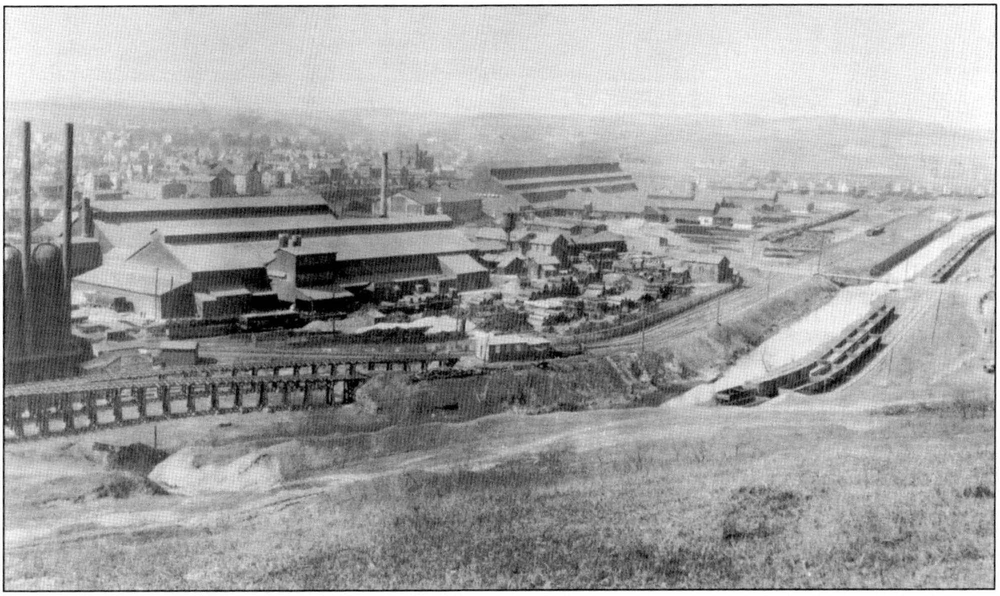

The US Cast Iron Pipe and Foundry was the largest industry in Scottdale, employing nearly 1,500 workers. It was incorporated in 1885 by members of the Loucks and Overholt families. This panoramic view from Pigeon Hill illustrates the size of the operation, which occupied land from the Charlotte Furnace to Ruth Lumber Company. (Courtesy Joseph Hawk.)

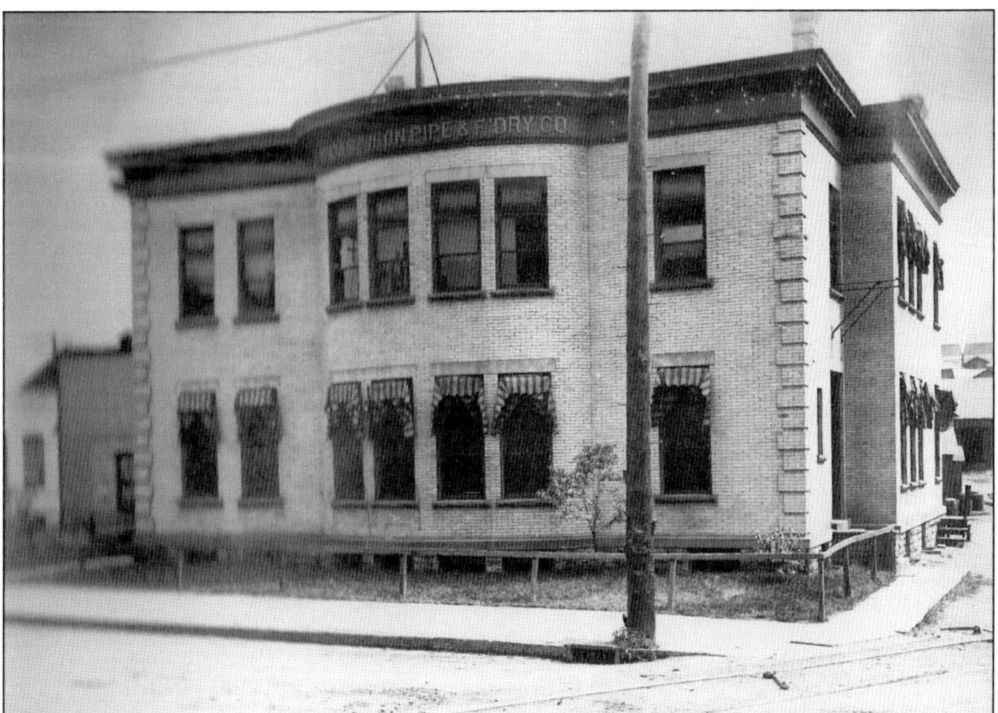

This is the US Cast Iron Pipe and Foundry office on Bridge Street, which became the headquarters of Duraloy when it relocated from West Virginia to Scottdale in 1937. (Courtesy Joseph Hawk.)

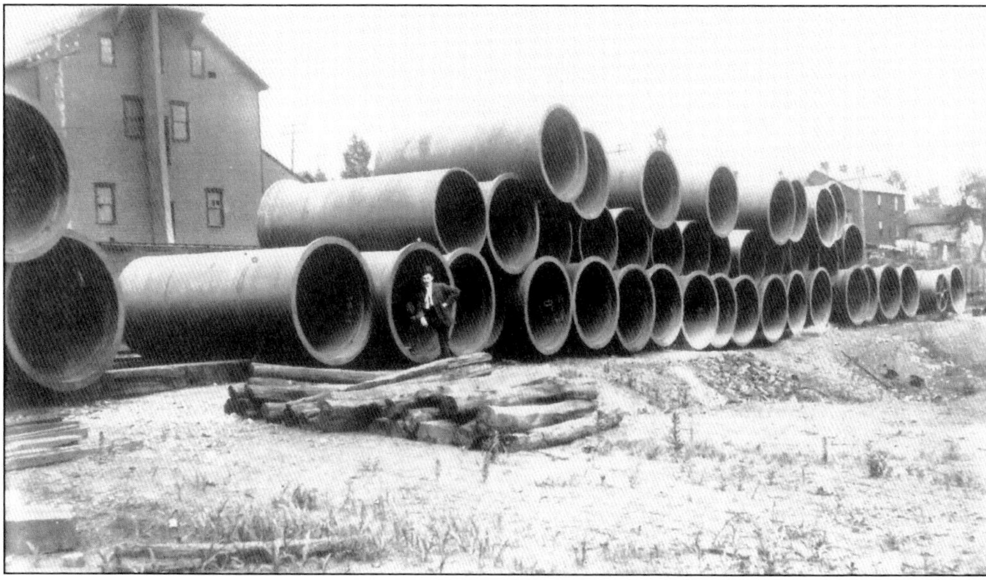

This image shows the size of the pipes manufactured in the mill, which ranged from 3 to 72 inches in diameter. Cast-iron pipe was in high demand at the time because cities and municipalities were building water, sewer, and gas systems. (Courtesy Joseph Hawk.)

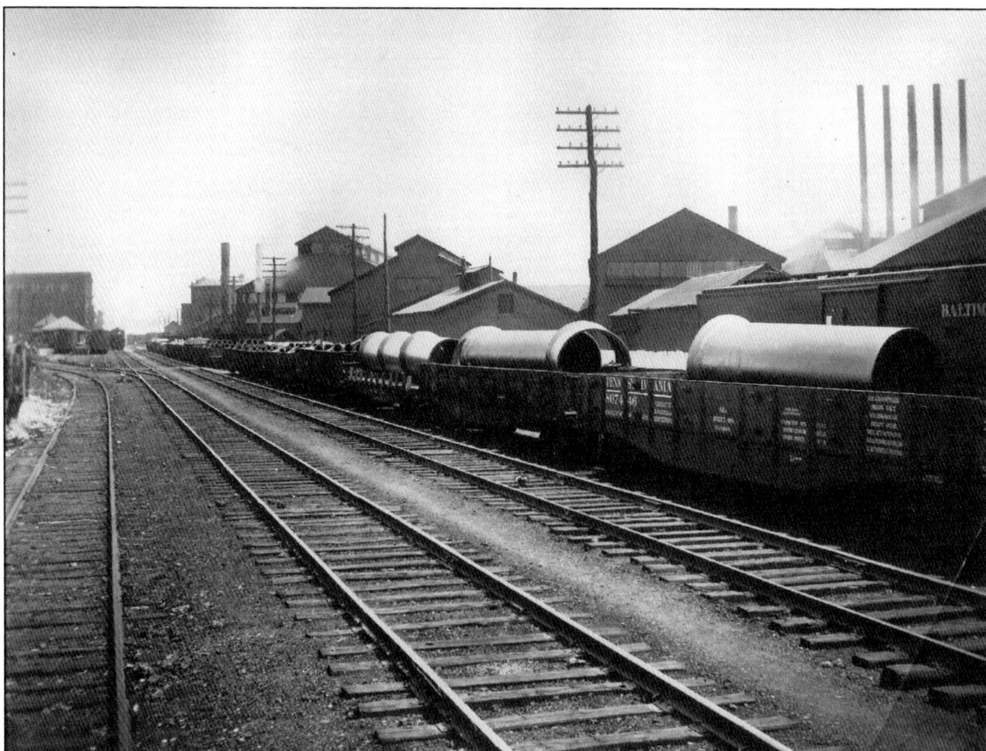

A train loaded with pipes appears to be ready to depart Scottdale for the Pennsylvania Railroad Yard at Youngwood—a trip the train made on a daily basis. (Courtesy Joseph Hawk.)

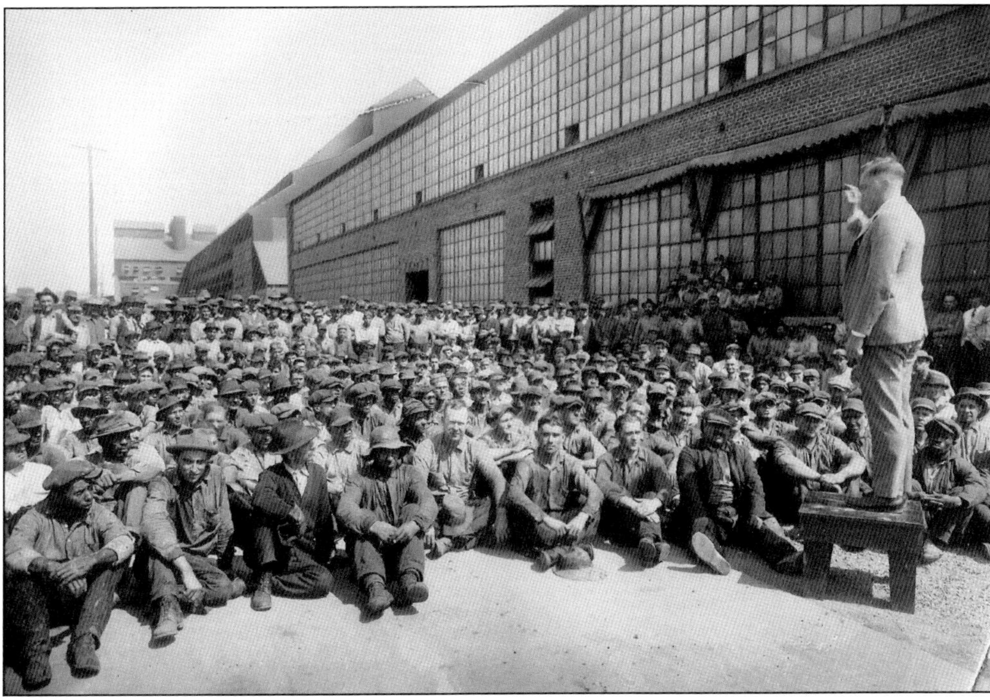

This picture, taken before hard hats, safety glasses, and steel-toed shoes were required, shows a noontime safety meeting at the pipe mill. (Courtesy Joseph Hawk.)

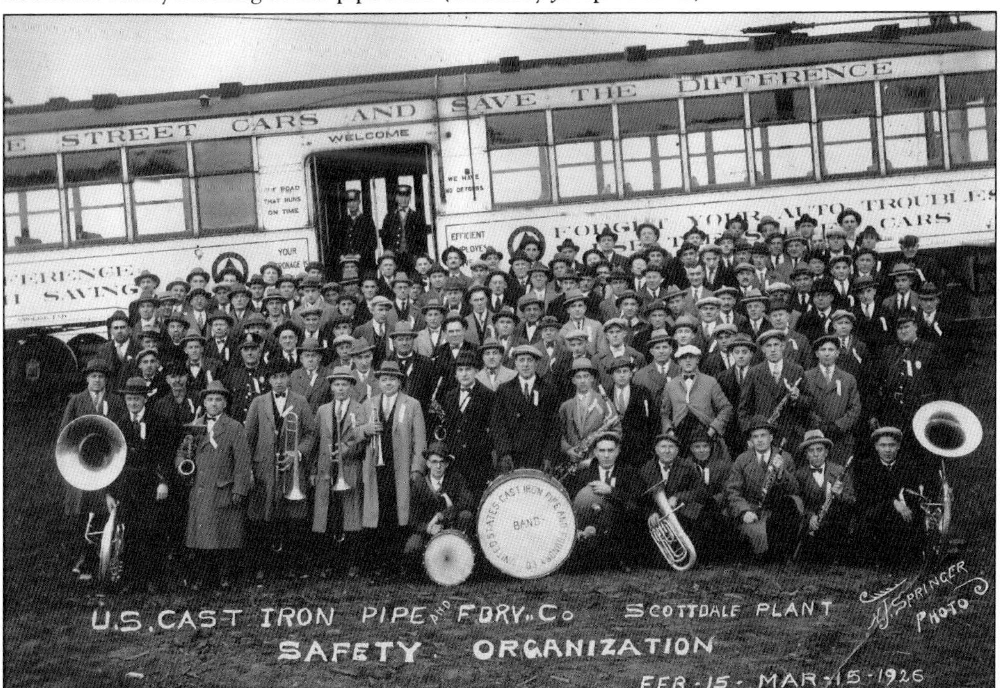

A safety organization at the pipe mill prepares to board a West Penn trolley for a parade or rally. Note the two trolley operators standing in the doors of the train car. In later years, the cars were modified so that they could be operated with one motorman. (Courtesy Mary Ann Zozula.)

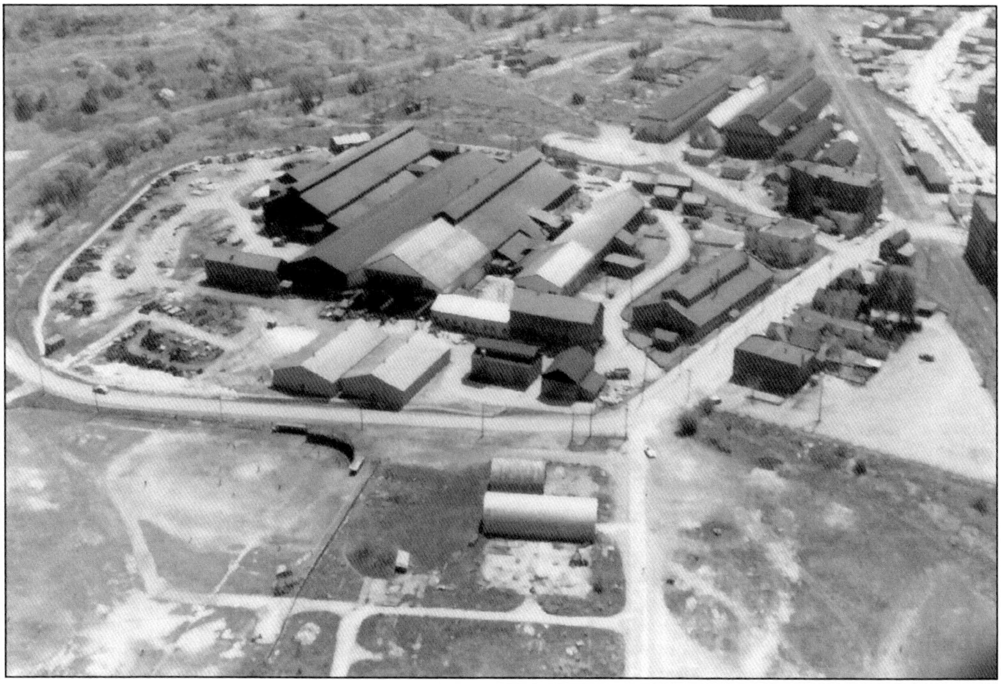

This 1955 aerial view shows Duraloy, which occupied Plant A of the pipe mill. Over the years, Duraloy has consolidated its operations in Scottdale. Duraloy is an industry leader in manufacturing high-alloy castings and fabrications. The R.E. Uptegraff Manufacturing Company appears near the upper right corner, adjacent to the Pennsylvania Railroad tracks. Uptegraff, which manufactures specialized electrical transformers, occupied some of the buildings originally constructed for the Scottdale Rolling Mill. (Courtesy Chuck King.)

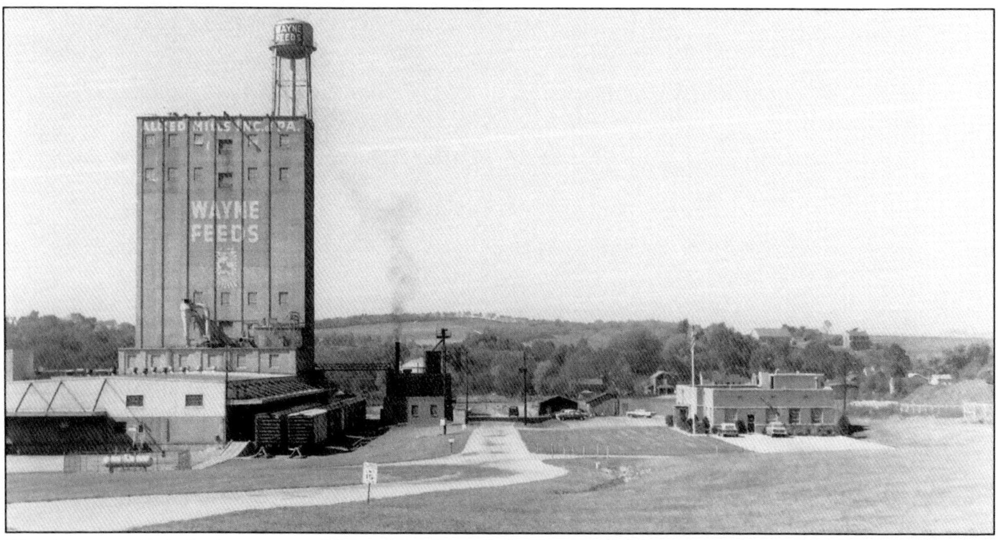

The Everson Polish American Club played mush ball on a field next to the H.C. Frick (US Steel) Car Shops. In 1954, Allied Mills, Inc., purchased the property and constructed a modern feed mill in order to produce its Wayne Feed brands closer to Eastern markets. In 1997, the mill was acquired by Doane Pet Care. Ownership was transferred in 2010 to Megnablend, Inc., a custom chemical company. (Courtesy Michael Banaszak.)

Two

Living, Shopping, and Moving Around

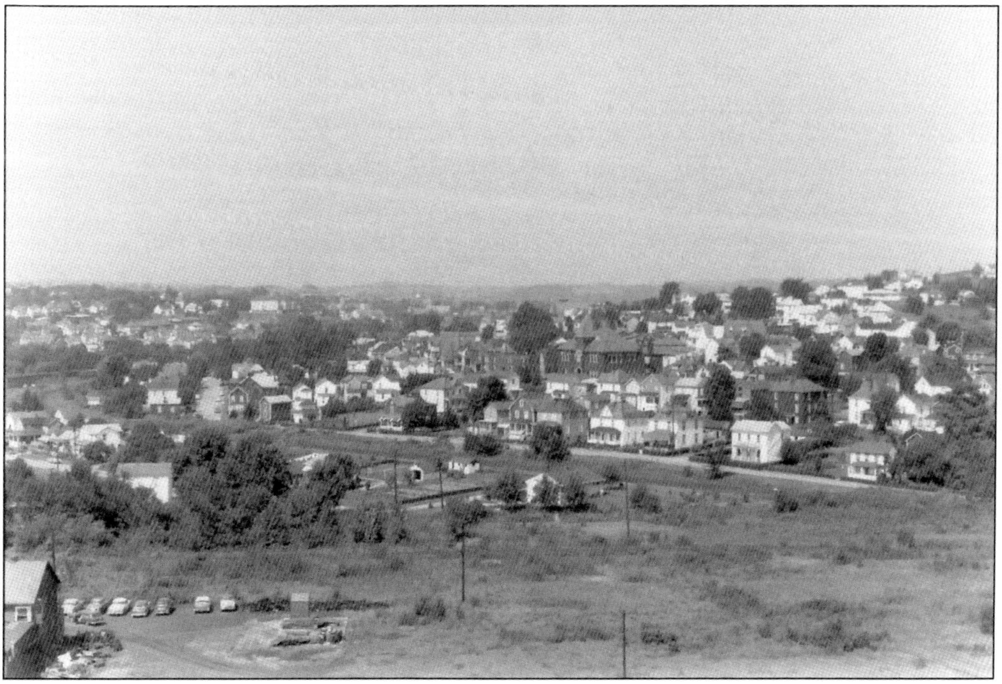

Here is a mid-1950s aerial view of Everson on the right showing nearly all of Graff Street in the foreground. The Everson Grade School, which was located on the corner of Jones and Brown Streets, is the largest building depicted slightly right of center. The car shop parking lot is visible on the lower left and a section of Scottdale appears in the upper left, showing the old high school. (Courtesy Michael Banaszak.)

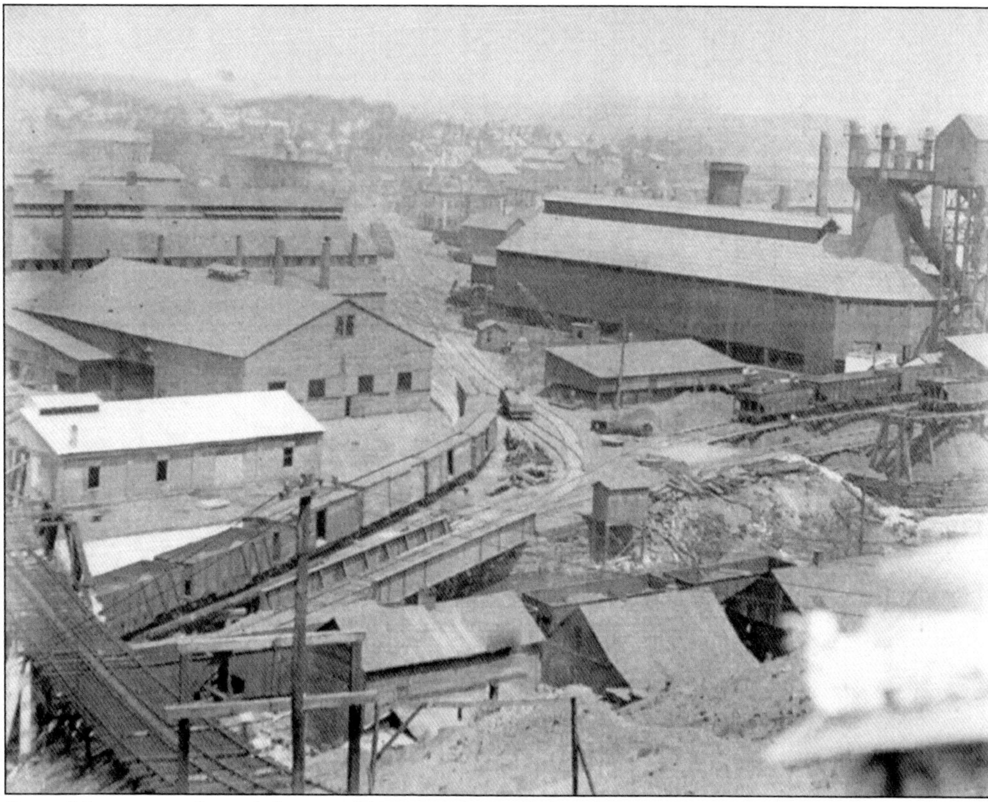

Part of downtown Scottdale is visible around 1910 behind the smoke generated by the Charlotte Furnace on the right and the Scottdale Rolling Mill on the left.

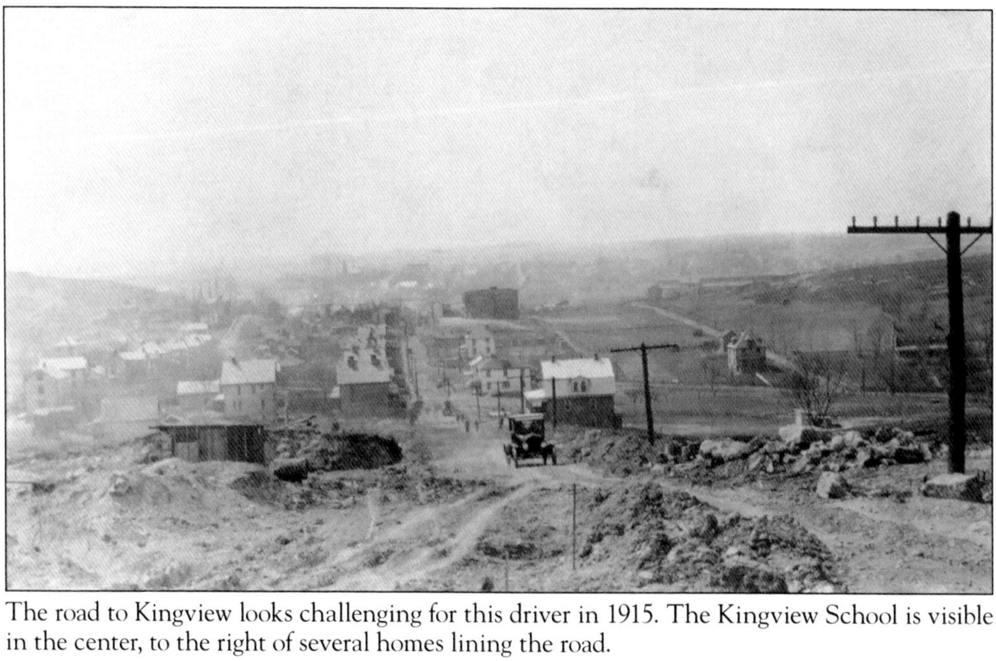

The road to Kingview looks challenging for this driver in 1915. The Kingview School is visible in the center, to the right of several homes lining the road.

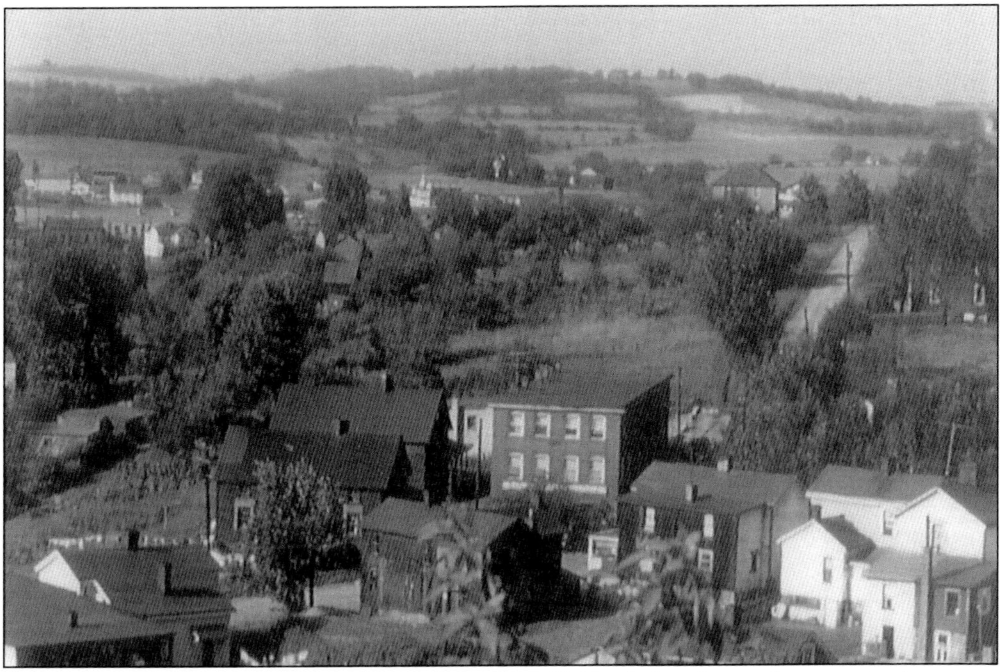

The section of Kiefertown pictured here shows Felix Zaffina's distribution business in the center surrounded by homes owned by the Price, Brown, DeSantis, and Smith families. (Courtesy Thelma Evans.)

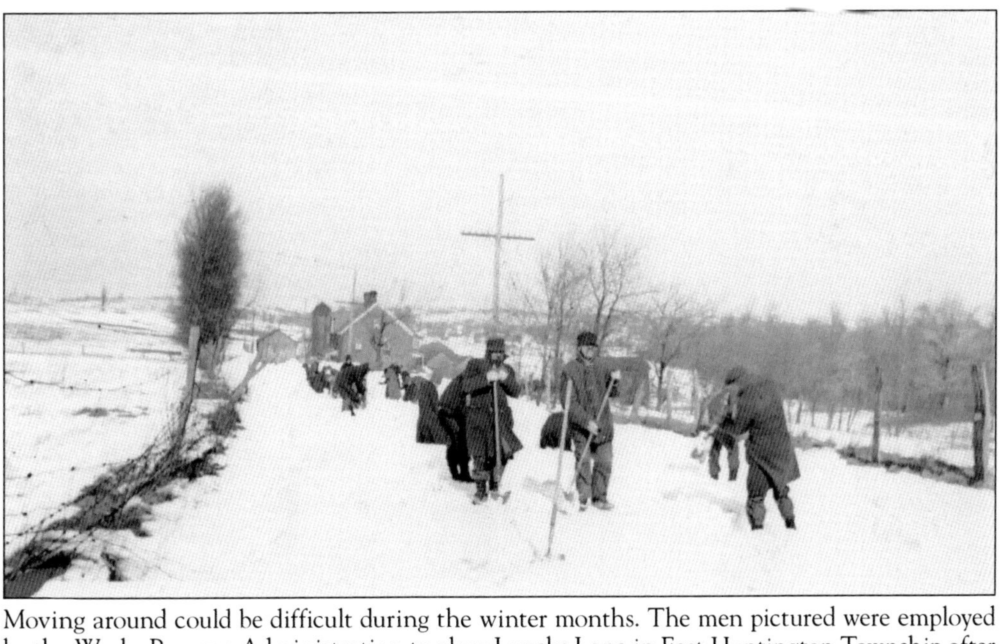

Moving around could be difficult during the winter months. The men pictured were employed by the Works Progress Administration to clear Loucks Lane in East Huntington Township after a 1936 snow storm. The men received approximately $52 per month for work on public projects. (Courtesy George Santmyer family.)

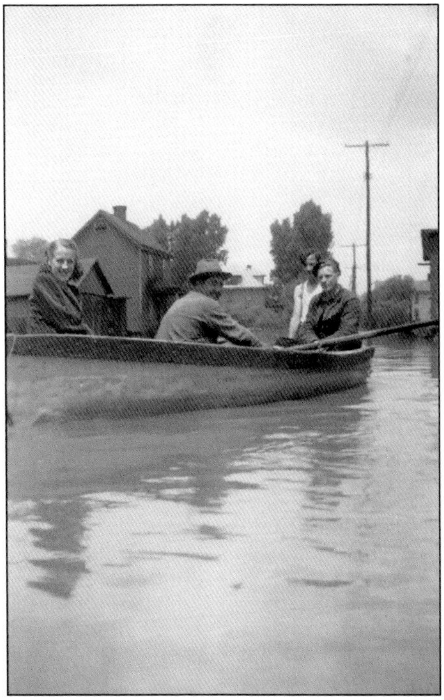

Dorothy Siwula (left) and Bruno Kmieciak (in the dark coat) needed this boat to get around South Everson when Jacobs Creek overflowed its banks in 1936. High water in the "bottom" was a recurring event before flood control projects were completed in the 1990s. (Courtesy Sharyn Kmieciak.)

Swedetown residents were stranded when Jacobs Creek flooded their neighborhood on North Scottdale Road in 1927. (Courtesy Joseph Hawk.)

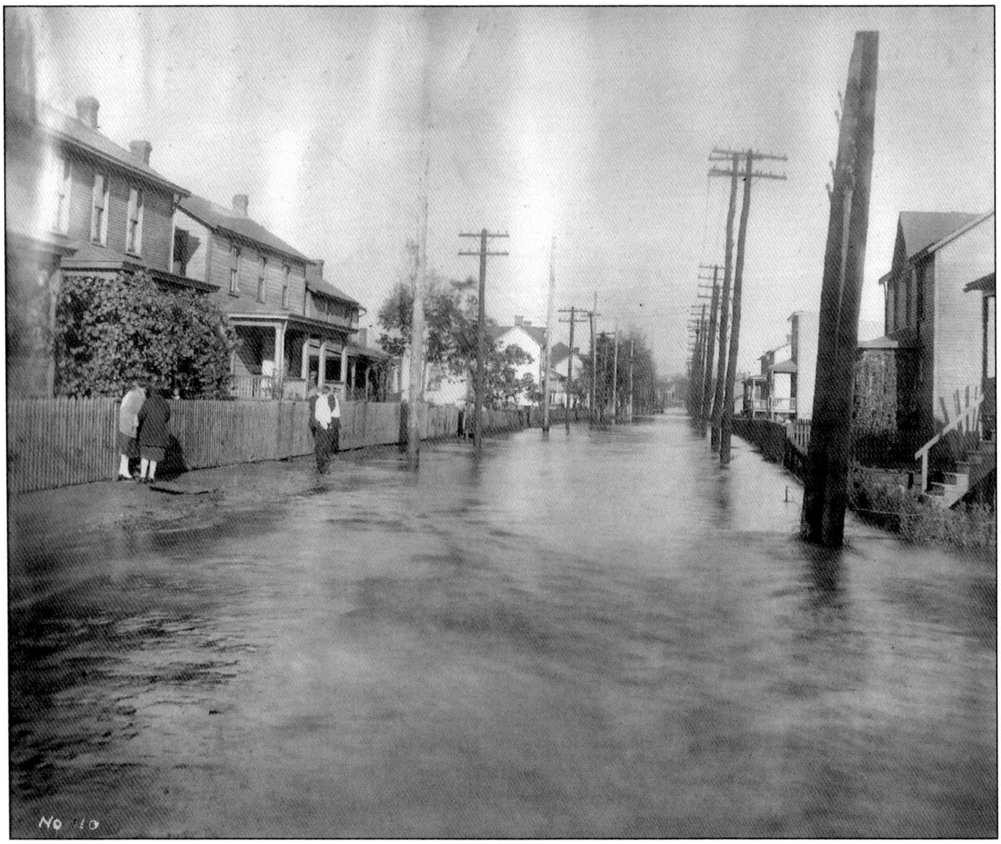

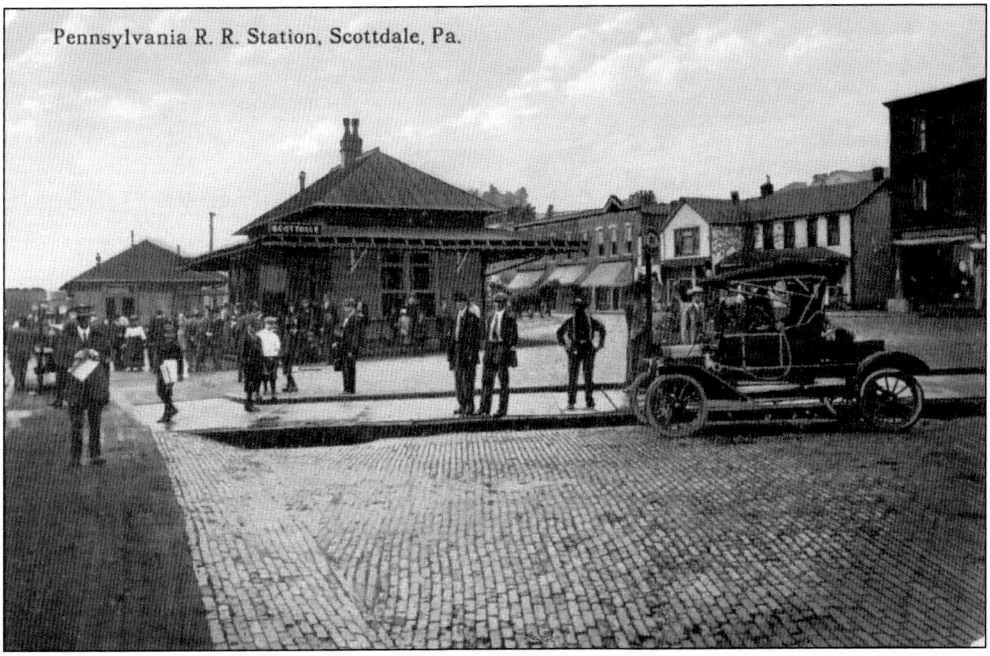

From the Pennsylvania Railroad passenger station, located on the corner of Pittsburgh Street and Broadway, one could travel to Greensburg and connect with the main line between New York and Chicago.

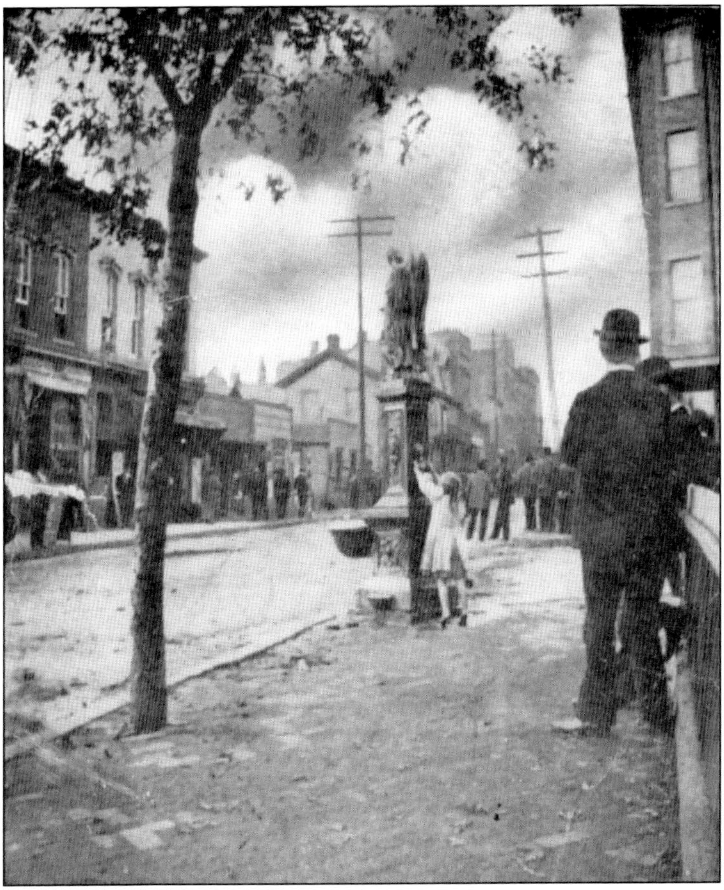

This drinking fountain, pictured on the same corner around 1893, became a cherished memory for generations of Scottdale residents. The basin facing the street provided water for animals, and a faucet on the sidewalk offered refreshment for pedestrians.

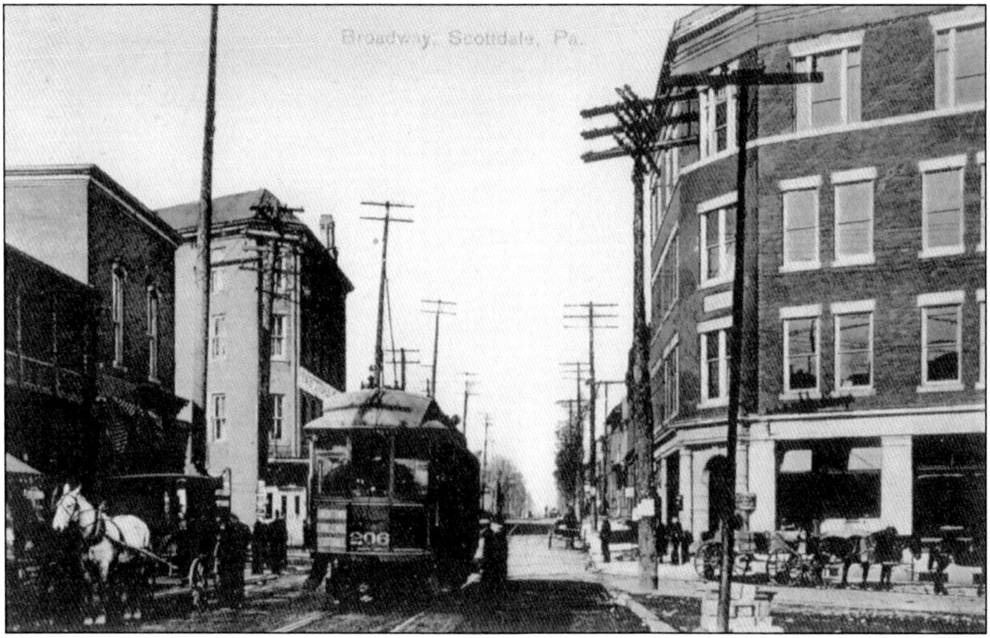

The Broadway National Bank, pictured on the right around 1895, and the Scottdale House, across the street, were prominent landmarks near the Pennsylvania Railroad train station at the intersection of Broadway and Pittsburgh Street.

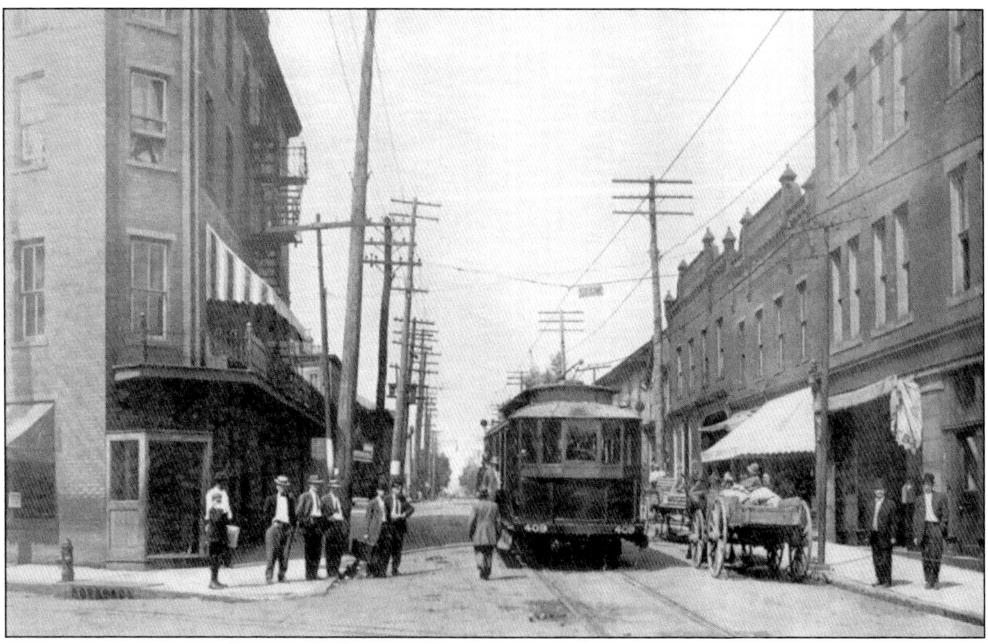

Commuters wait for the approaching trolley at the same intersection in 1910. At right is Reid's Block, which contained a number of stores initially built and operated by E.H. Reid. Reid was also president of the Broadway National Bank.

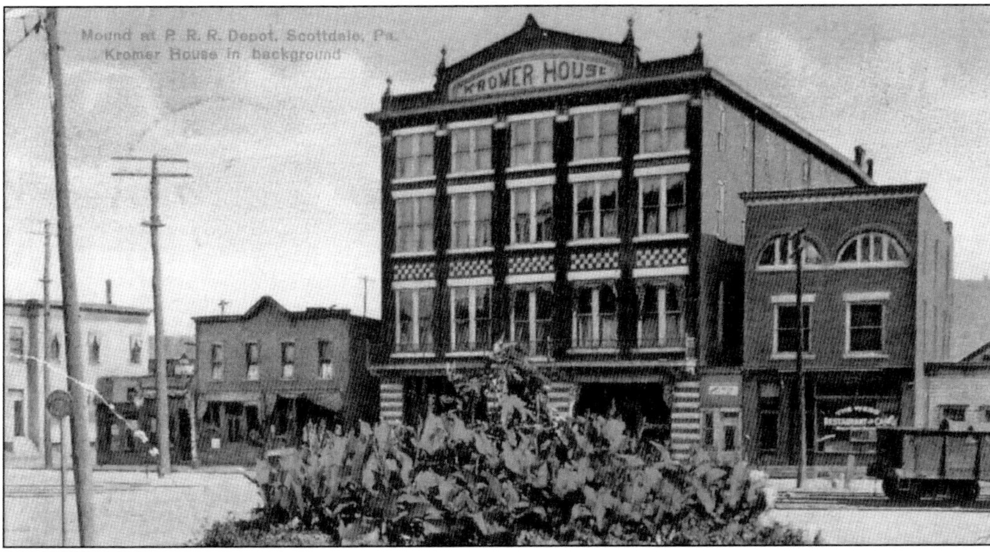

The Kromer House was one of six hotels in Scottdale. It was built by Nicholas Kromer, who emigrated from France in 1869. The establishment was promoted as the largest and most up-to-date hotel in Scottdale. The management promised gentlemanly treatment, handsome parlors, and fine sleeping apartments. Before entering business in Scottdale, Kromer operated the Eureka House in Everson, and in 1907, he acquired the Columbia Hotel in Alverton.

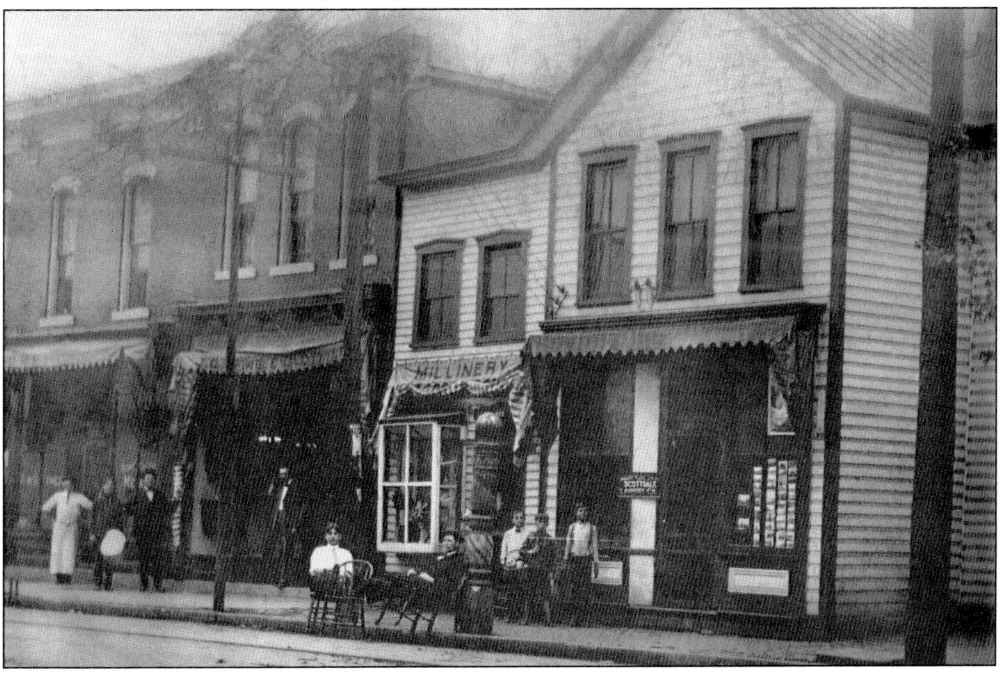

This was the scene across from the Scottdale train station on Broadway around 1900. It was known as Campbell's Block and included Campbell's Meat Market, depicted on the far left, followed by J.C. Gamble Clothiers, an unidentified millinery store, and a barbershop. In later years, the meat market became the location of the Fraternal Order of Eagles. The AC Products discount store was on the lot formally occupied by the clothing store. (Courtesy Scottdale Bank and Trust Company.)

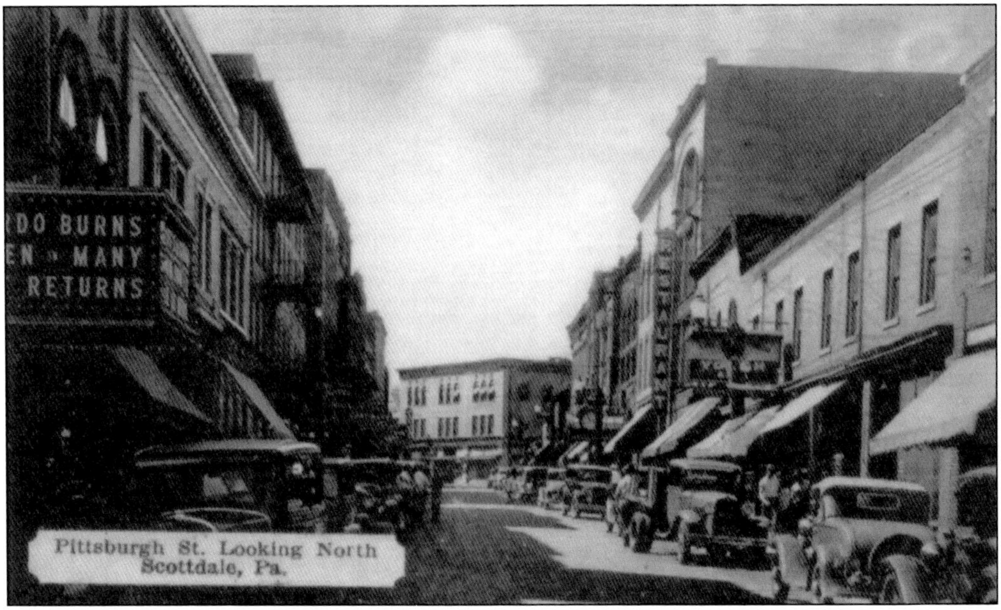

This image shows Pittsburgh Street in 1934, before the traffic pattern was limited to one direction. The Yough Bowling Alley is shown at right. The Strand, pictured at left, featured George Burns starring in *Many Happy Returns*. (Courtesy Westmoreland County Historical Society.)

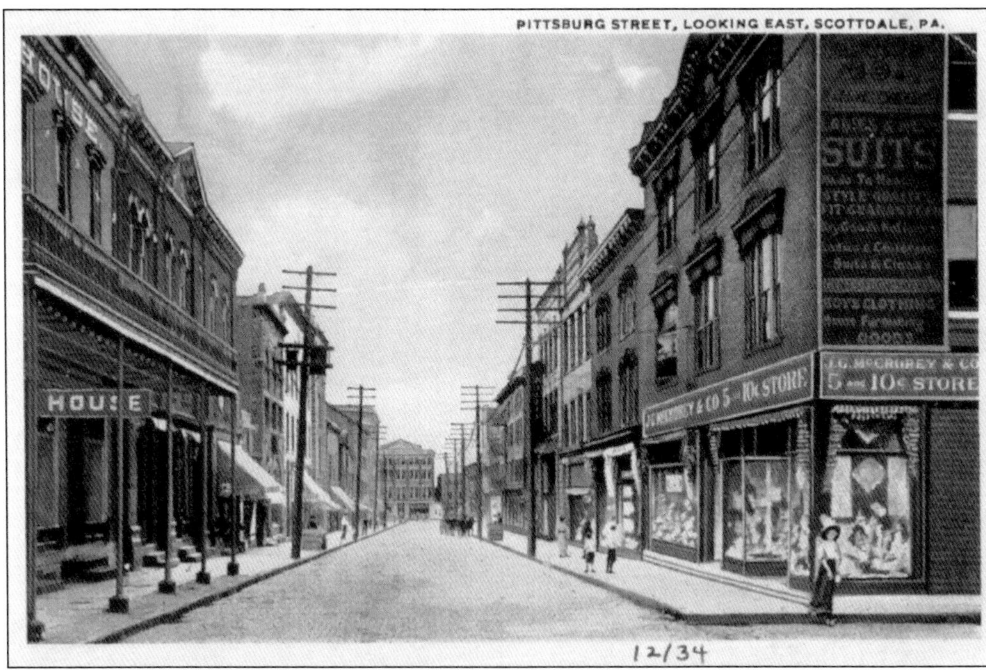

This 1890 view of Pittsburgh Street looks east toward the Kromer House. The first five-and-dime store, established by John G. McCrorey (Crory) in 1887, is at right, with the Hill House partially visible across the street. After the latter property was demolished in the late 1960s, the space became the location of the Scottdale Bank and Trust Company. The former McCrorey lot is currently occupied by Scottdale Elks Lodge No. 777 (BPOE).

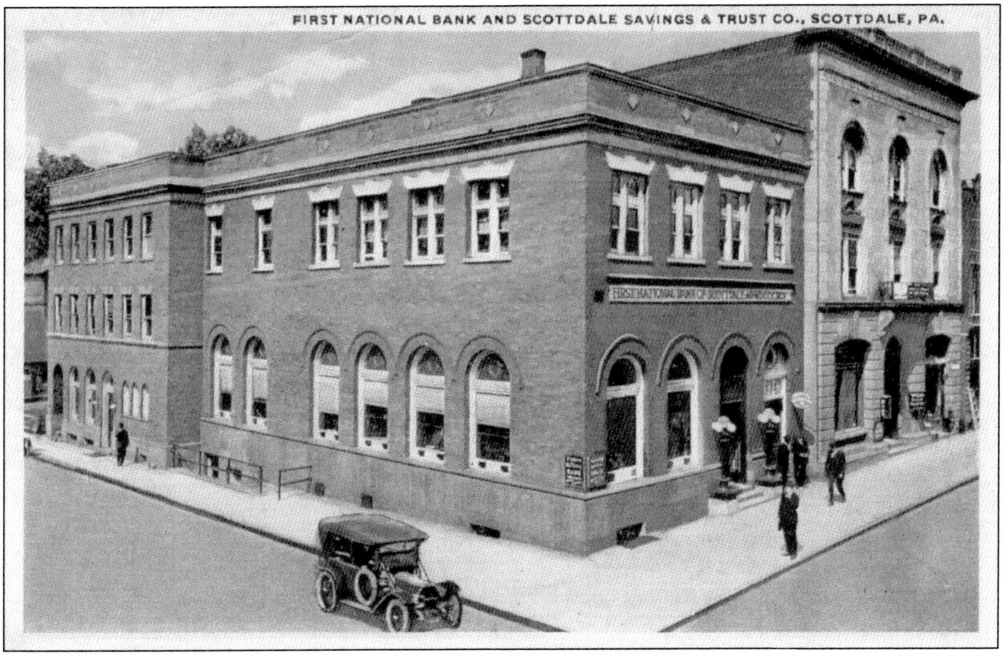

The First National Bank and the Scottdale Savings and Trust Company are pictured in 1910. The First National Bank claimed that it was the largest financial institution in Westmoreland County and the second-largest bank in the nation in terms of capitalization before 1929. The Scottdale Savings and Trust Company, established in 1901, was one of the few financial institutions in the area that remained open during the bank moratorium declared by Pres. Franklin D. Roosevelt in 1933.

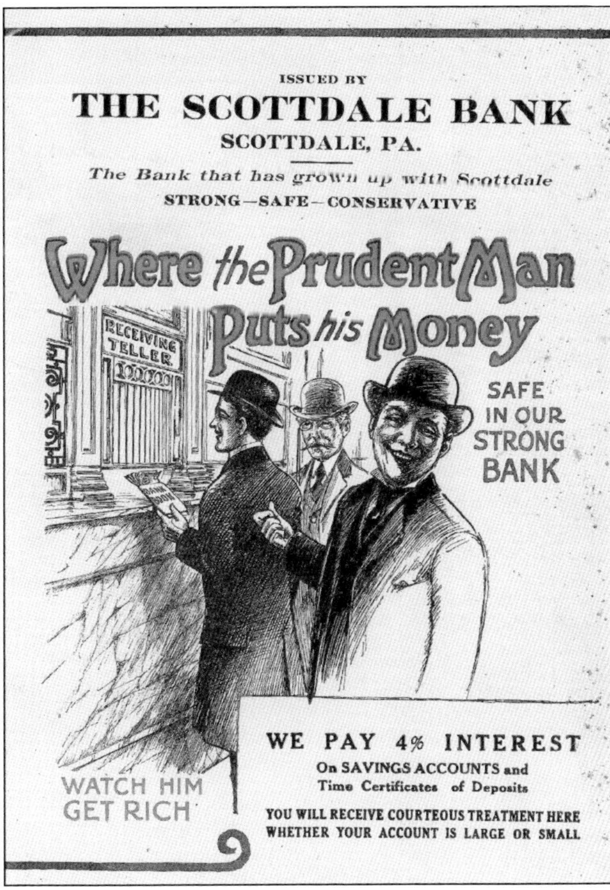

In 1882, J.R. Stauffer and P.S. Loucks organized the Scottdale Bank on Pittsburgh Street. As noted in the image, they offered four-percent interest on savings accounts in order to attract depositors, who could also "watch [people] get rich."

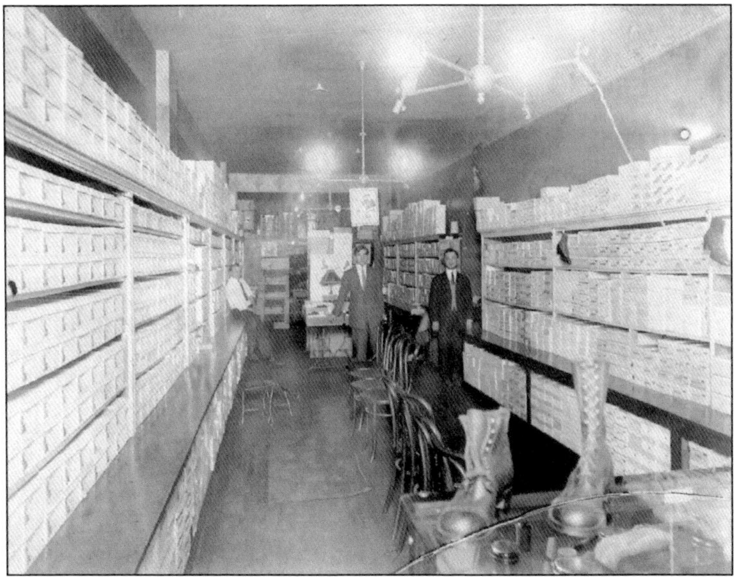

This image shows the shoe department in Mark's and Goldensen's Clothing Store, located at 117 Pittsburgh Street. Lee Goldensen is standing in the center, Israel Marks is on the right, and the other person is unidentified. The business operated as Mark's and Sons after 1950 and closed in 1967. A video store is now in this location.

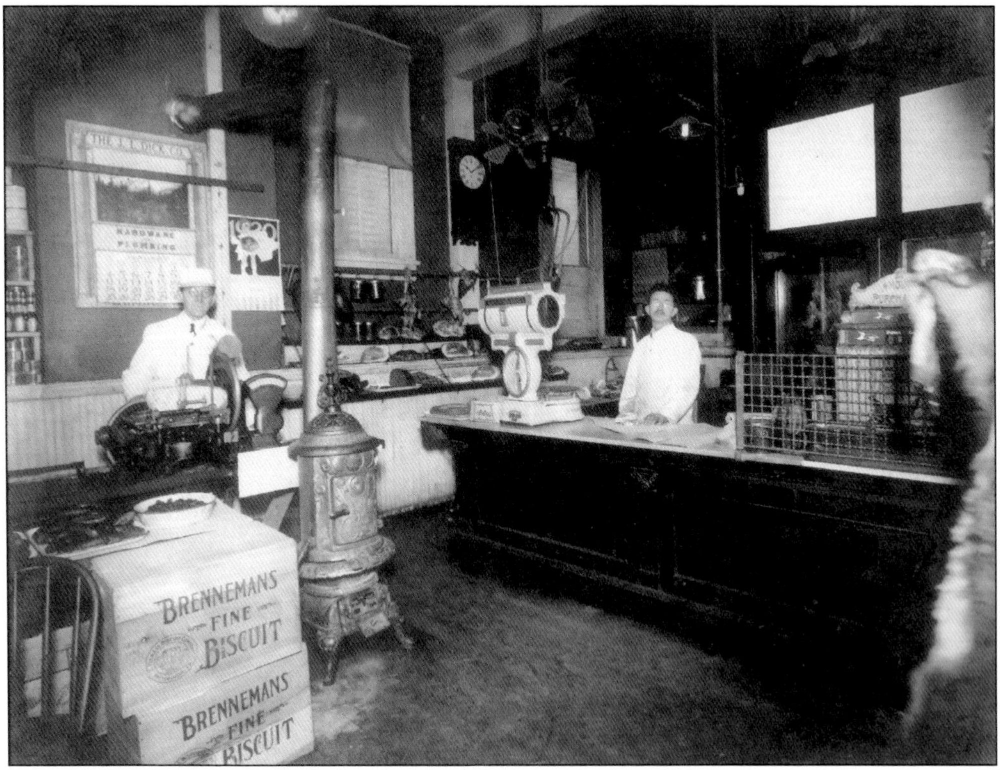

Charles Berkey (left), who was born in Somerset County, opened this butcher shop in 1917 at 152 Pittsburgh Street, across from the from the First National Bank. An employee, ? Snowden, is at right. (Courtesy Elsie Ellis.)

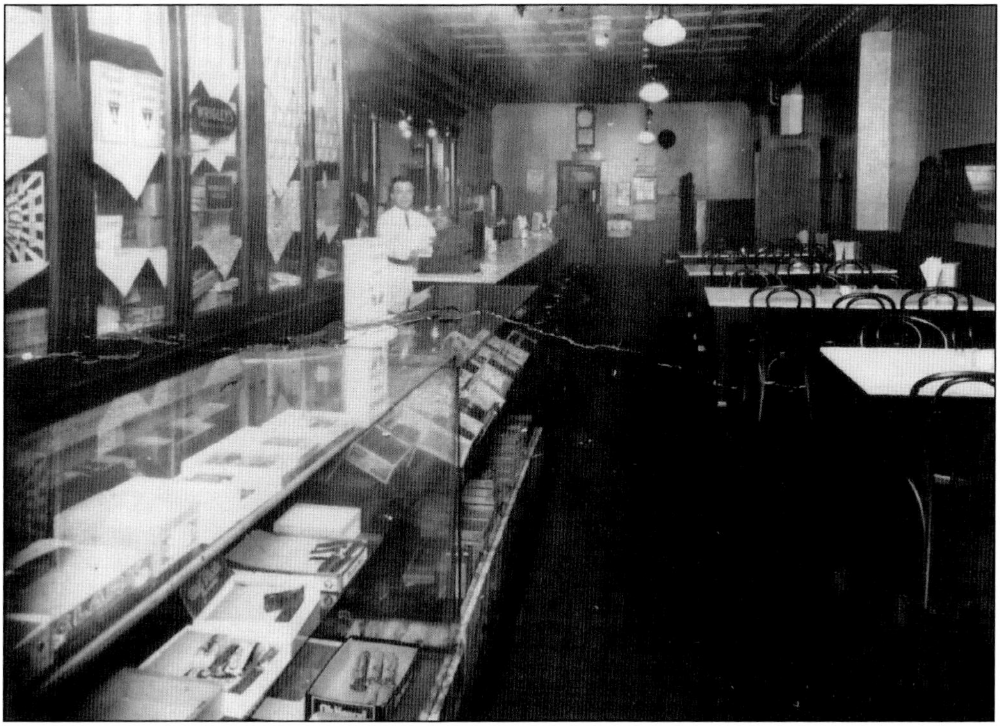

Ira Crawford stands behind the counter in his restaurant, located at 16 North Broadway, around 1928. The popular establishment operated between 1920 and 1944. (Courtesy Crawford family.)

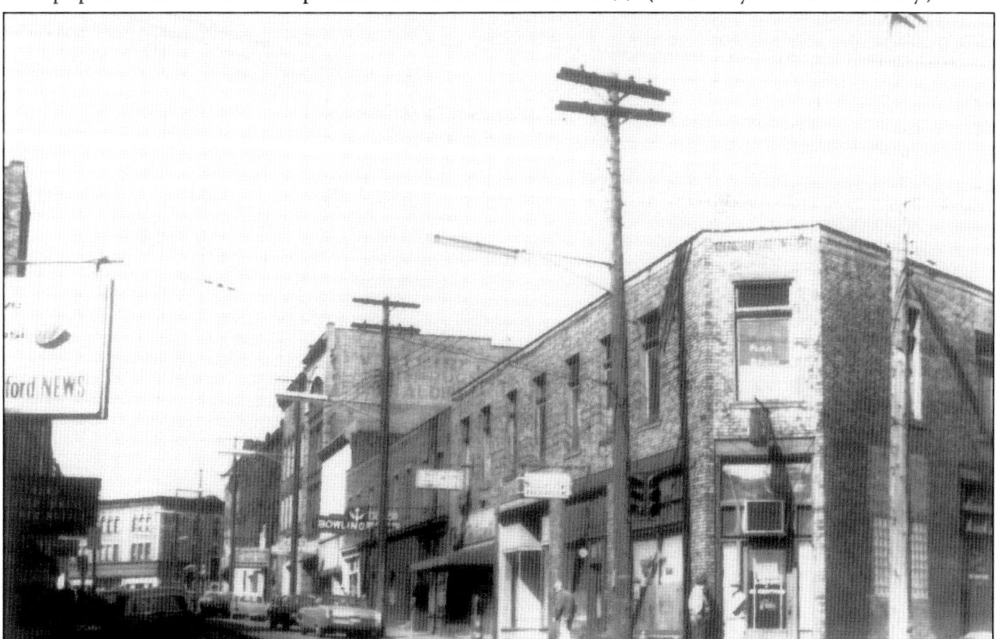

This picture of Pittsburgh Street was taken just before the block was demolished in 1968 for redevelopment. The building in the foreground replaced the Scottdale House after it was destroyed by fire in 1926. (Courtesy Scottdale Bank and Trust Company.)

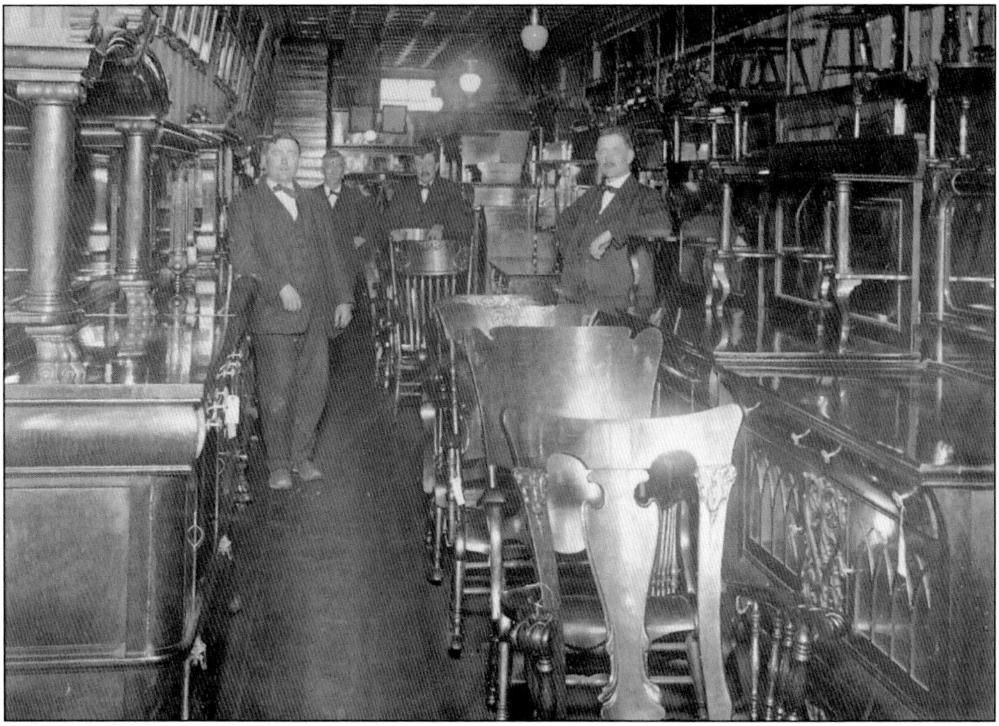

William Ferguson (right) established Ferguson's Furniture Store and undertaking business with James Owens in 1900. After the partnership dissolved in 1910, Ferguson continued to operate the businesses with his two sons, John and George. The furniture store, shown above, consisted of three floors on Pittsburgh Street. William Ferguson also served as burgess (mayor) and was the first president of the Scottdale Chamber of Commerce. (Courtesy Robert Ferguson.)

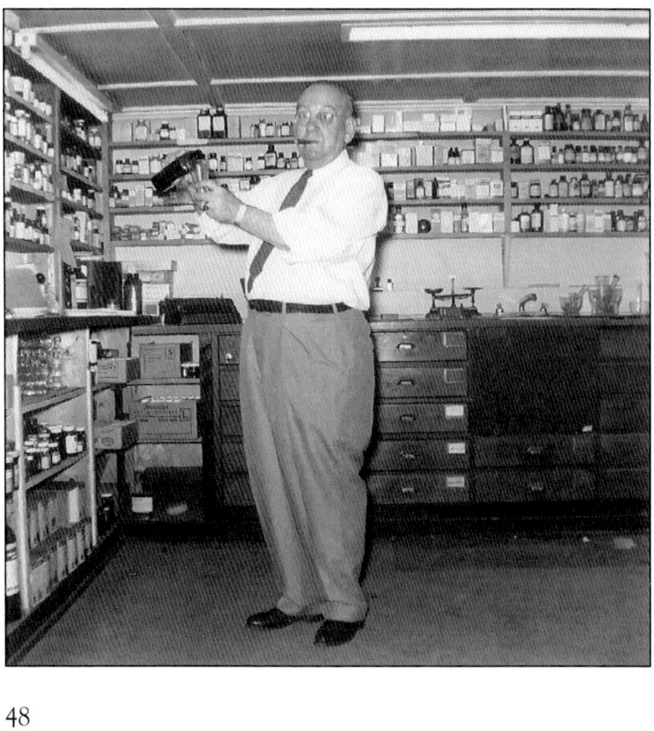

Pharmacist James Lipps, known as "Daddy Day," is shown filling a prescription at Burns Drug Store in 1958. In addition to the pharmacy, Burns Drug Store operated a soda fountain that attracted lunch crowds and students who came by after school. (Courtesy Hilda Schuster.)

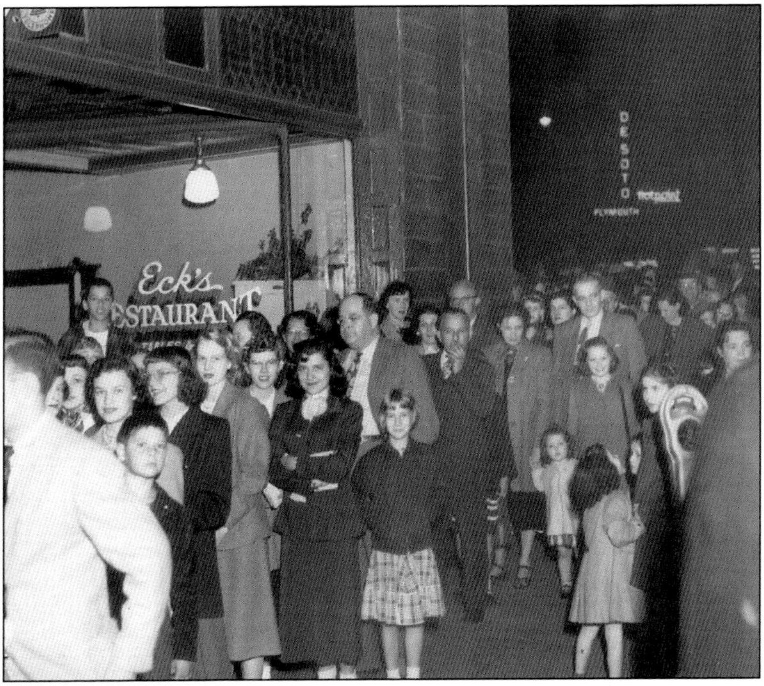

This crowd was waiting to enter the First National Bank on the evening of October 20, 1950. The bank was hosting a party and distributing gifts in celebration of "Know Your Bank Week." The line reportedly extended from Stoner Street to the A&P Store on Chestnut Street. Note the signs in the background advertising the products of Kepner Motors. (Courtesy Marilyn Gaut.)

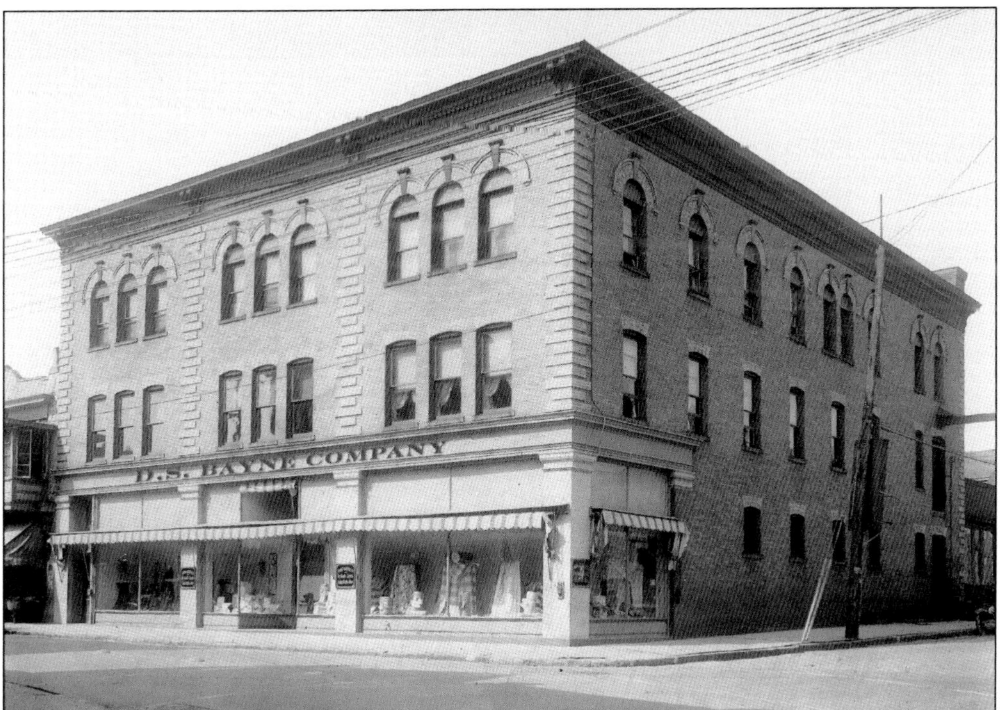

The corner of Pittsburgh and Spring Streets was home to the N.S. Parker Department Store, an Acme Market, and McCrorey's. In this 1929 photograph, the building was occupied by the D.S. Bayne Company, which offered a variety of merchandise ranging from carpets and fabrics to clothing. (Courtesy Carol Tacconi.)

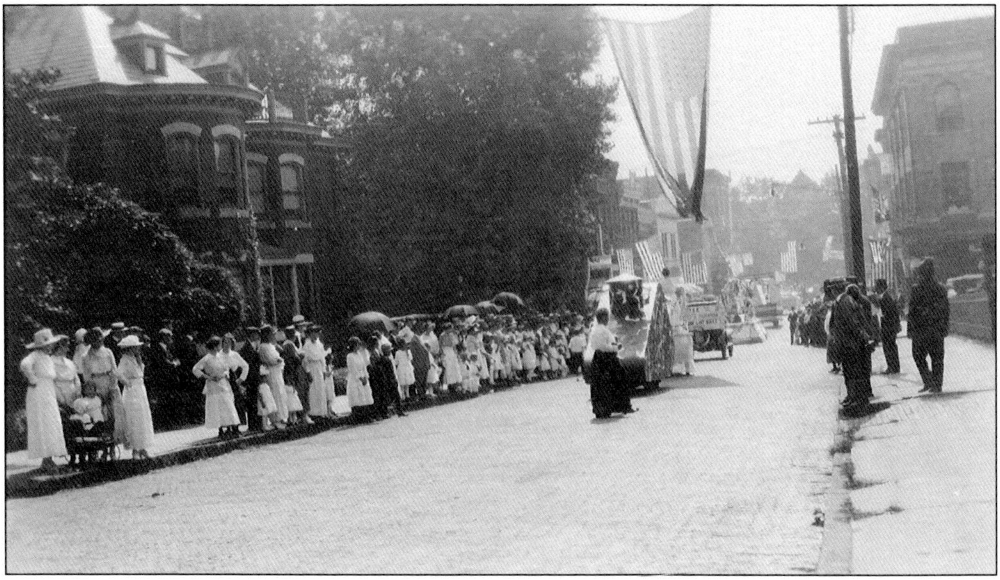

A c. 1910 Fourth of July parade passes the elegant residence of Abraham C. Overholt on Pittsburgh Street. The peaked roof of the Arcade Theatre is partially visible in the distance, to the right of the second utility pool. Overholt was an officer in the First National Bank of Scottdale and president of the National Foundry and Pipe Works.

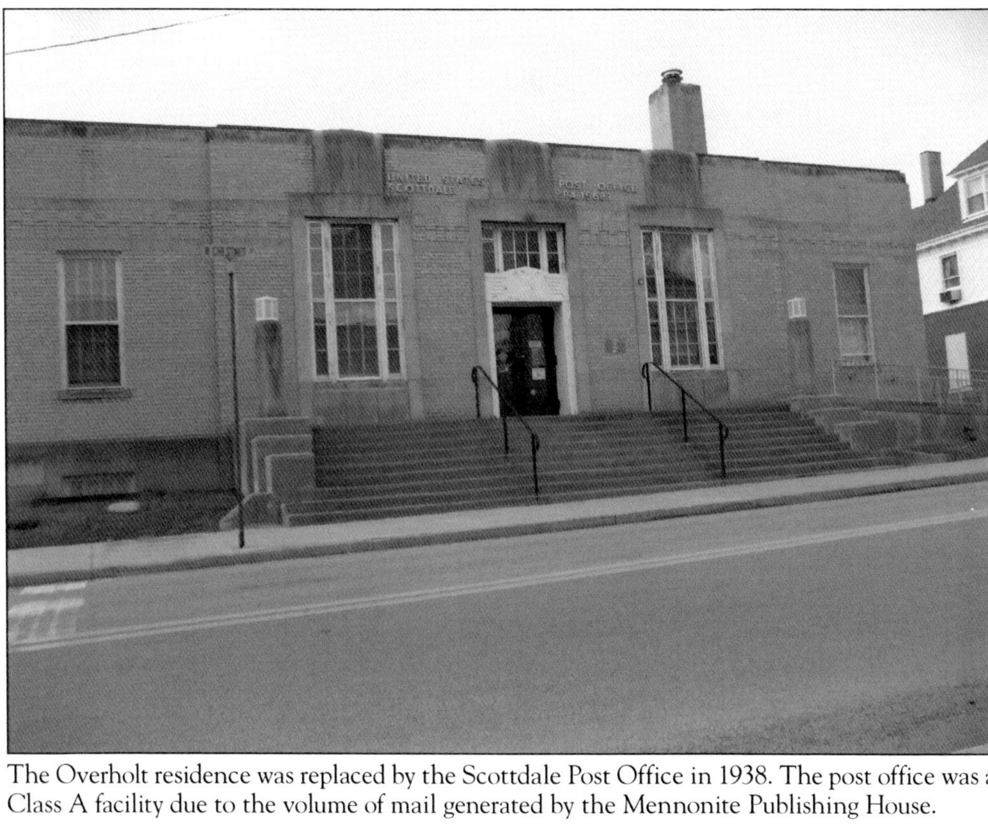

The Overholt residence was replaced by the Scottdale Post Office in 1938. The post office was a Class A facility due to the volume of mail generated by the Mennonite Publishing House.

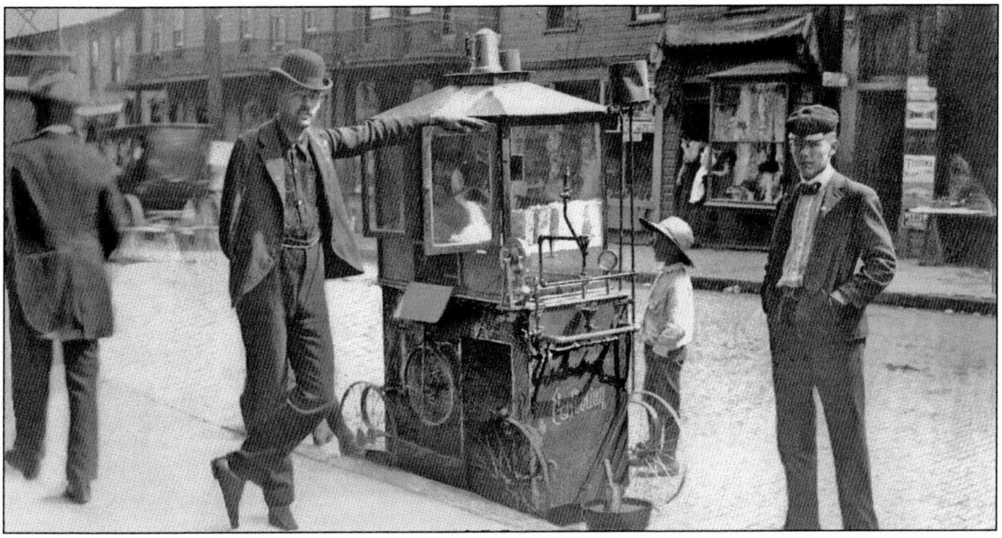

William Seaman, also known as "Popcorn Bill," is pictured here around 1900 on Broadway with his popcorn maker, which he pushed on the streets of Scottdale and neighboring Mount Pleasant. In 1919, the small concession evolved into Seaman's Wholesale Company, which distributes confectionery, tobacco, and paper products throughout several counties in Western Pennsylvania. (Copyright William Seaman Jr.)

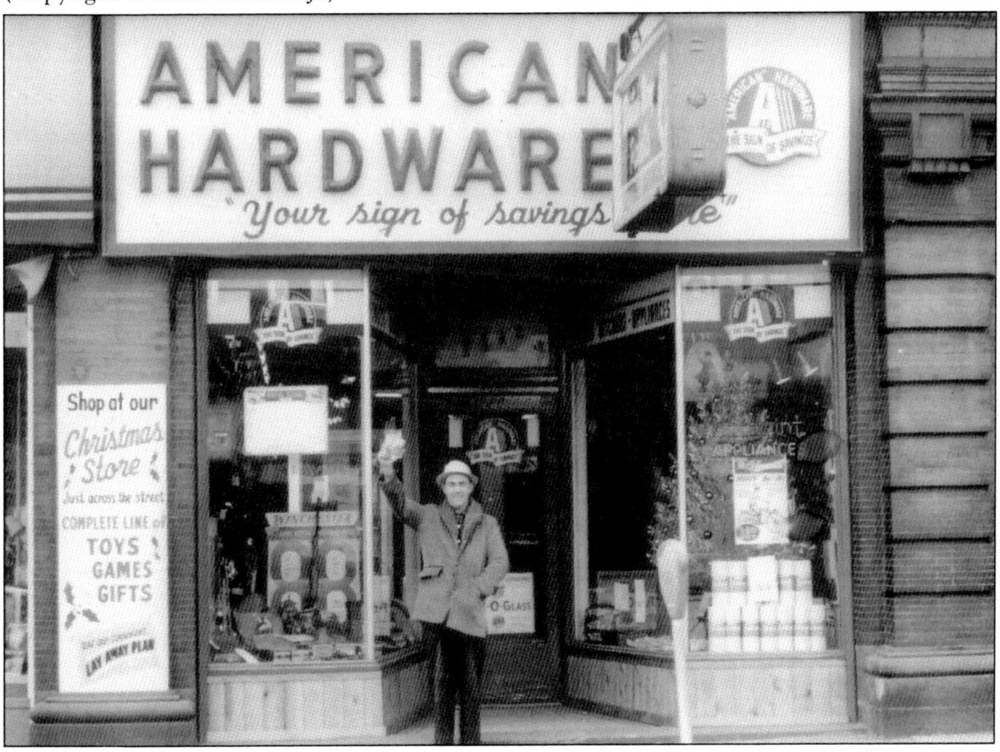

The American Hardware Store, located in the Eicher Graft building at 237 Pittsburgh Street, was owned by Don Zimmerman. He opened in 1950 during the Christmas season and subsequently expanded the store to include hunting and fishing supplies. The business closed in the late 1970s. (Courtesy Don Zimmerman family.)

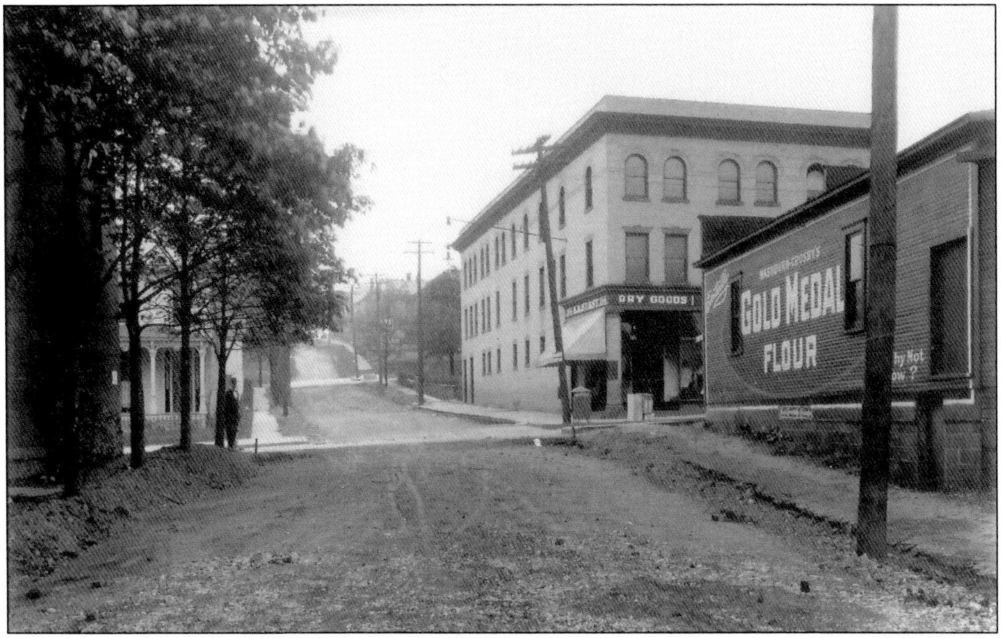

The Hurst Department Store dominates this 1915 scene on the corner of North Hickory and Pittsburgh Streets. The building was erected by Henry Hurst, whose family was prominent in the Mount Pleasant area. Apartments occupied the top floors. Frank Kapr purchased the property and replaced the building with a family garden, which is a popular spot for reflection, summer outings, weddings, and prom pictures. (Courtesy Scottdale Bank and Trust Company.)

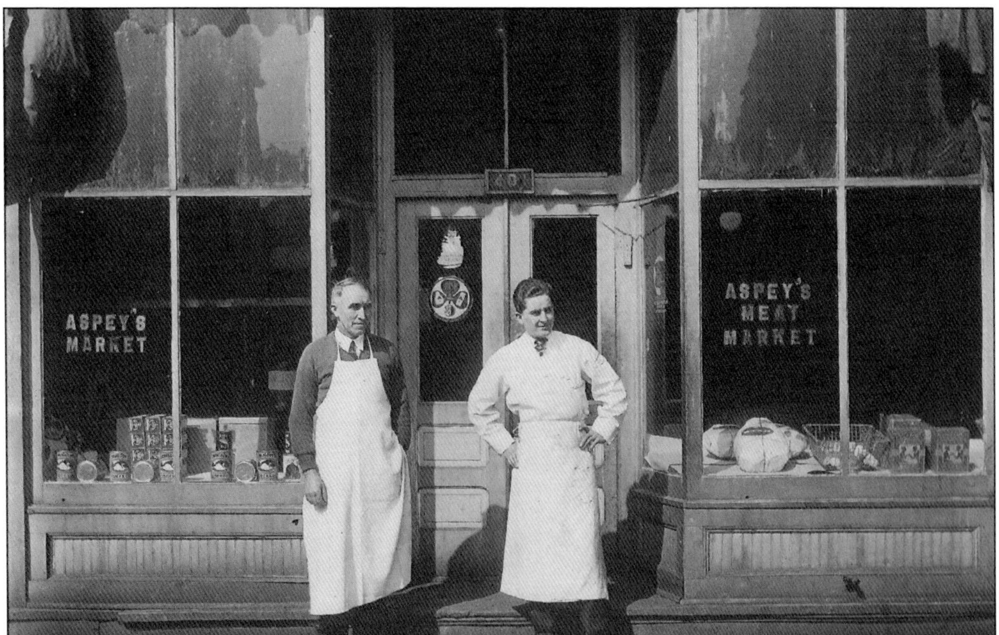

The building advertising Gold Medal Flour (shown in the previous picture) was the location of Aspey's Market at 401 Pittsburgh Street. Pictured in front of the building around 1925 are Oliver Aspey (left) and Patrick Shean. (Courtesy Joseph Hawk.)

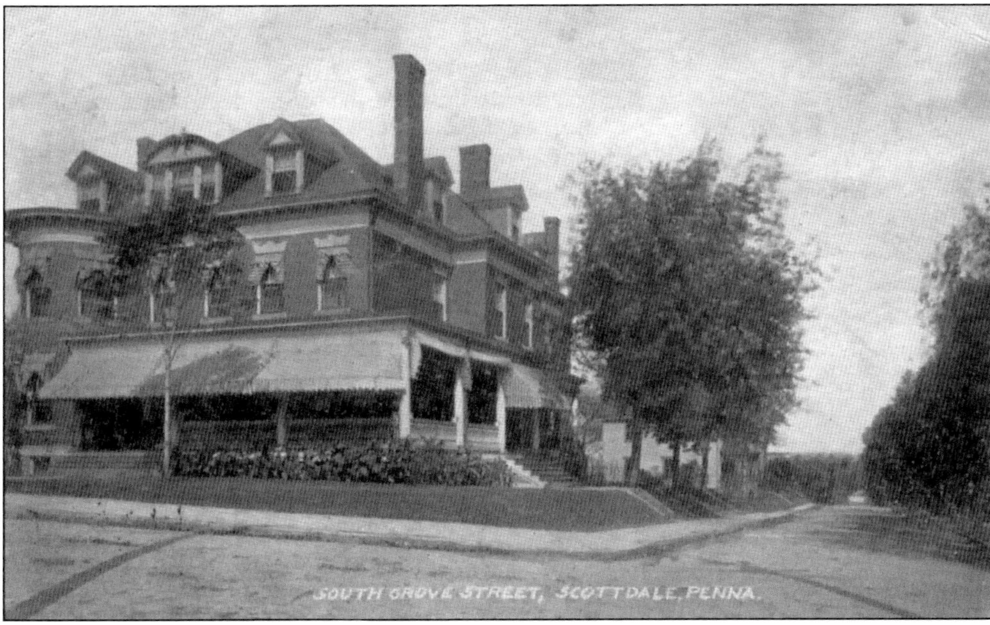

Abraham L. Keister occupied this spacious home on the corner of North Pittsburgh and Grove Streets. This picture dates from 1910. Keister was a president of the First National Bank and a founding director of the Scottdale Electric Light and Power Company and the Old Meadow Rolling Mill. He also served as U.S. Representative from the 22nd Congressional District of Pennsylvania between 1912 and 1914. The property is currently owned by James Hill.

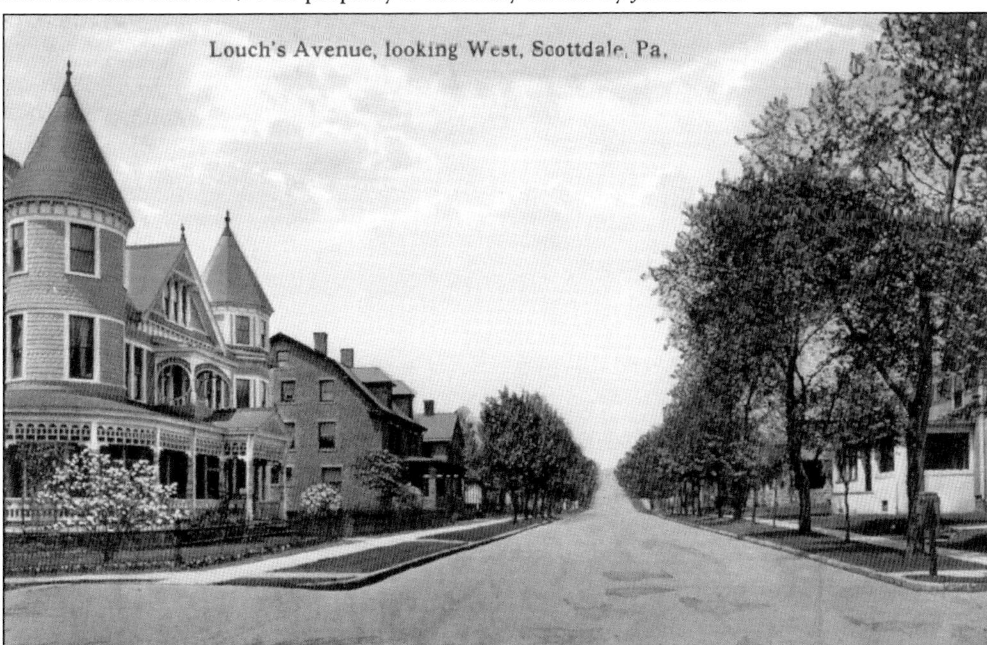

Other prominent businessmen lived within a short distance of Pittsburgh Street. At left is the c. 1910 Loucks Avenue residence of Walter Glasgow, assistant general superintendent of the H.C. Frick Coke Company. He was also the first secretary of mines and served two Pennsylvania governors, John S. Fisher and Gifford Pinchot. Currently, the house is owned by R. Grabiak.

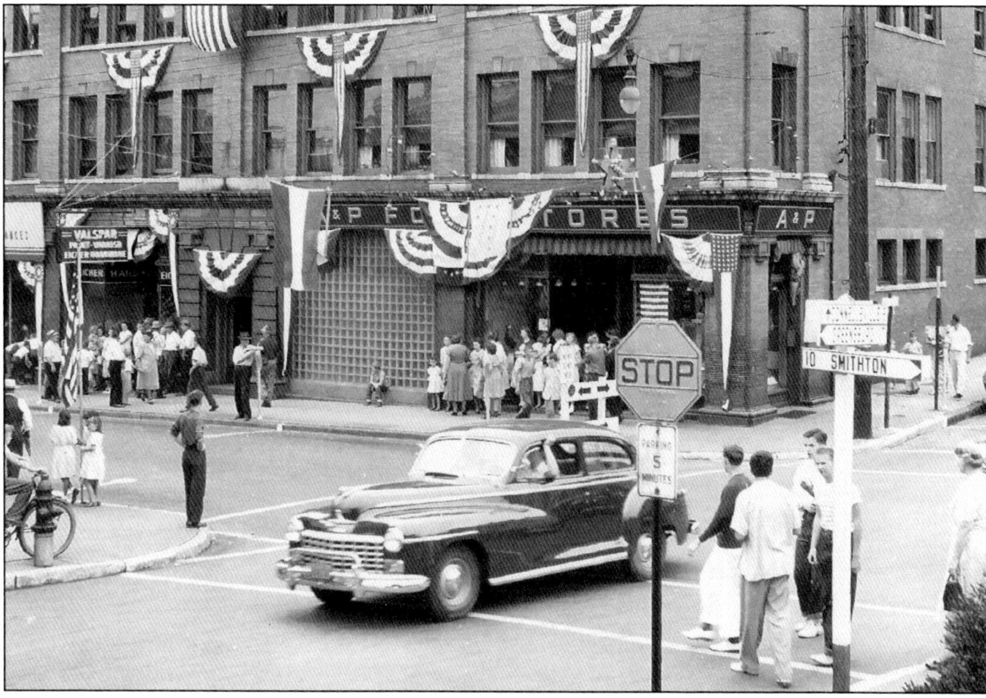

The A&P Store on the corner of Pittsburgh and Chestnut Streets was decorated for Scottdale's 75th-anniversary celebration in 1949. (Courtesy Chuck King.)

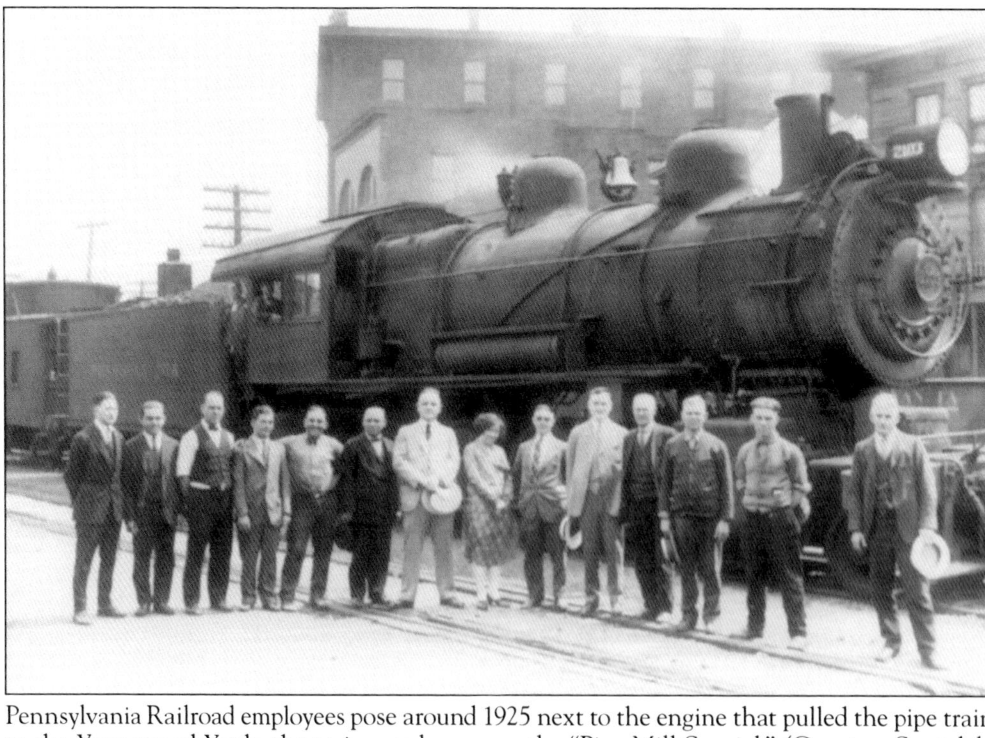

Pennsylvania Railroad employees pose around 1925 next to the engine that pulled the pipe train to the Youngwood Yards; the train was known as the "Pipe Mill Special." (Courtesy Scottdale Bank and Trust Company.)

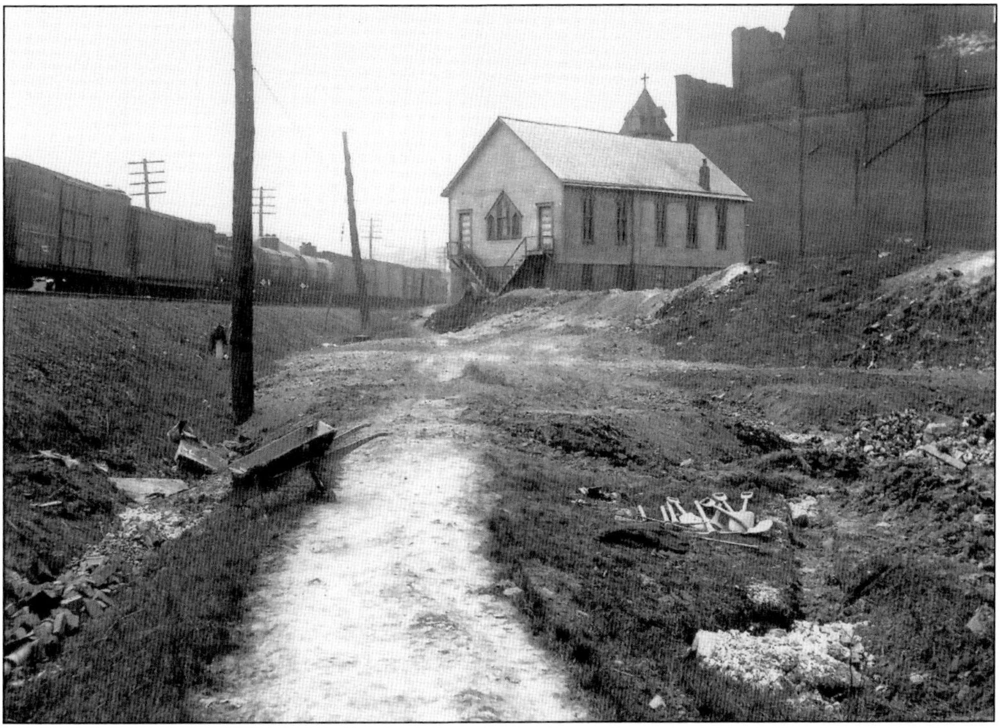

This April 5, 1926, photograph shows the Morningstar Baptist Church and the remaining walls of the Scottdale Brewery before Broadway was extended from Park Avenue to North Chestnut Street. The brewery was destroyed by fire several years before this photograph was taken. (Courtesy Scottdale Bank and Trust Company.)

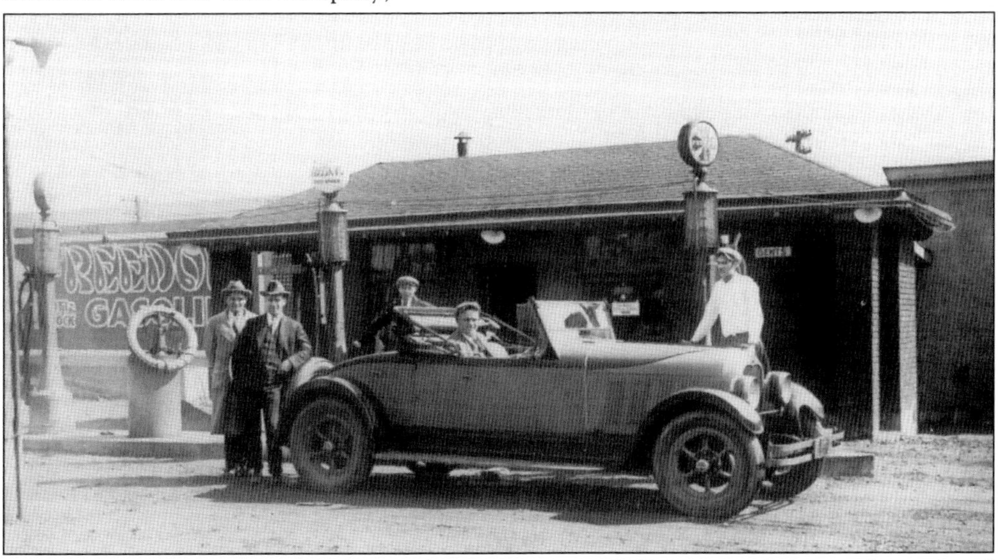

Broadway was a convenient fuel stop when it was part of US Route 119. It was the preferred location for gas stations, auto repair shops, and car dealerships. This c. 1929 image shows the Freedom gas station on North Broadway that was operated by Charley Wiley, who is standing behind the front of the car wearing a white shirt. The car's owner, "Pug" Cafferty, is behind the wheel. (Courtesy Scottdale Bank and Trust Company.)

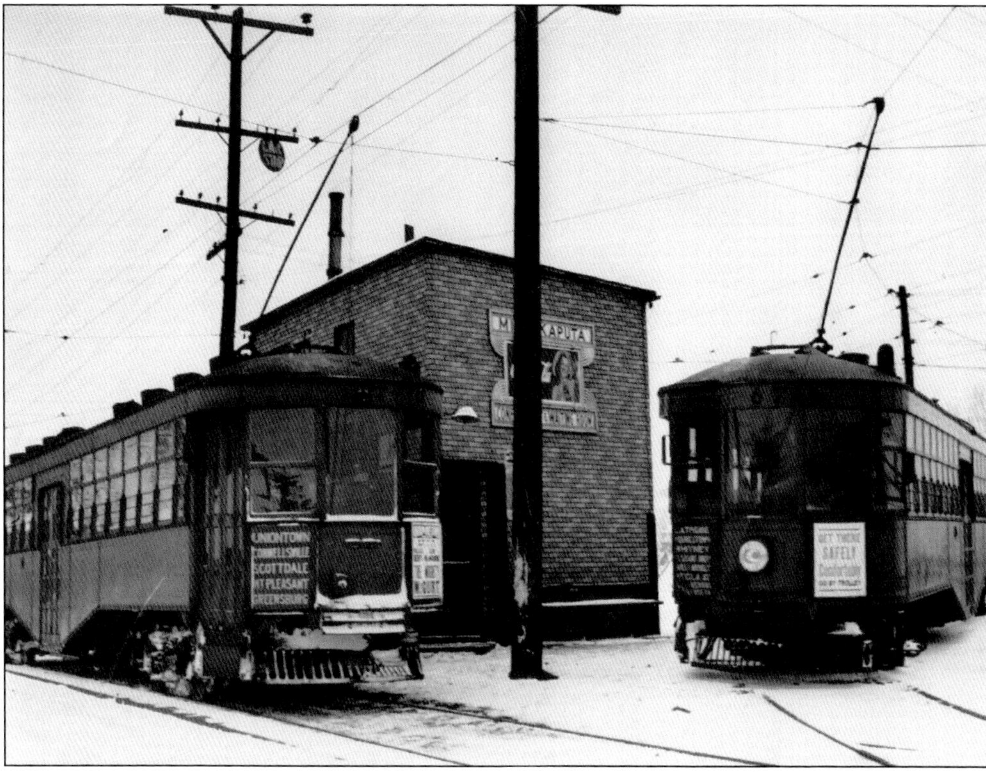

West Penn streetcars meet around 1938 on North Broadway at a waiting room next to the US Casket Company. The car on the right is en route to Latrobe via Mount Pleasant, Whitney, and Hecla. It will also stop at West Overton and Iron Bridge. The other car, from Connellsville, is heading north through Alverton, Tarrs, Ruffsdale, New Stanton, and Youngwood to its scheduled destination in Greensburg.

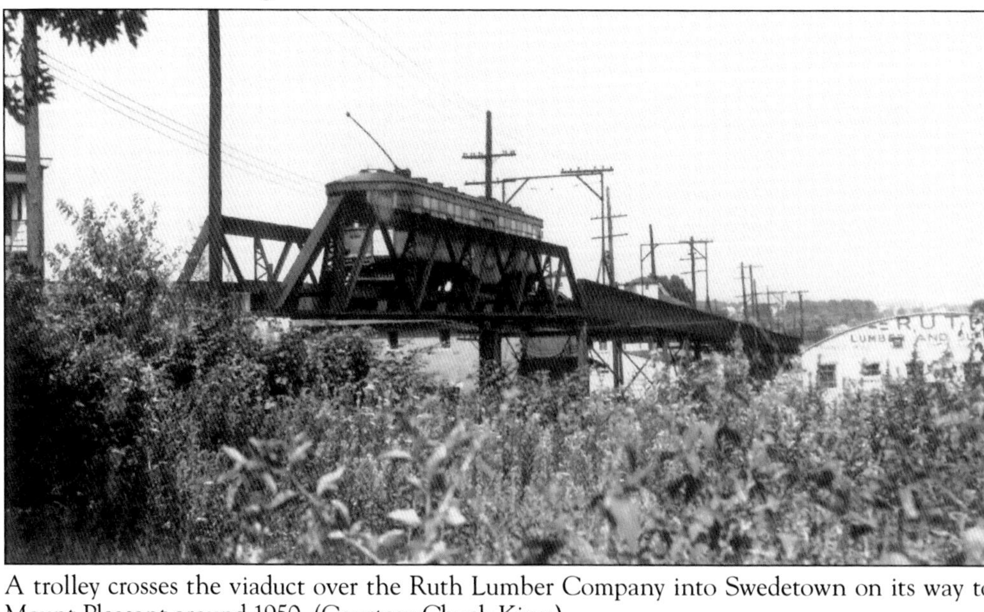

A trolley crosses the viaduct over the Ruth Lumber Company into Swedetown on its way to Mount Pleasant around 1950. (Courtesy Chuck King.)

Pictured around 1929, the silos at the Ruth Lumber Company, below the streetcar viaduct, held sand, gravel, and coal ready for distribution. In addition to the silos, Ruth operated a planing mill and constructed many buildings in the region, including tenement houses for the H.C. Frick Coke Company. The lumber company was started in 1873, owned briefly by Jacob S. and Peter Loucks, and sold to J.W. Ruth in 1888. (Courtesy Carol Tacconi.)

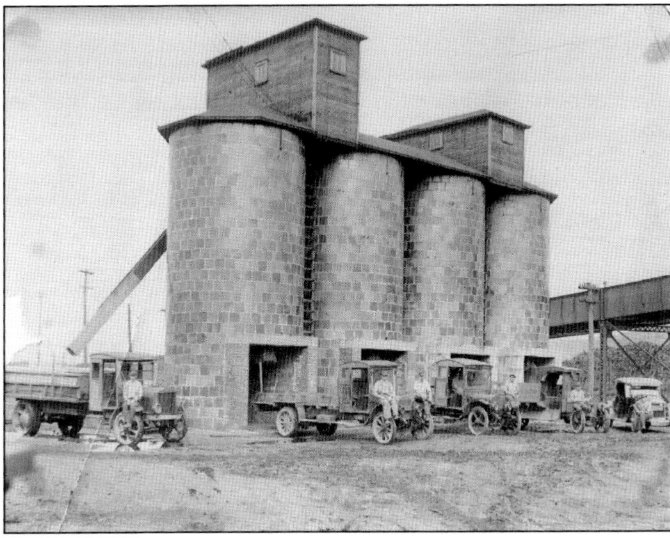

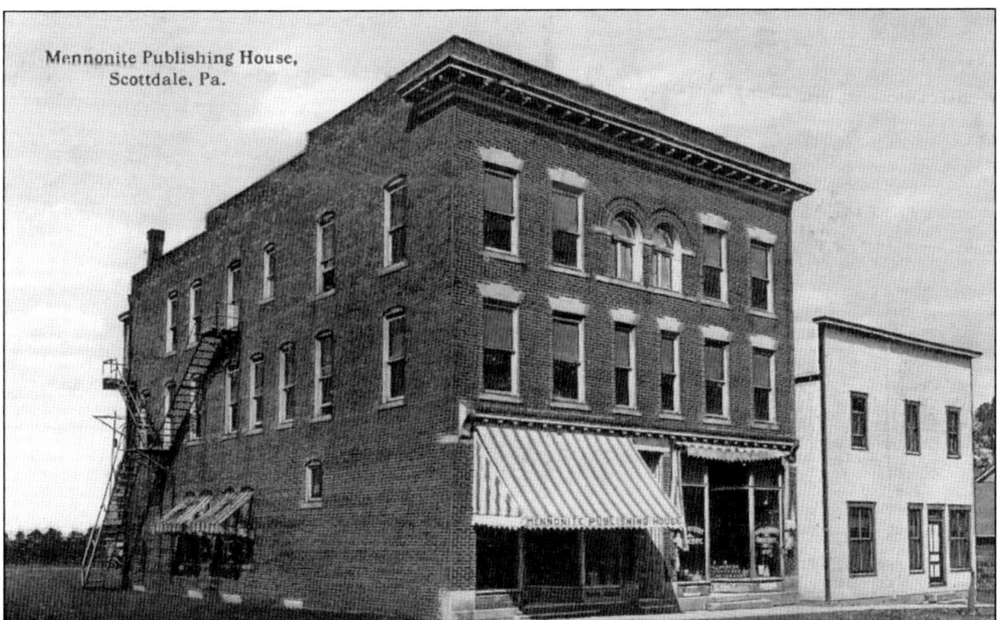

The Mennonite Publishing House was established by Rev. Aaron Loucks in 1908 with support from the local Mennonite community. Within a short period of time, it became the printing center for the religious denomination, employing approximately 250 individuals. Its copyright, the Herald Press, became recognized throughout the world. This is the company's first building, located at 616 Walnut Street.

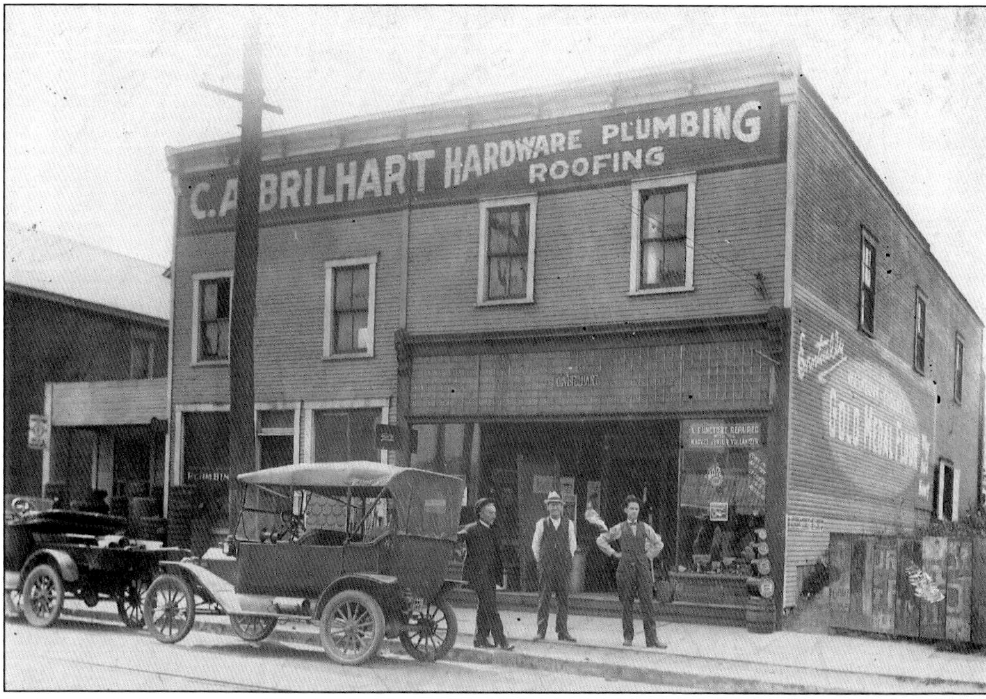

In this 1920 photograph, Charles Anthony (C.A.) Brilhart stands between two unidentified men in front of his establishment on South Broadway. Reportedly, the current brick structure was built covering the original one (shown here) in order to keep the business open during the rebuilding process. (Courtesy James Brilhart.)

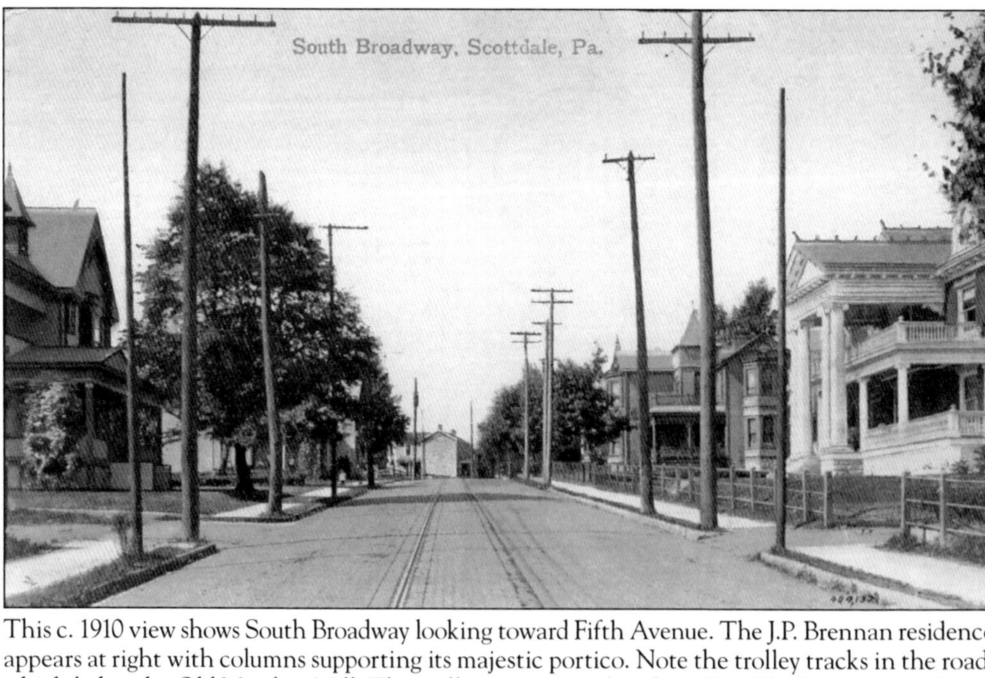

This c. 1910 view shows South Broadway looking toward Fifth Avenue. The J.P. Brennan residence appears at right with columns supporting its majestic portico. Note the trolley tracks in the road, which led to the Old Meadow Mill. The trolley route was closed in 1931. The Brennan residence is currently owned by Patricia Hill.

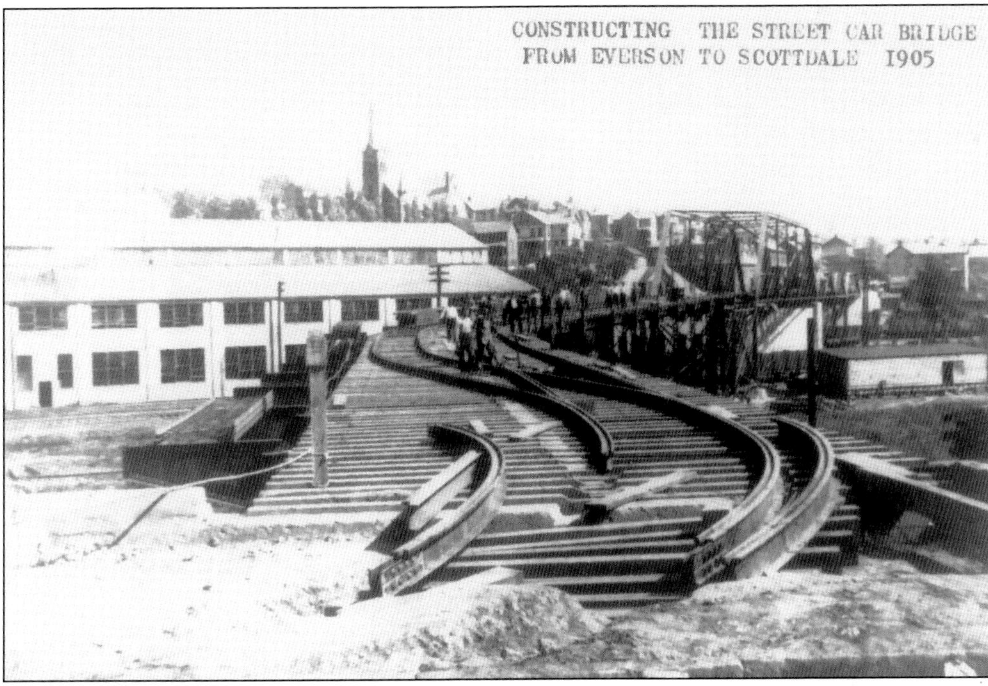

Workers lay tracks during the construction of the West Penn Bridge, which connected Brown Street in Everson with South Broadway in Scottdale. For many years, the bridge was limited to streetcar traffic. A pedestrian walkway and a paved surface for vehicular traffic were added later.

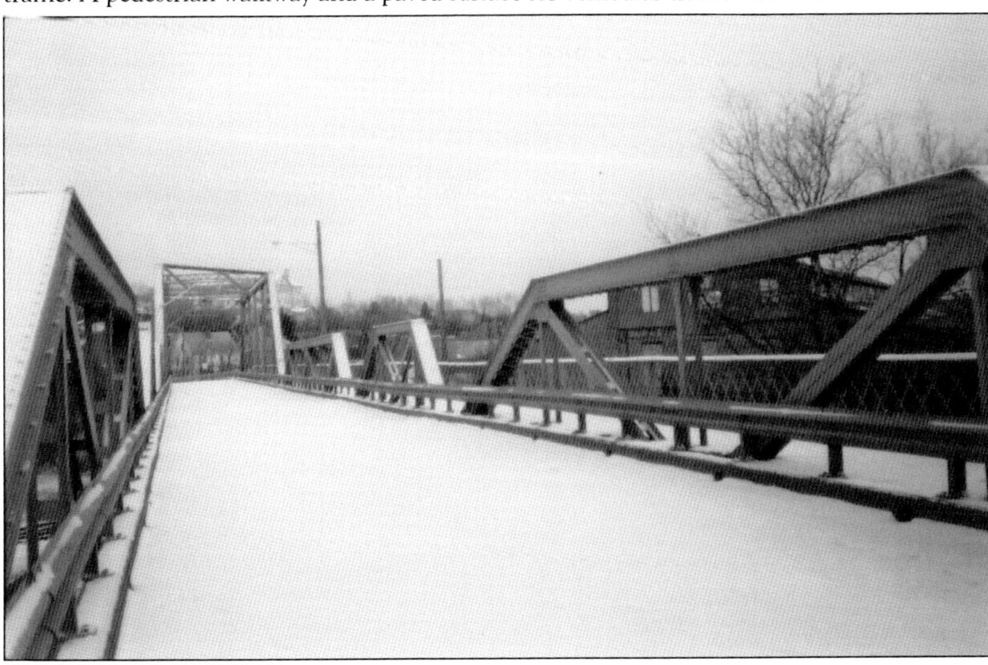

After West Penn ceased operations on its main line between Uniontown and Greensburg in 1952, the bridge was rebuilt with a concrete deck and reinforced steel, as shown above. In 1988, it was declared unsafe and was demolished; a new structure opened in 1990. (Courtesy Michael Banaszak.)

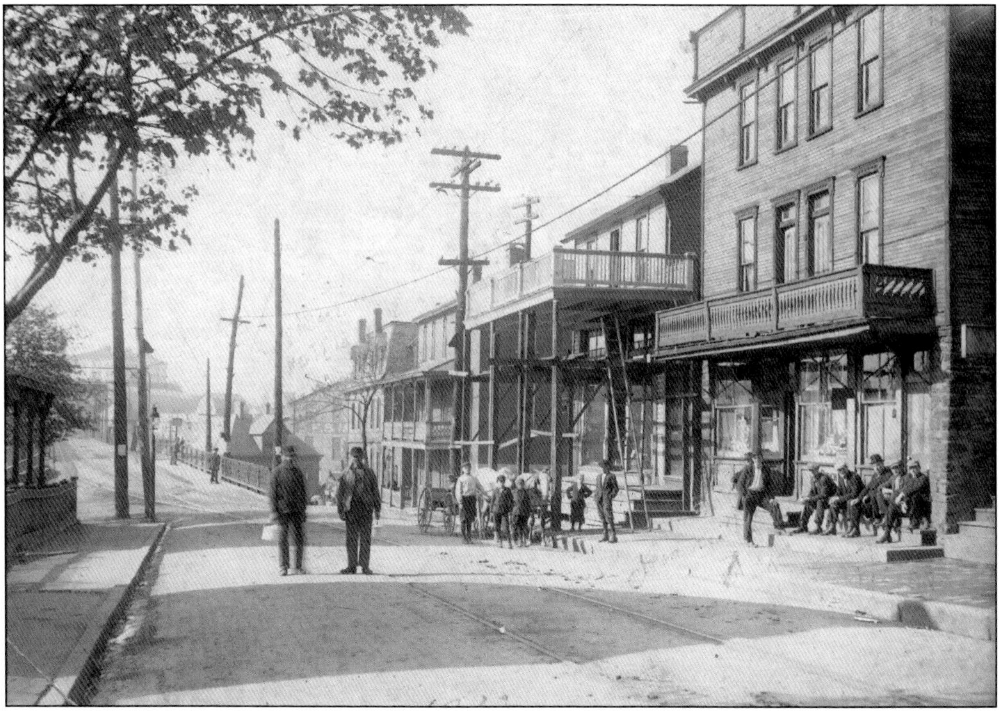

Brown Street was the main road through Everson after the construction of the West Penn bridge. In this 1912 image, Winsek's store is visible in the foreground, followed by John Ryan's grocery store on the corner of Vance and Brown Streets. The original Pisula family residence is next to the bridge, beyond the first utility pool, followed by the Everson House. The Everson House was one of three hotels in the borough.

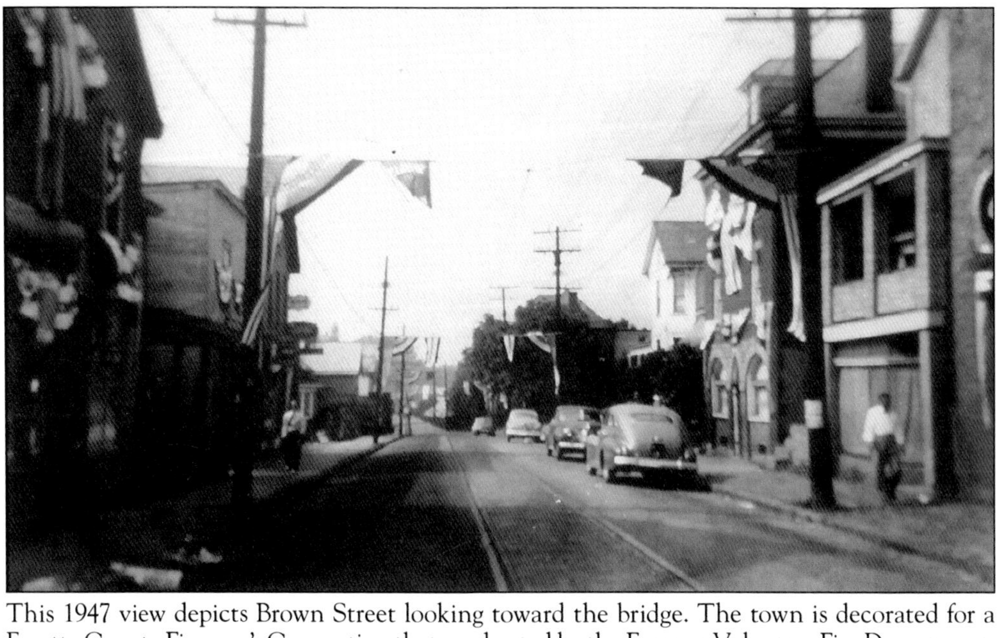

This 1947 view depicts Brown Street looking toward the bridge. The town is decorated for a Fayette County Fireman's Convention that was hosted by the Everson Volunteer Fire Department. (Courtesy John Farrah family.)

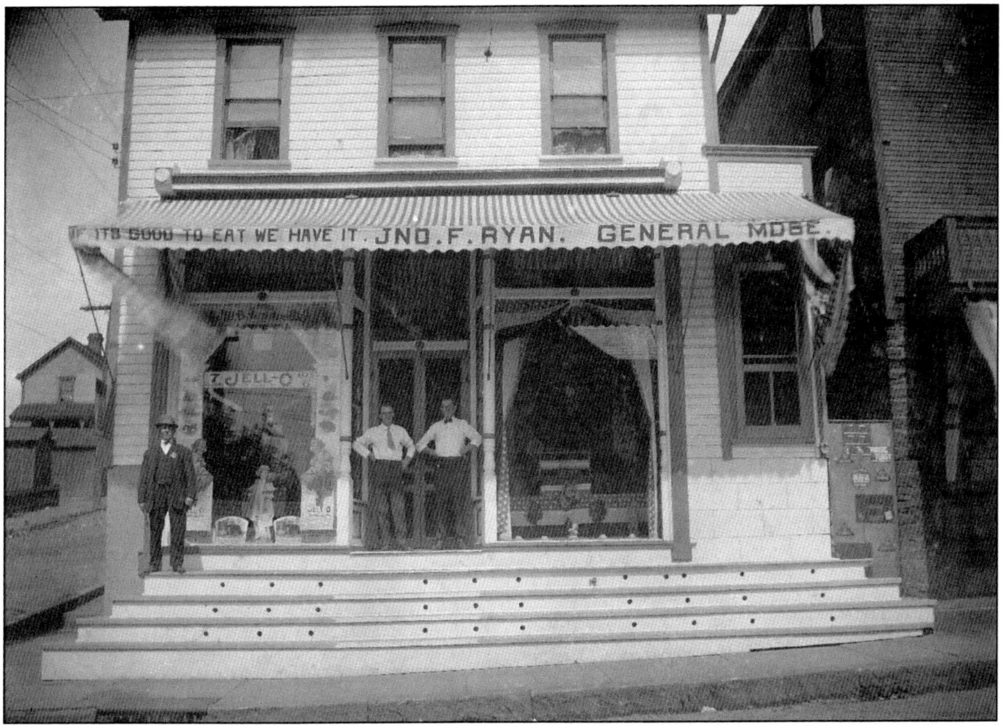

This c. 1900 photograph shows John Ryan's grocery store before the porch was built over the sidewalk. (Courtesy Marion Mitrisin.)

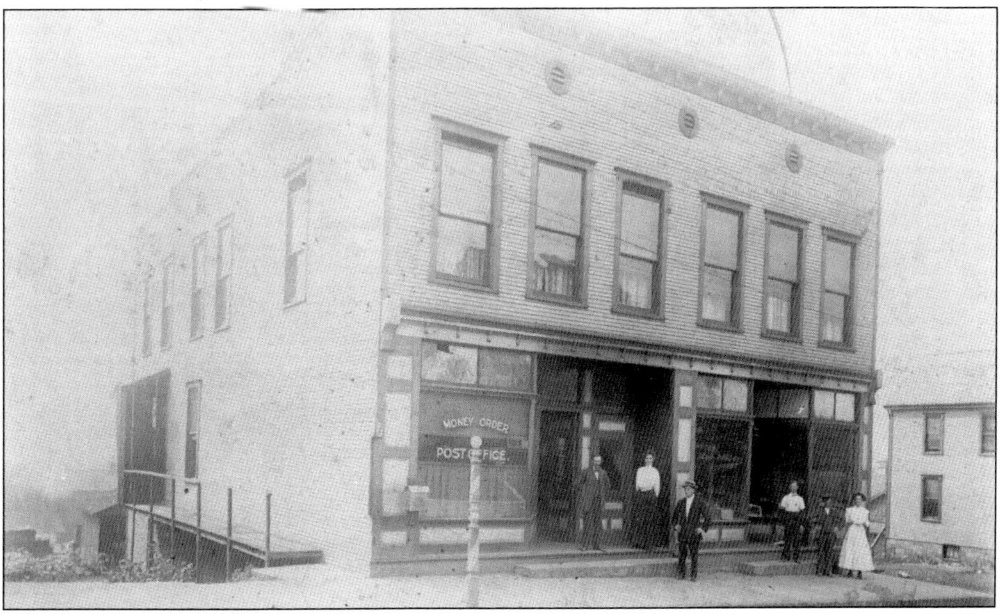

In this 1903 photograph, Everson postmaster William Reese, standing next to the post office door, and his clerk, Elizabeth Hill, pose in front of the first Tyrone Club building on Brown Street. The club was later expanded to three floors that included a bowling alley, pool room, meat market, and dance hall in addition to the post office. In 1942, the building was destroyed by a fire that threatened the main business district.

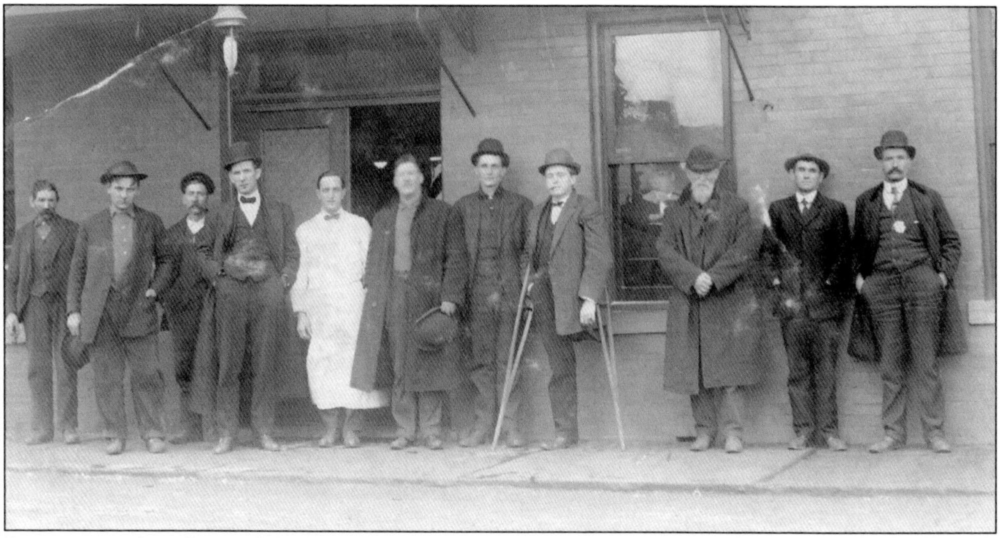

Patrons stand in front of the barroom entrance to the Eureka Hotel, which was located on the corner of Graff and Vance Streets. The hotel advertised a daily rate of $1.50, which included a free bath. The man wearing an apron is the bartender, Mart Shimshock. Charles O'Neil stands on crutches, and police chief Adam Brown is at far right. The other men are unidentified.

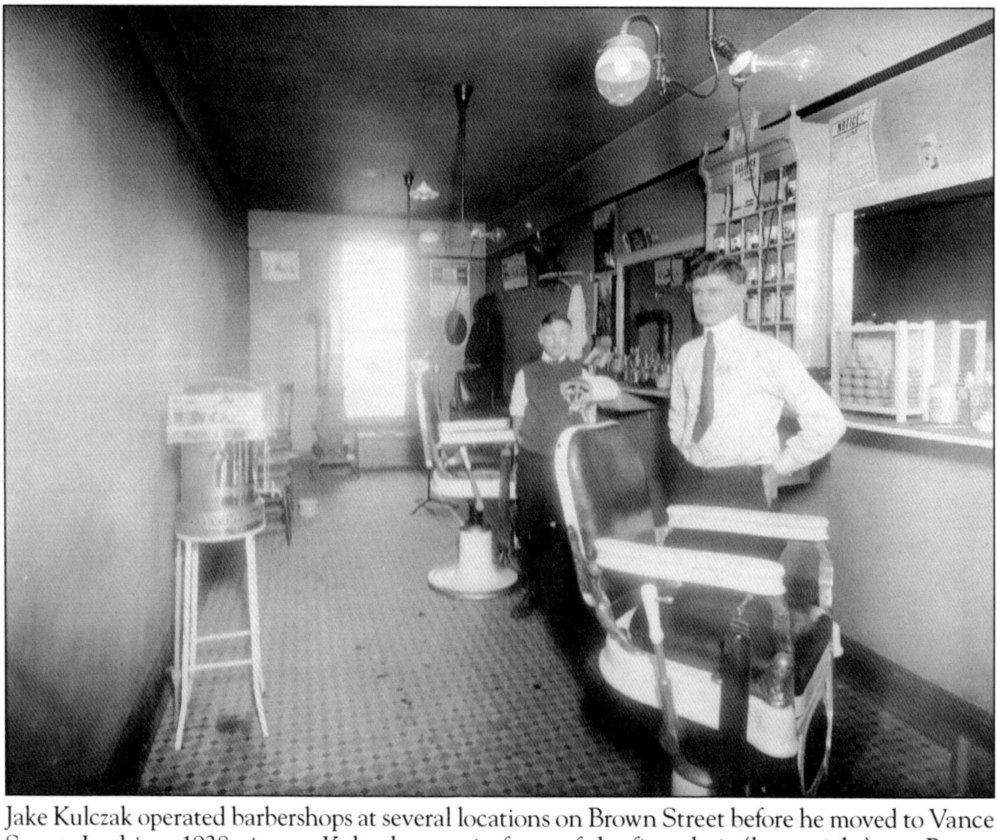

Jake Kulczak operated barbershops at several locations on Brown Street before he moved to Vance Street. In this c. 1938 picture, Kulczak poses in front of the first chair (lower right) at a Brown Street location. The second barber is Frank Swed.

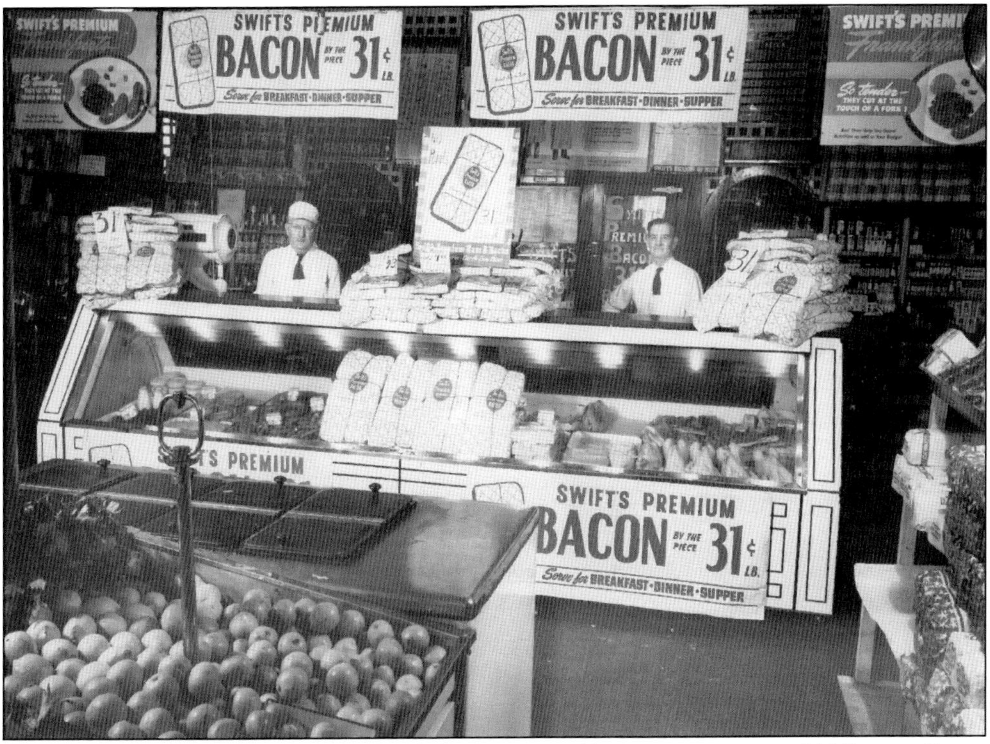

Thomas O'Donnell (left) stands behind the counter of his grocery store at 346 Brown Street around 1942 with employee Richard Parker. During the Great Depression, O'Donnell supplied food to a soup kitchen operated by Everson borough residents for the homeless and unemployed. When O'Donnell retired, the grocery business was operated by William Campbell as a Clover Farm Store.

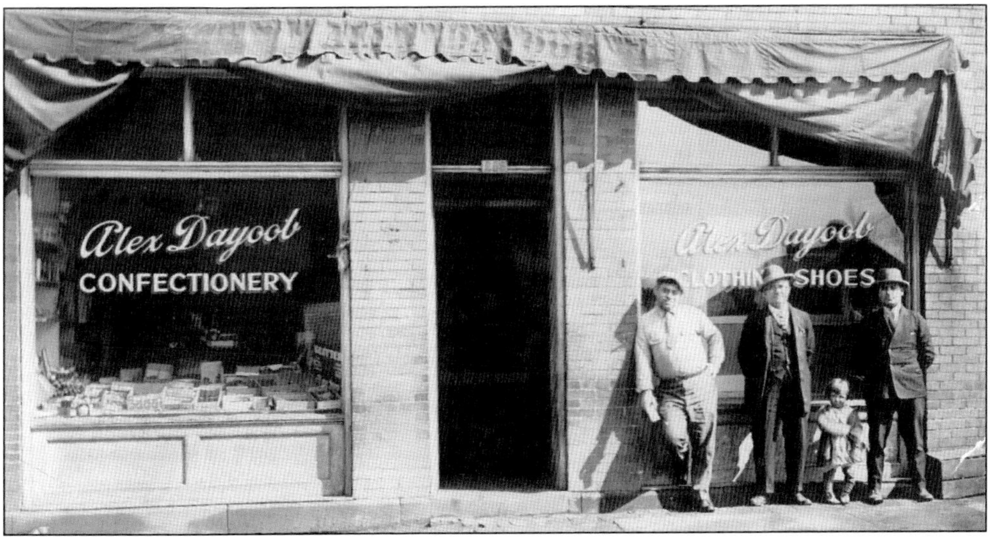

Alex Dayoob (left) leans near the entrance to his candy and clothing store at 253 Brown Street with friends Weimer Baird (center) and Albert Nasser (far right) around1939. The child is unidentified. Dayoob was representative of immigrant families from Lebanon who established businesses in the coke region.

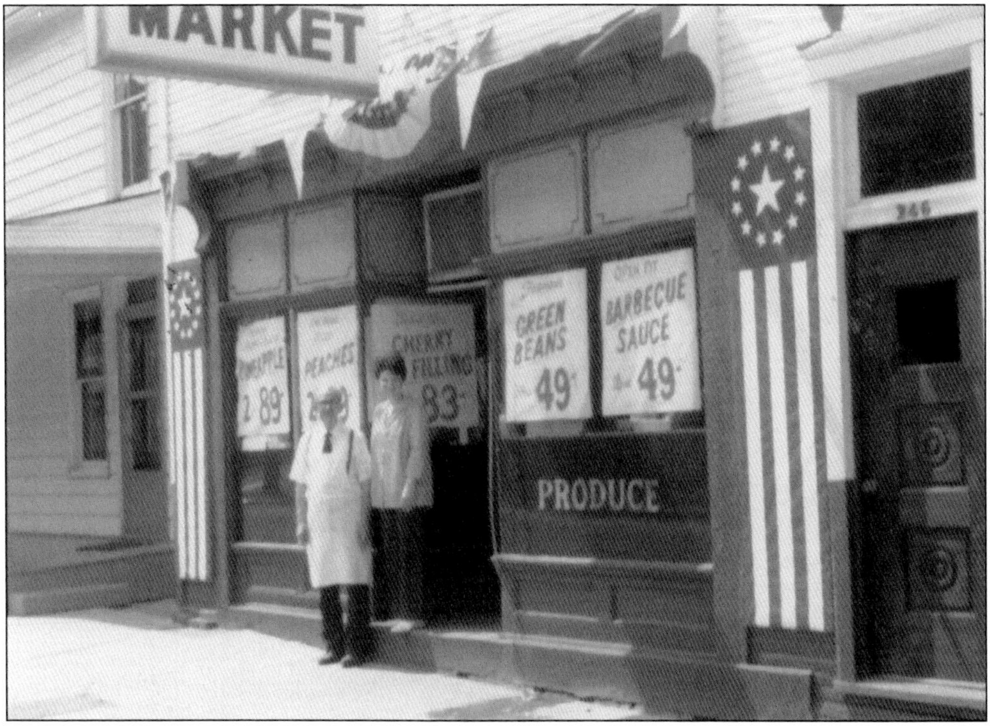

Marion Nowicki is pictured with Loretta Sowinski in front of his grocery store on Brown Street. The front is decorated for the 1976 bicentennial celebration. Nowicki and his wife, Helen Zgorecki, managed an American Store on the site before opening an independent market. (Courtesy Marion Nowicki family.)

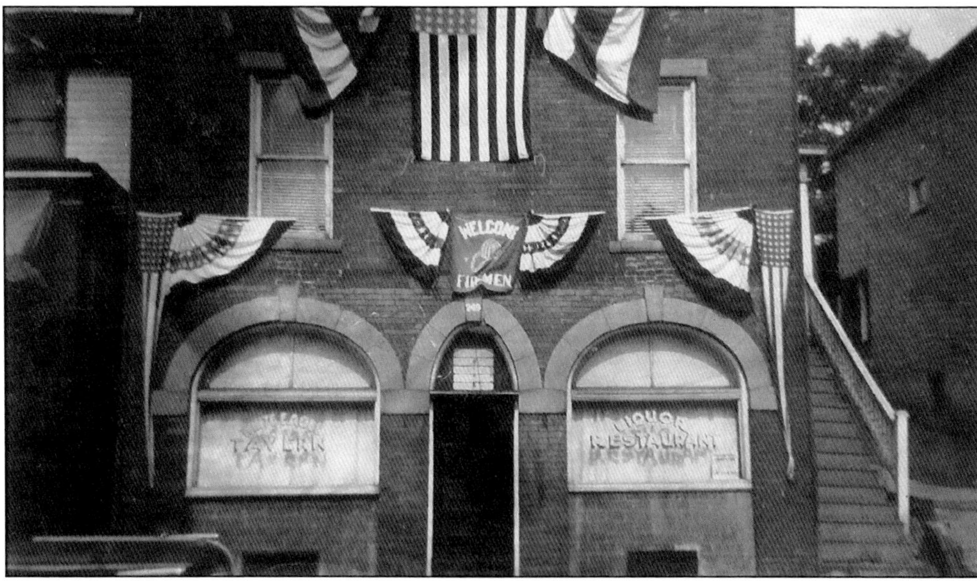

The White Eagle Tavern, pictured here in 1947, was located across Brown Street from Marion's Market. It was operated by Joseph Potocki. After Potocki's death, James and Regina Shandorf continued the business. Before the tavern, the location was home to a Keystone Grocery Store. (Courtesy John Farrah family.)

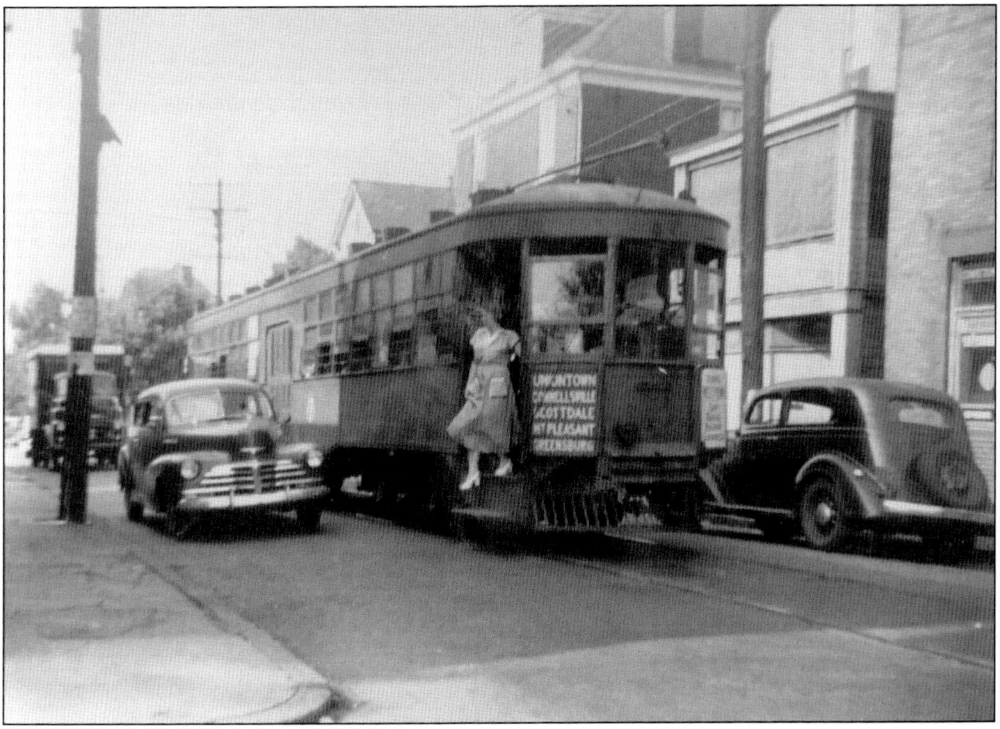

A West Penn streetcar stops to discharge a passenger at the corner of Brown and Shipley Streets in 1941. The car was en route to Connellsville.

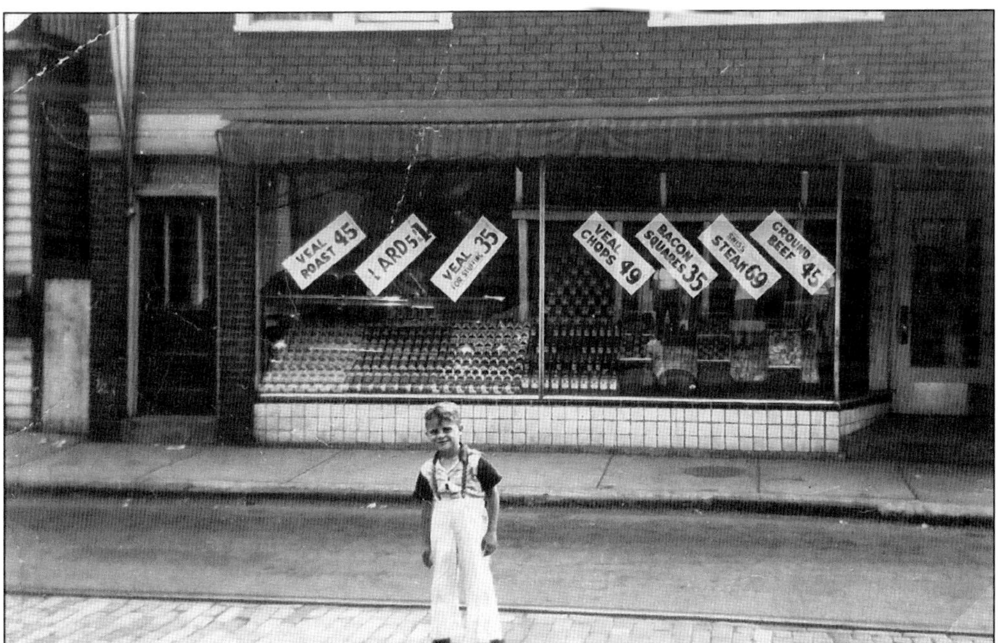

Daniel Farrah stands in the front of the Central Meat Market in 1947. It was operated by John Stankowitz and was known later as the "Red and White Store." (Courtesy John Farrah family.)

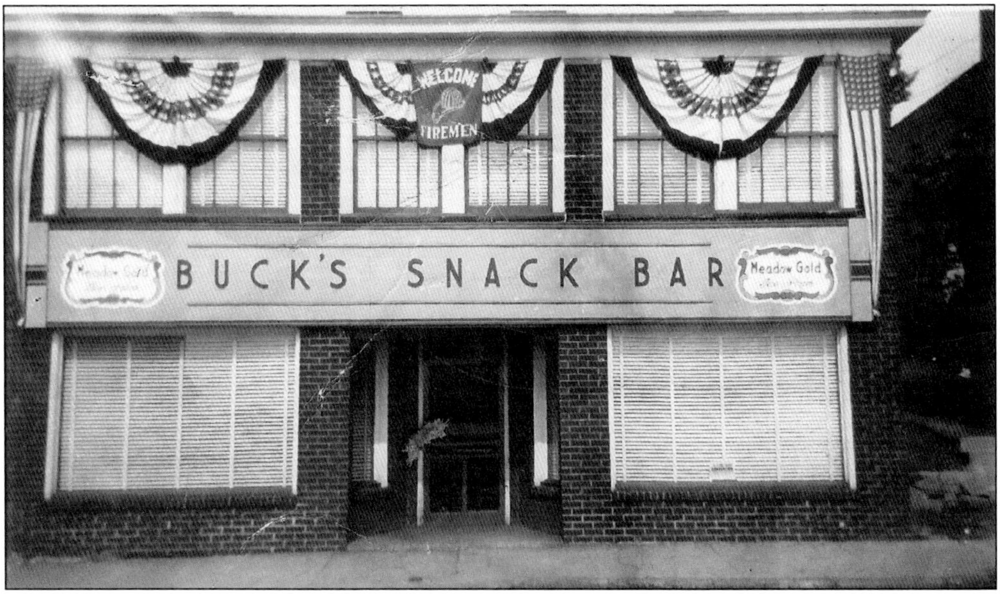

Buck's Snack Bar was the place to go for milk shakes, ice cream, and hot dogs. It was owned by Stanley Wujczk and operated by Michael and Stella Boaza. It closed in the early 1970s. This is now the residence of Michael Banaszak, who restored the basement interior to resemble the original snack bar. (Courtesy John Farrah family.)

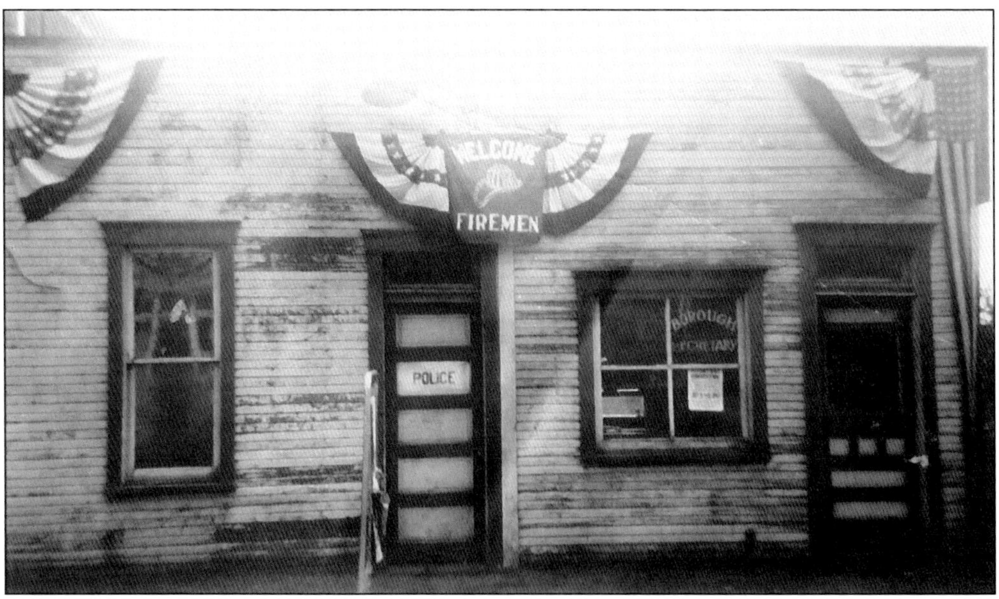

This is the old Everson borough building, which was next to O'Donnell's Store, before the municipal office was moved to its current location at 232 Brown Street in 1957. The old building was subsequently demolished, and the property is currently a vacant lot. (Courtesy John Farrah family.)

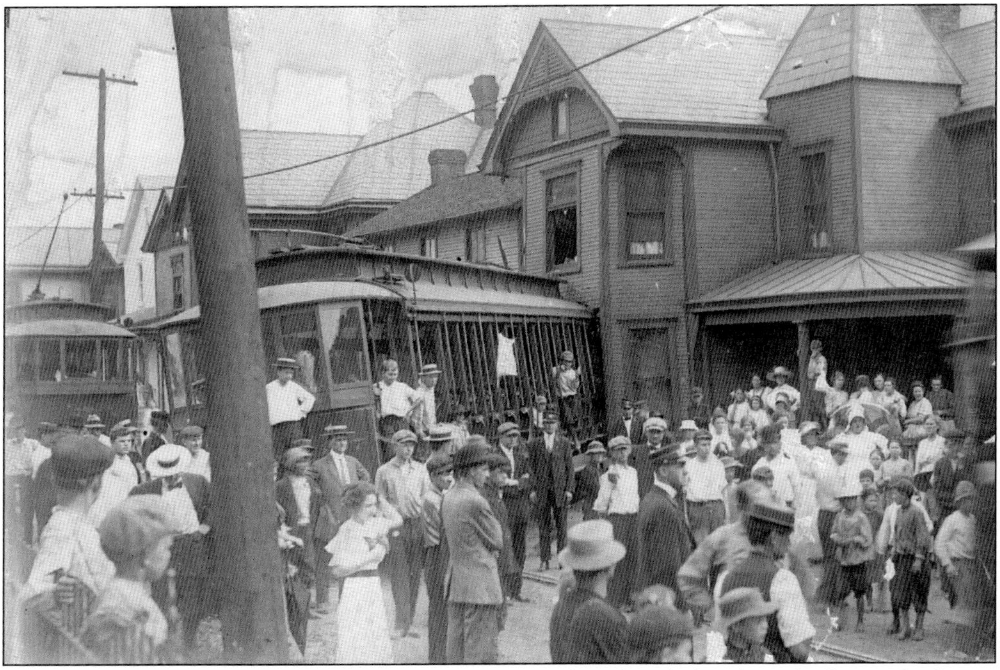

This c. 1925 image shows a West Penn summer car that derailed and crashed into the living room of the Berlin family residence at 504 Brown Street. Reportedly, Nell Berlin, a school music teacher, was playing the piano at the time of the accident.

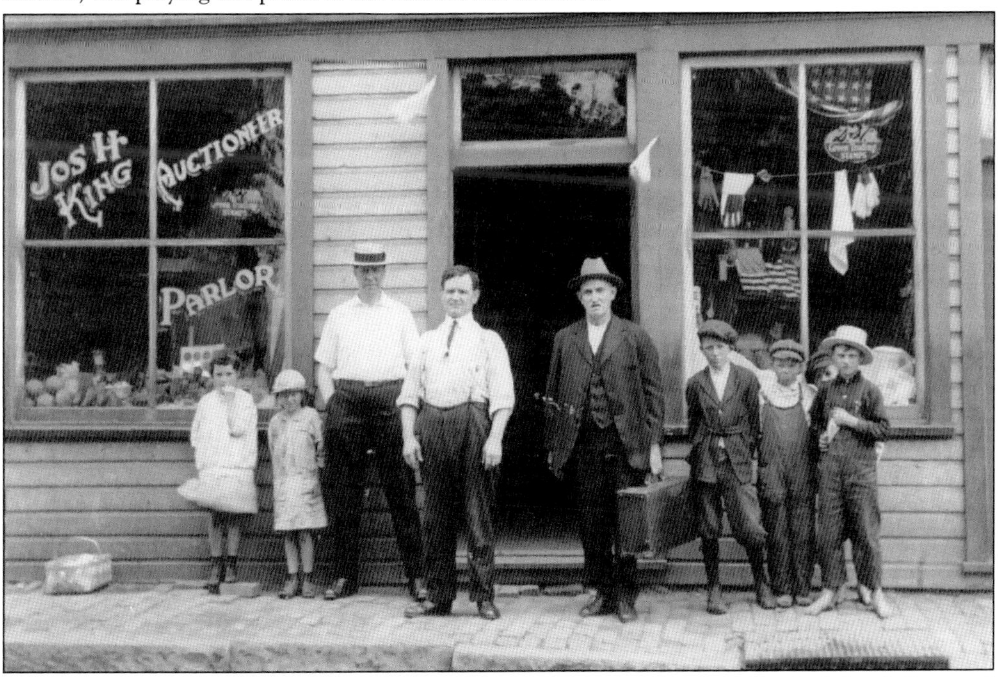

King's Store, shown here around 1912, was across from the Everson Grade School. Pictured here are, from left to right, Theresa King, Katherine O'Shea, "Red" Berlin, Joseph King, and an unidentified salesman. Thomas O'Shea is the second boy to the right of the salesman. The other young men are unidentified.

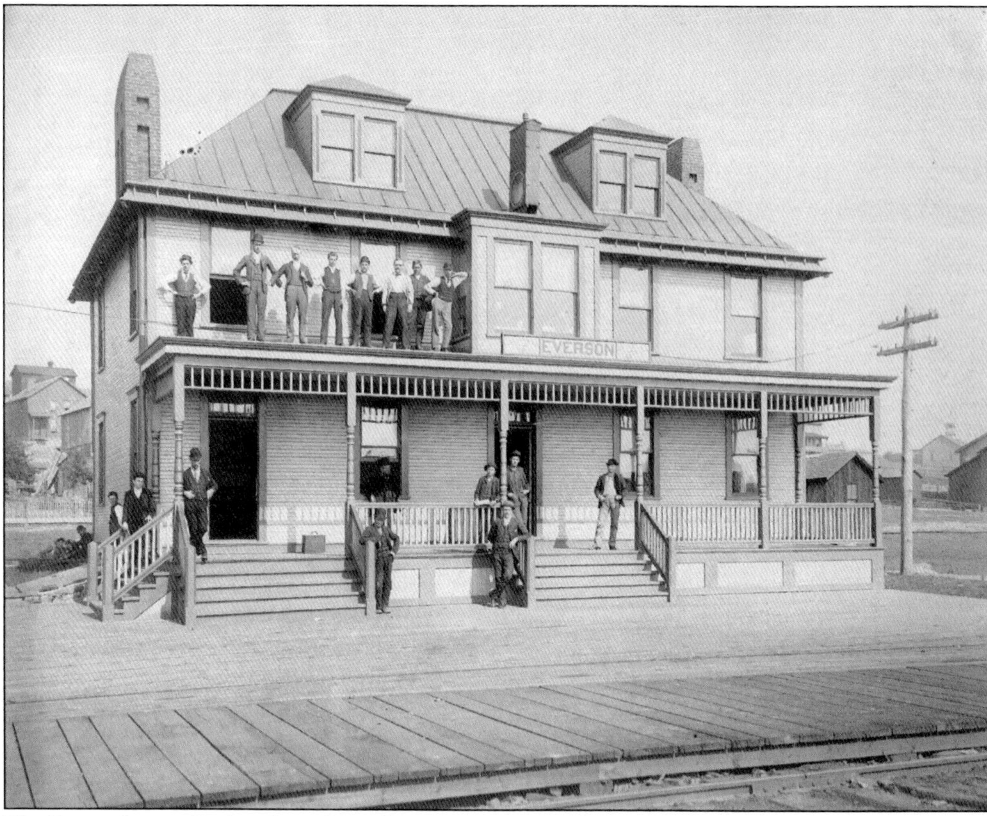

The Pennsylvania Railroad conducted passenger service from this station on Graff Street, pictured around 1920, until the mid-1930s. The building was later purchased by the Everson Veterans of Foreign Wars and remodeled for their first post.

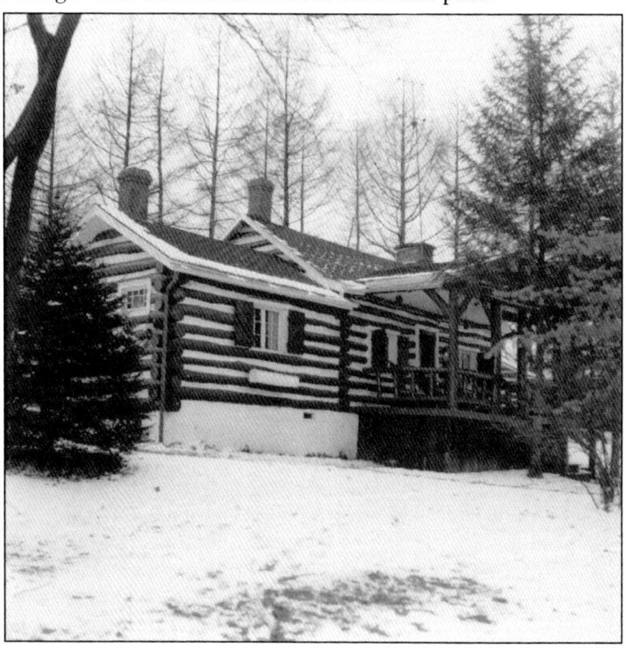

In 1939, Stanley Kubiak built this log cabin in the Everson Valley, which was a popular destination for Sunday visits and picnics. (Courtesy Marion Nowicki family.)

Three

Serving and Protecting

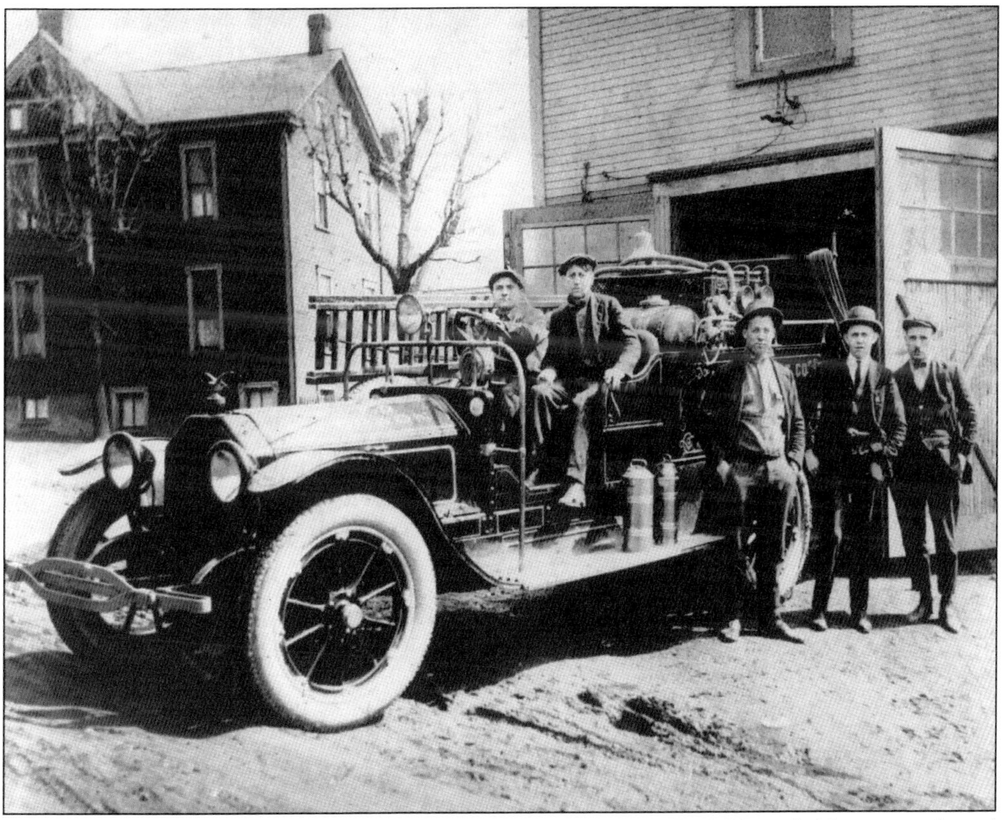

Everson organized a volunteer fire company on January 22, 1909. Dr. Milton A. Noon was elected chief, and John O'Brien was chosen as president. Pictured here in 1920 is the department's first motorized vehicle—a modified Peerless Style F car. The driver is Howard Morehead. Seated next to him is Chief Oswald Orish. Standing next to the car are "Short" Harshman (left), William Whaley (center), and Ray Clites.

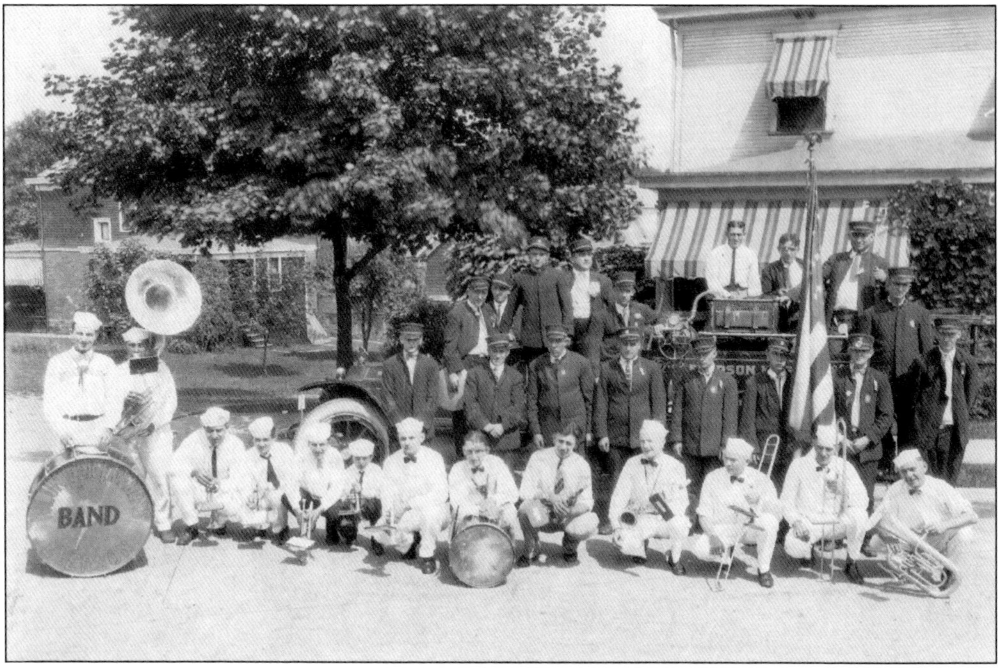

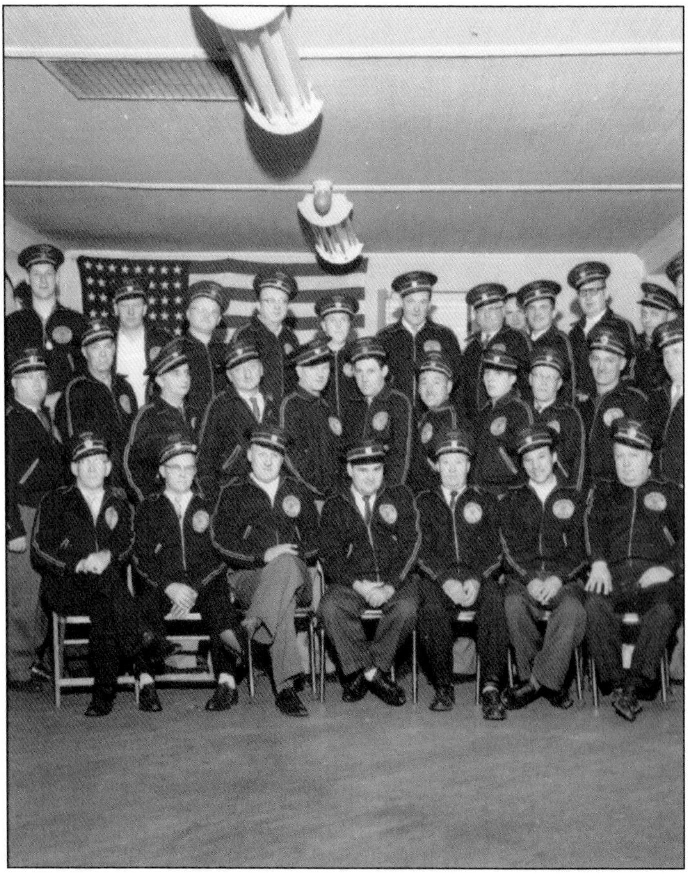

The Everson Volunteer Fire Company and its band pose for a picture at the 1927 Western Pennsylvania Fireman's Convention in Greensburg.

This 1955 picture of the Everson Fire Company was taken in the old fire hall on the corner of Painter and Jones Streets. Lester Wilhelm, who served as chief for nearly 20 years, is seated at far left. (Courtesy James Smith.)

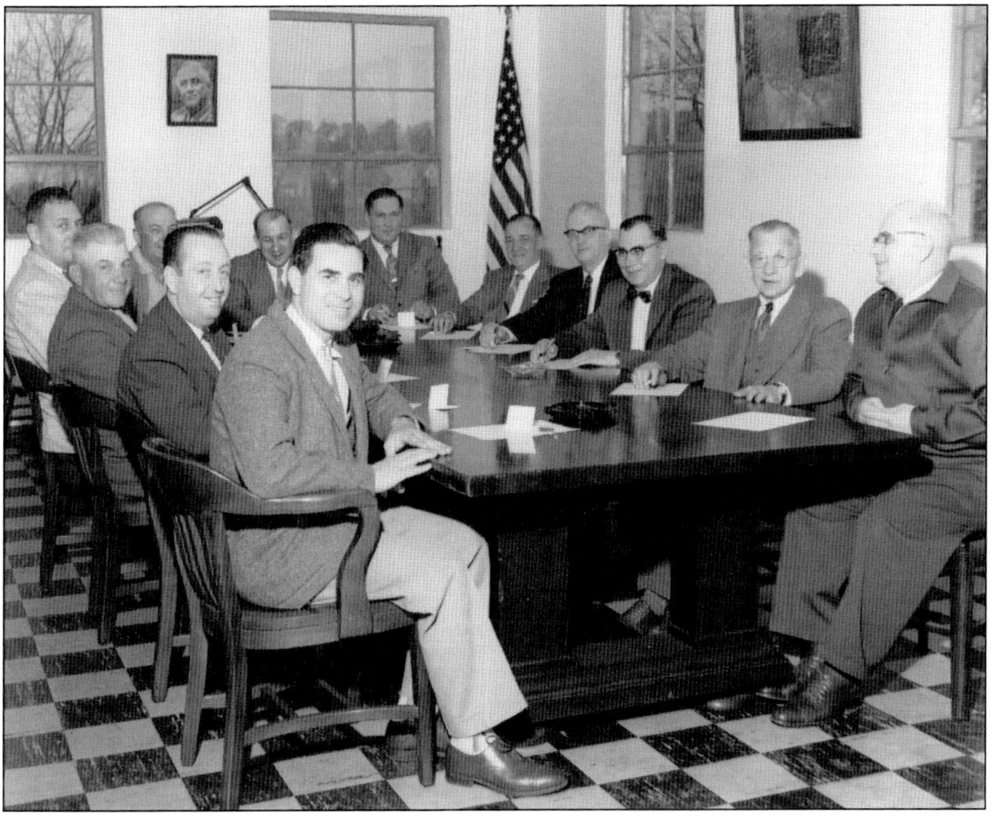

The Everson Borough Council and other officials pose before a meeting in 1957. Seated around the table, clockwise beginning with the first chair on the left, are Wilber Watson, Abbey Shaffer, ? Pisula, unidentified, Steve Mitrisin, George Farrah, Robert Nawrocki, Charles Remaley, mayor Frank Menes, unidentified, Joseph Banaszak, and Walter Szczekocki. Farrah served as borough secretary and justice of the peace for over 35 years. (Courtesy Michael Banaszak.)

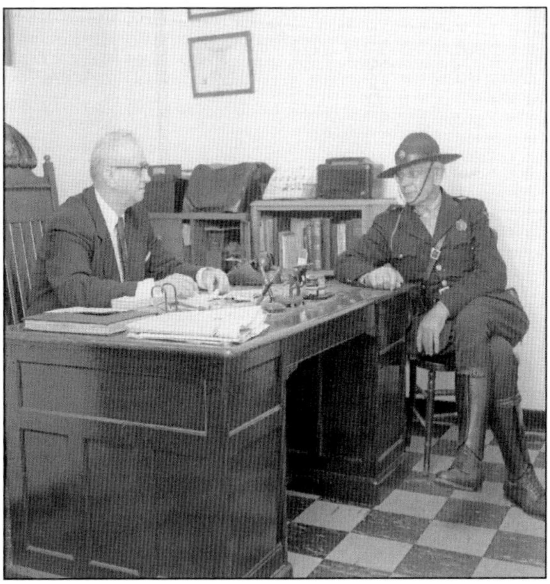

In this image, Mayor Frank Menes (left) meets with longtime police chief Stanley Kubiak. Menes served as burgess (mayor) for 21 years. Kubiak was chief for 35 years and after his retirement became a justice of the peace for Upper Tyrone Township. Kubiak was also active in Boy Scout Troop 4, serving as Scoutmaster for 25 years. (Courtesy James Smith.)

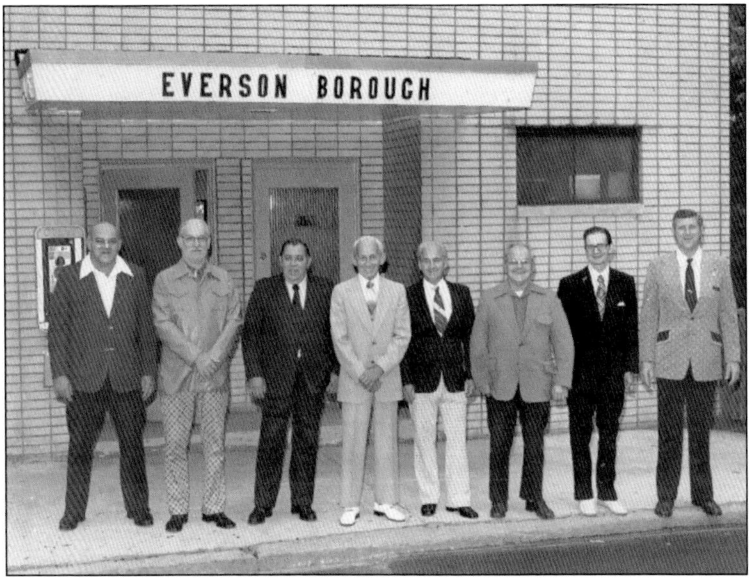

Officials pose in front of the borough building in 1978. From left to right are Frank Zoracki, John Szolek (council president), Louis Tressatti, Edward Luczka, Joseph Eckman (mayor), Adam Kravice, John Kacala, and Vincent Santarel.

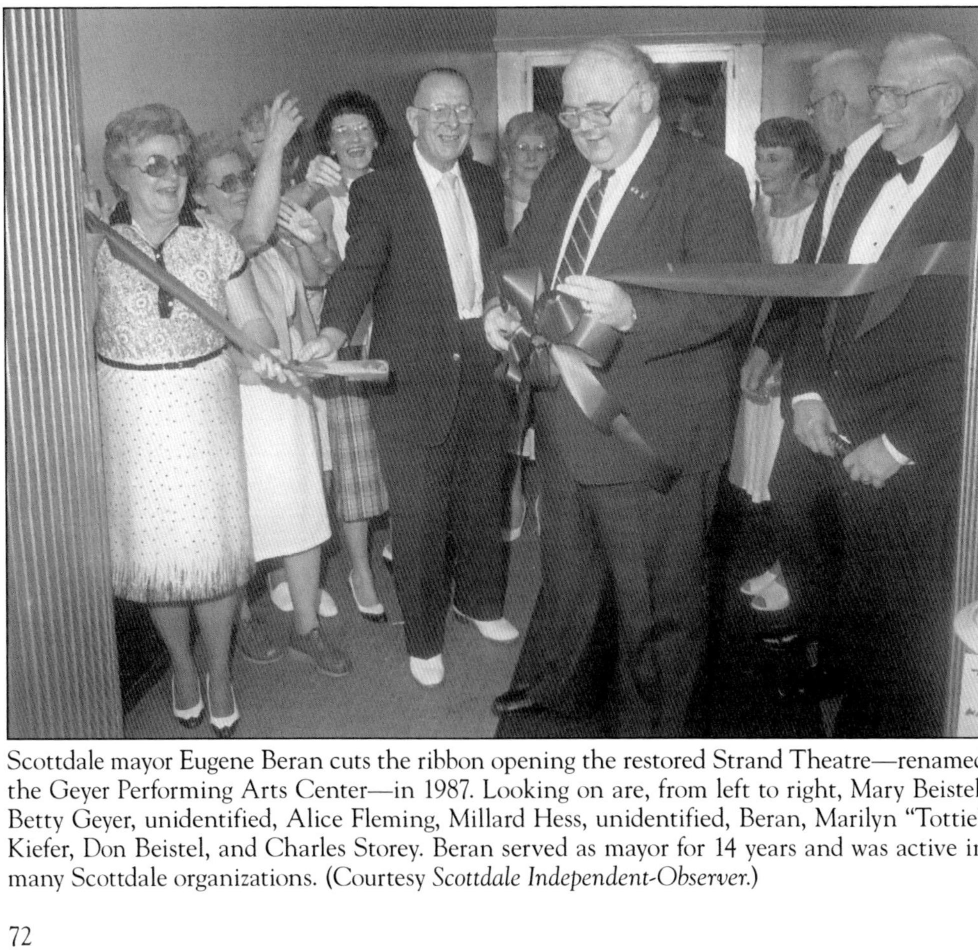

Scottdale mayor Eugene Beran cuts the ribbon opening the restored Strand Theatre—renamed the Geyer Performing Arts Center—in 1987. Looking on are, from left to right, Mary Beistel, Betty Geyer, unidentified, Alice Fleming, Millard Hess, unidentified, Beran, Marilyn "Tottie" Kiefer, Don Beistel, and Charles Storey. Beran served as mayor for 14 years and was active in many Scottdale organizations. (Courtesy *Scottdale Independent-Observer.*)

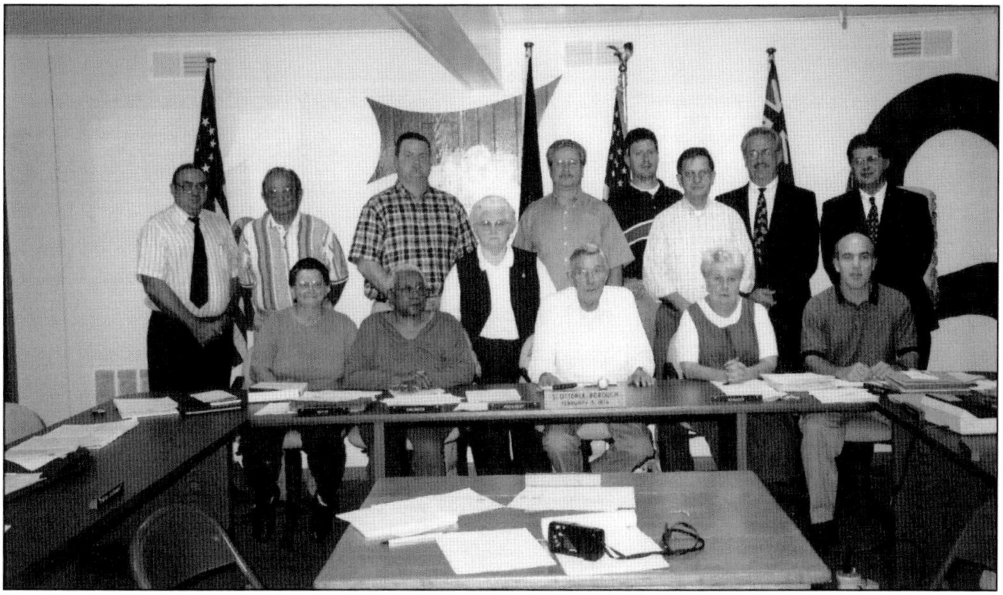

Scottdale municipal officials assemble for a photograph in 1997. Pictured here are, from left to right, (first row) June Ostroski, Patricia Walker, Frederick Eberharter (council president), Susan Killinger, and Barry Whoric; (second row) Donald Reho, Steven Matsey, Tim Carson (mayor), Ardis Smith, Clyde Stoner, Douglas Riley, Thomas Ermine, John Toohey, and Randy Klimchock. (Courtesy Borough of Scottdale.)

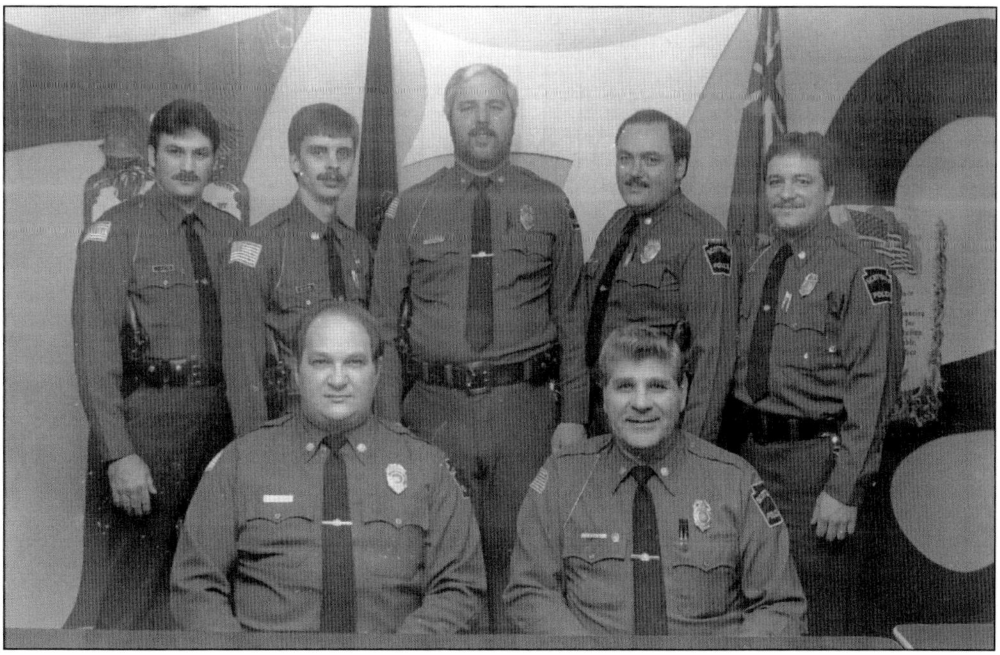

The first Scottdale police officer was hired in 1874. They were subsequently elected by the borough council on an annual basis until the enactment of civil service regulations in 1941. The 1990 police department is pictured here; they are, from left to right, (first row) Chief Tony Martin and Ralph Rich; (second row) Joseph Martin, Michael Grimm, Michael Thomas, Donald Dunn, and Randy Parfitt. (Courtesy *Scottdale Independent-Observer.*)

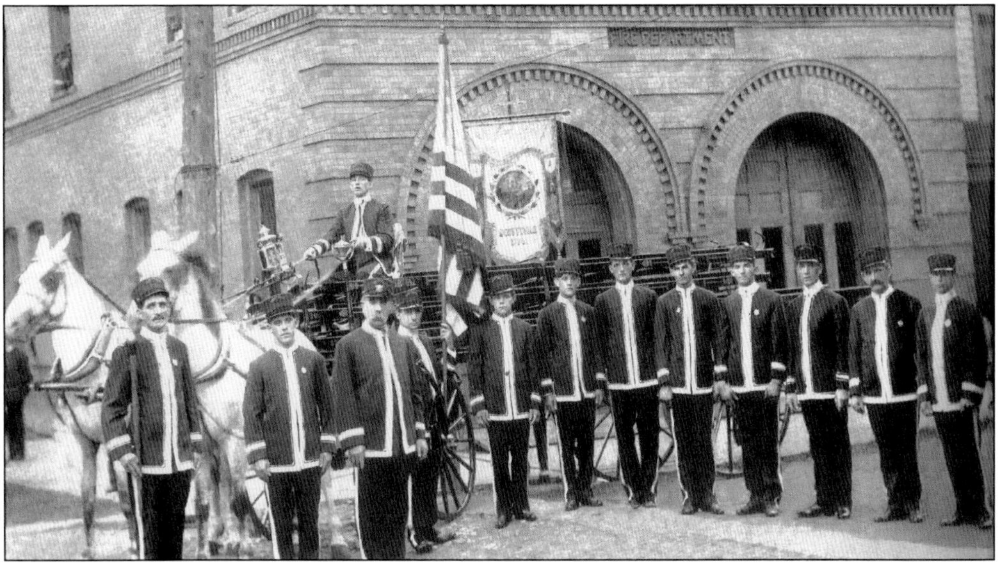

The Scottdale Fire Department was organized in 1886 after a series of fires threatened to engulf businesses on Pittsburgh Street. Hand-drawn equipment was used before Scottdale acquired this horse-drawn apparatus around 1905. (Courtesy Scottdale Fire Department.)

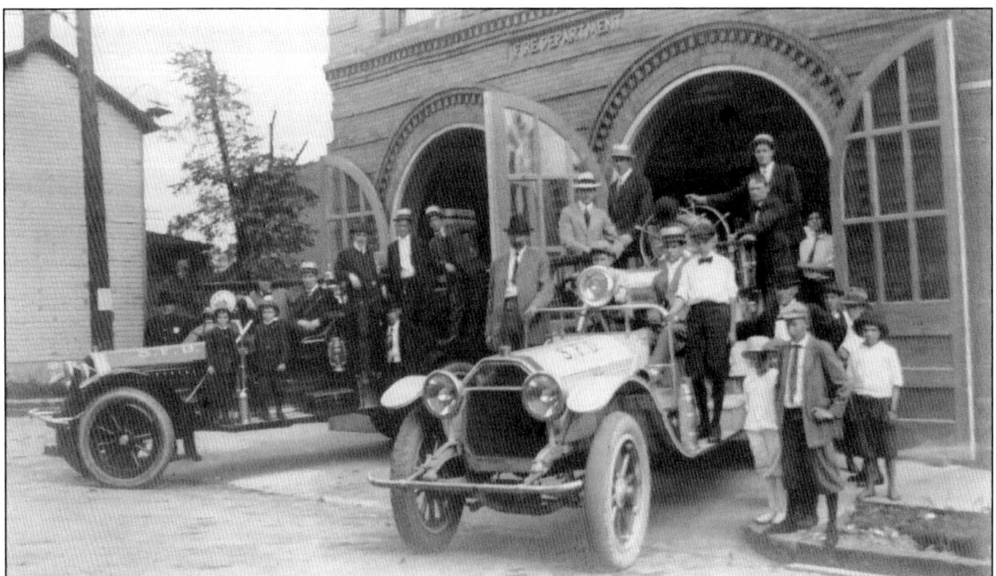

Residents admire the first motorized vehicles acquired by the fire department in 1917. The photograph was taken in front of the old central station, located on the corner of Everson Street and Grant Avenue. (Courtesy *Scottdale Independent-Observer.*)

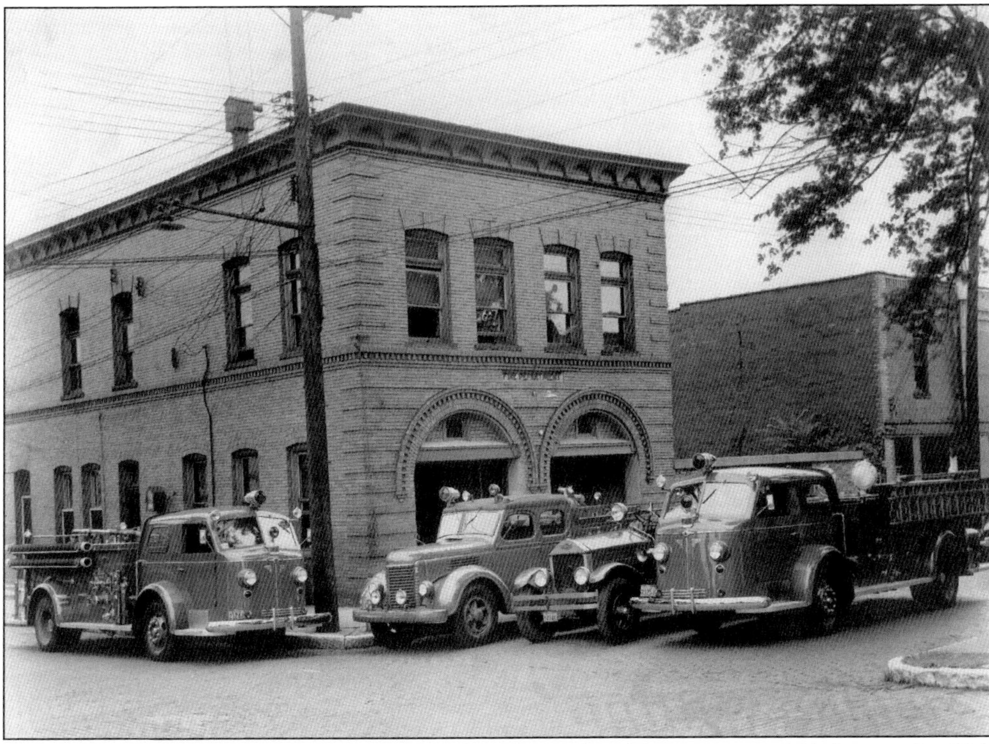

Modern firefighting equipment is displayed in front the old station in 1949 during the 75th anniversary of Scottdale's incorporation as a borough. (Courtesy Scottdale Fire Department.)

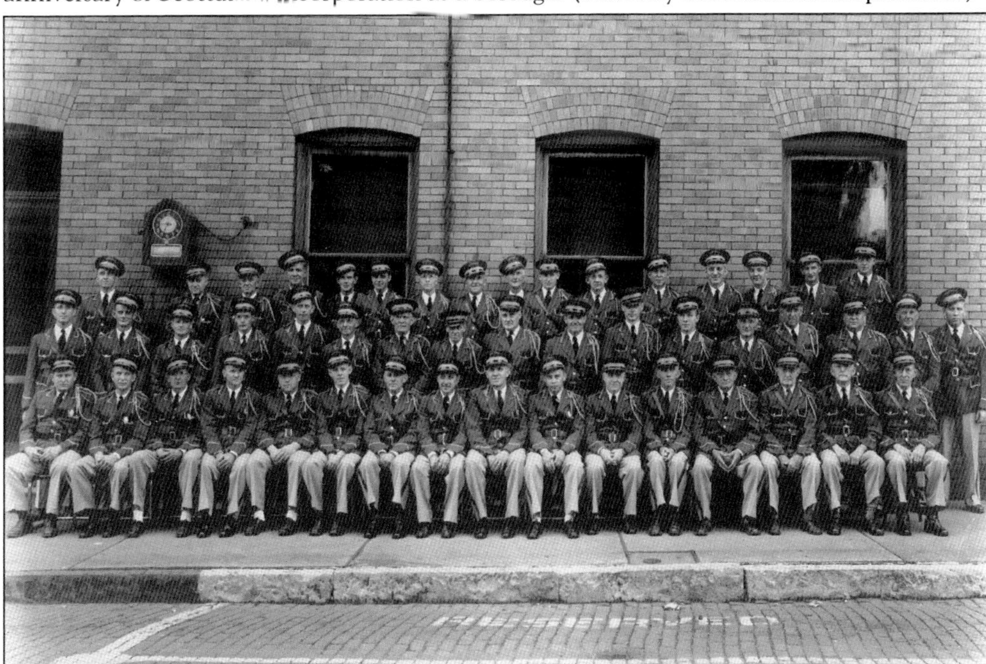

The Scottdale Fire Department posed in formal uniforms for this 1949 picture. (Courtesy Scottdale Fire Department.)

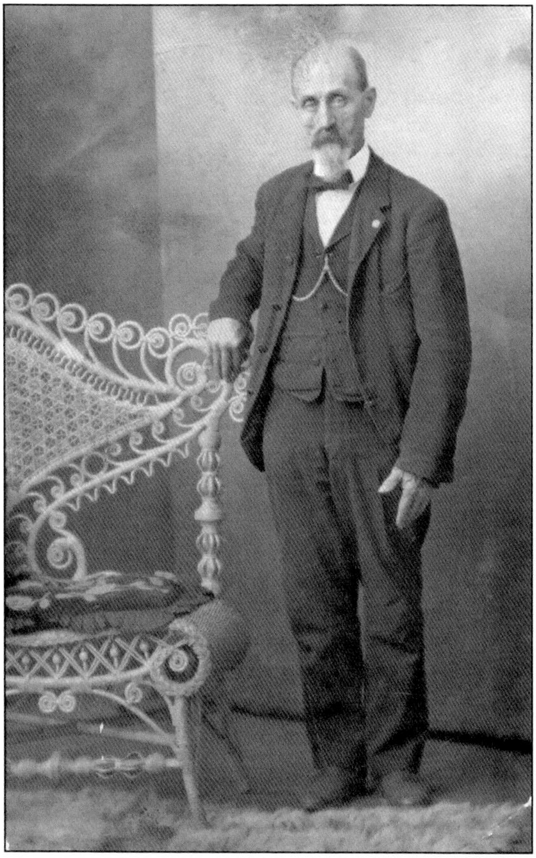

Daniel "Daddy" Kuhns, pictured around 1900, was a Civil War veteran and reportedly served in an honor guard at the funeral of Pres. Abraham Lincoln. Kuhns resided on Railroad Street in South Everson and reached 96 years of age.

This was the first honor roll erected by Everson residents in memory of veterans who served in foreign wars. It was located on the grounds of the Everson Grade School. When the property was purchased by the fire department for a new social hall, the steps were left intact, and they are visible today in front of the hall. A new honor roll was dedicated across from the original site on Brown Street. (Courtesy Marion Mitrisin.)

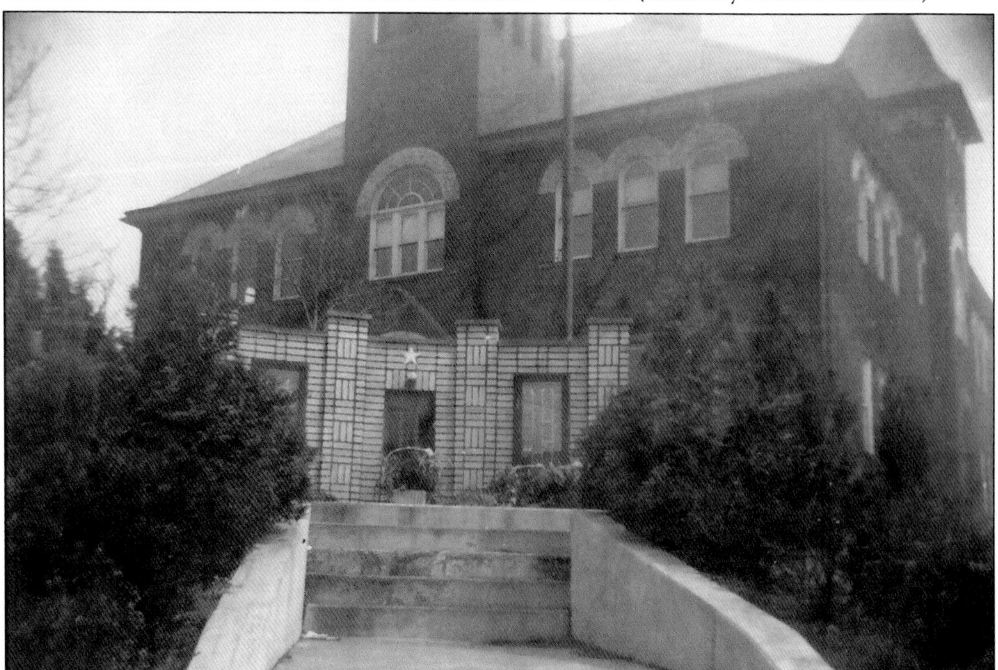

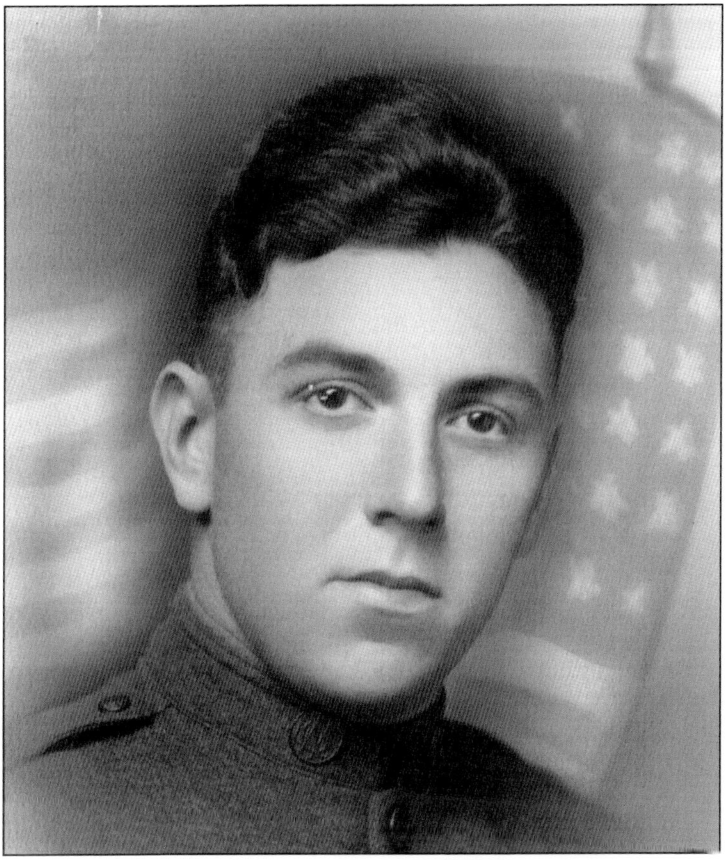

Wilbur Hamilton, who served in Headquarters Company, 110th Infantry, 28th Division in World War I, was the first Everson resident killed in a foreign war. Veterans of Foreign Wars Post 595 was named for Hamilton, along with Raymond Maloy from Scottdale. Hamilton was initially buried in France, but his remains were brought home to rest in the Scottdale Cemetery. The picture below shows his caisson and honor guard passing St. John the Baptist School on August 7, 1921, as part of a large funeral procession on South Broadway. (Both, courtesy Everson Veterans of Foreign Wars.)

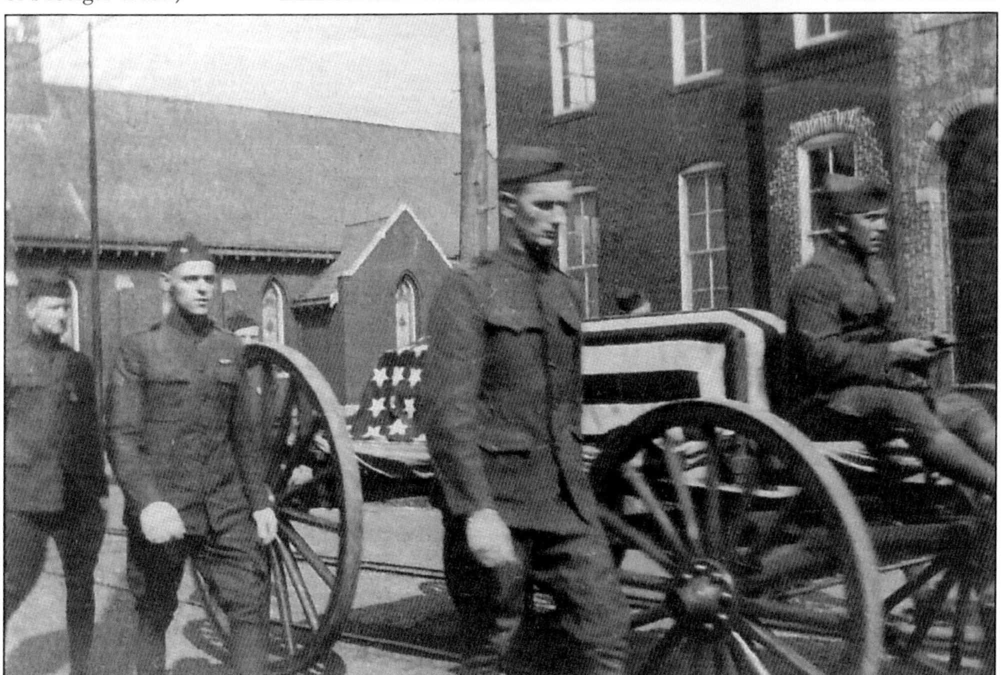

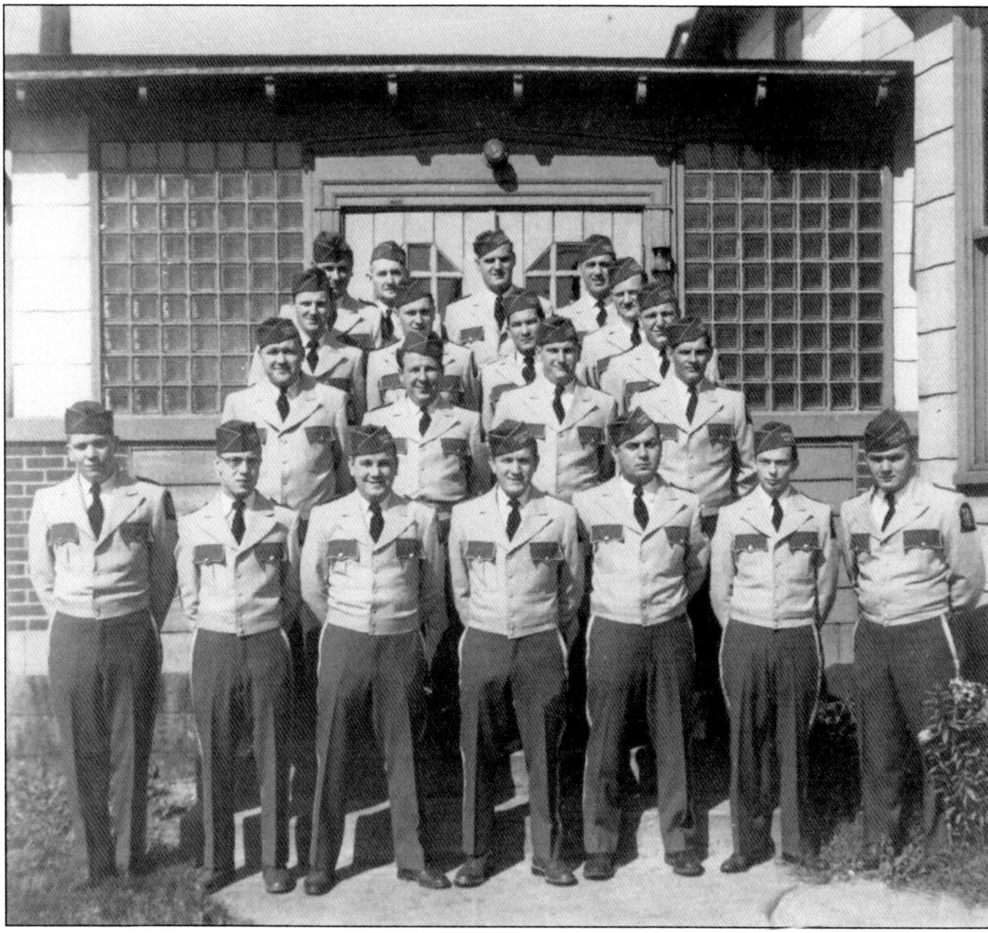

Members of Everson Post 595 gather around 1950 on the side steps of the old post in their new parade uniforms. (Courtesy Everson Veterans of Foreign Wars.)

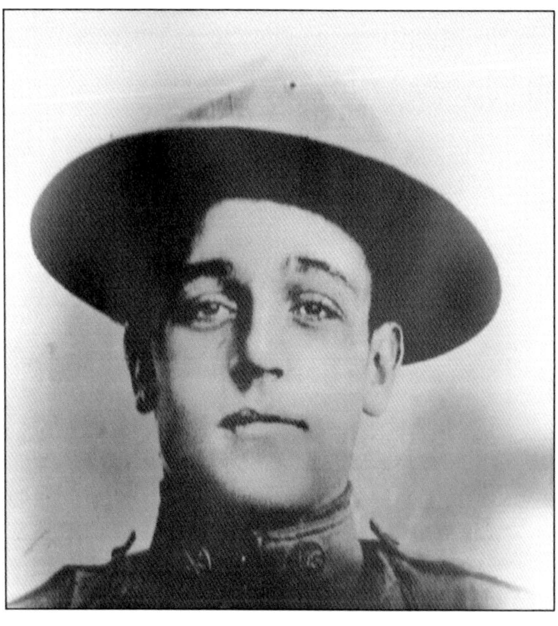

Raymond Maloy from Scottdale was killed by a high explosive in France on August 15, 1918. He served in the 110th Machine Gun Attachment, 28th Division. (Courtesy Everson Veterans of Foreign Wars.)

The doughboy monument honoring Scottdale veterans faced Pittsburgh Street and Broadway until it was moved to the grounds of the American Legion.

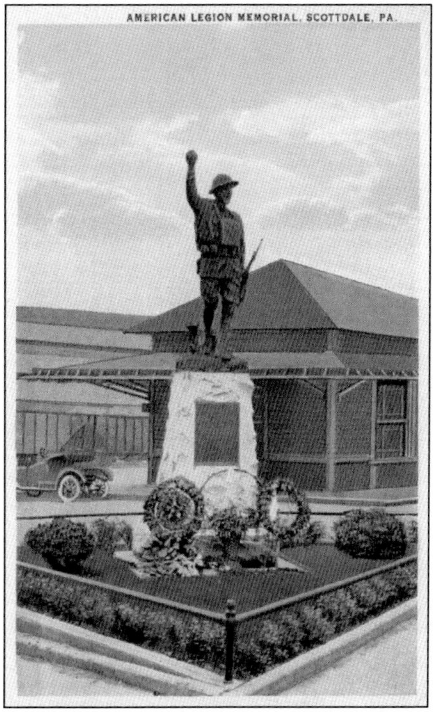

The Thomas Lewellyn American Legion Post Band is pictured in 1950 on the steps of the armory. The drum major, David Acres, is wearing his Scottdale High School Band uniform. (Courtesy Marilyn Gaut.)

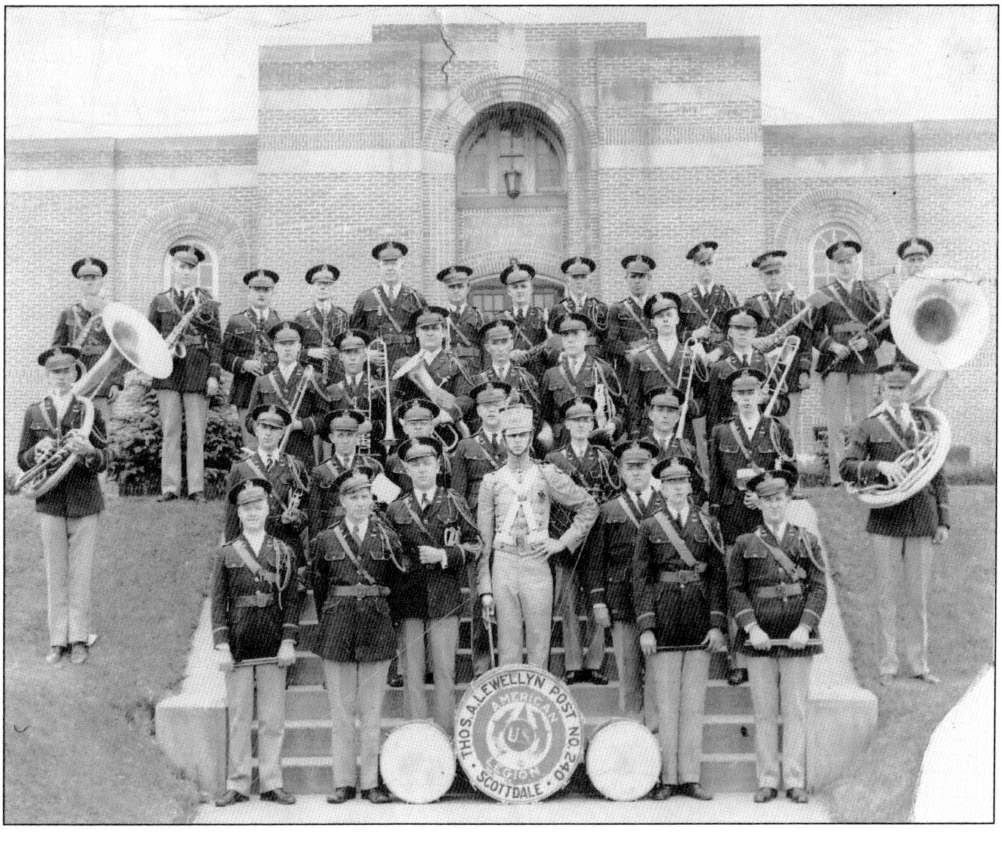

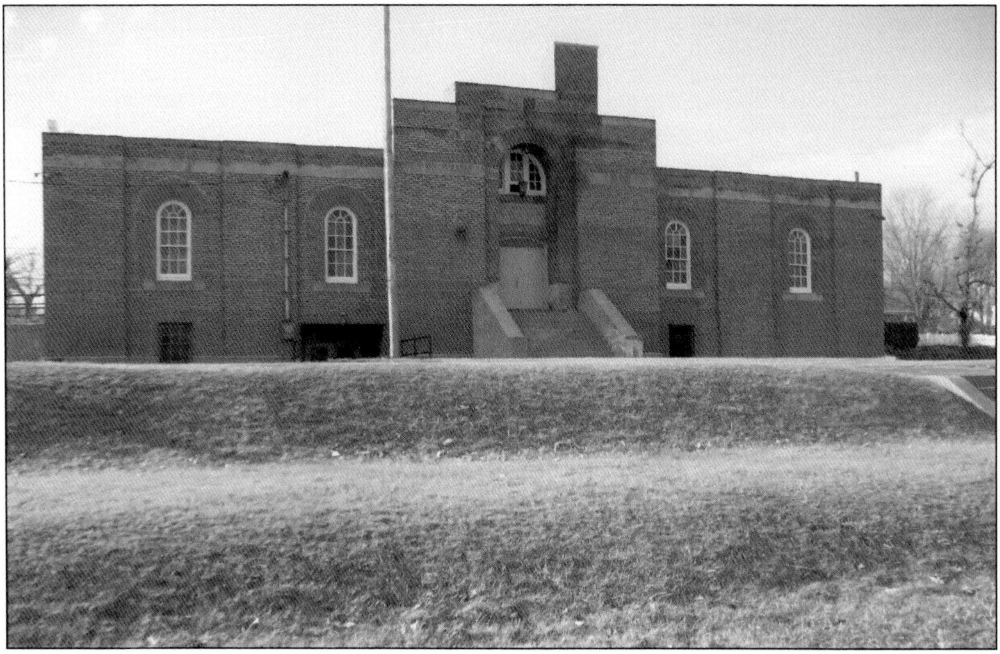

The Scottdale armory opened in 1930 and served as headquarters for the Supply Company, 110th Infantry, 28th Division. The unit, organized in 1873, served in two world wars, the Korean War, and Iraq. During World War II, it fought at Normandy and in the Battle of the Bulge. The company was reorganized in Mount Pleasant as a light infantry battalion in 2008.

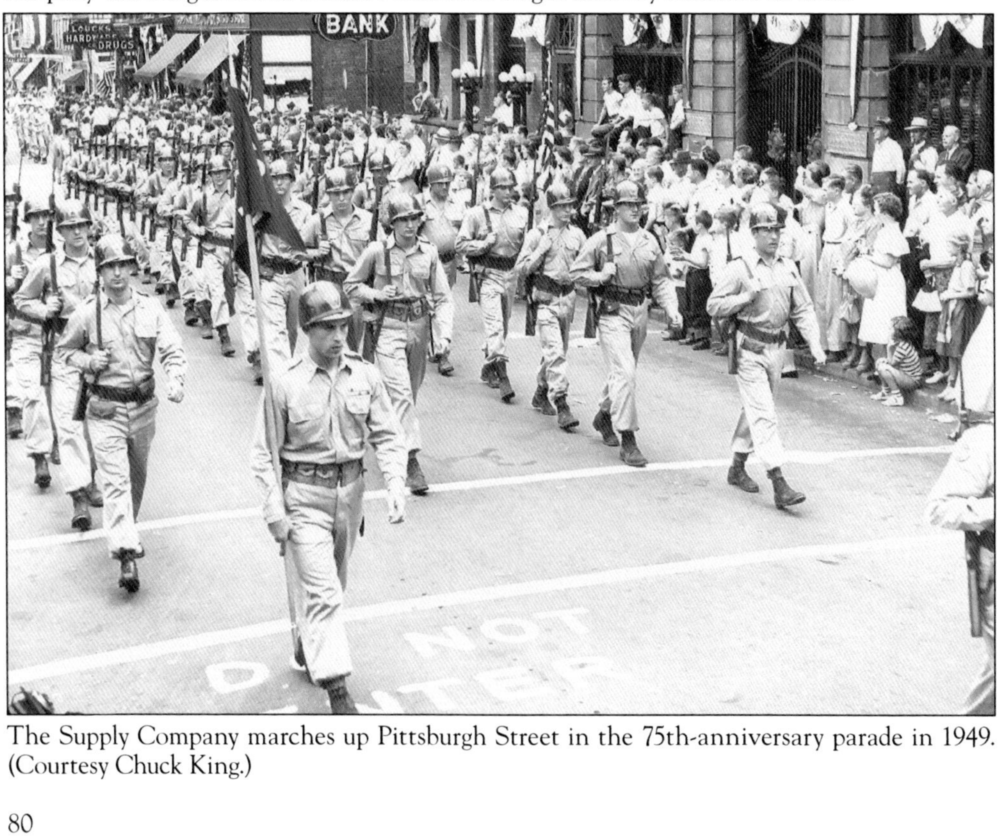

The Supply Company marches up Pittsburgh Street in the 75th-anniversary parade in 1949. (Courtesy Chuck King.)

Four

Learning and Coming Together

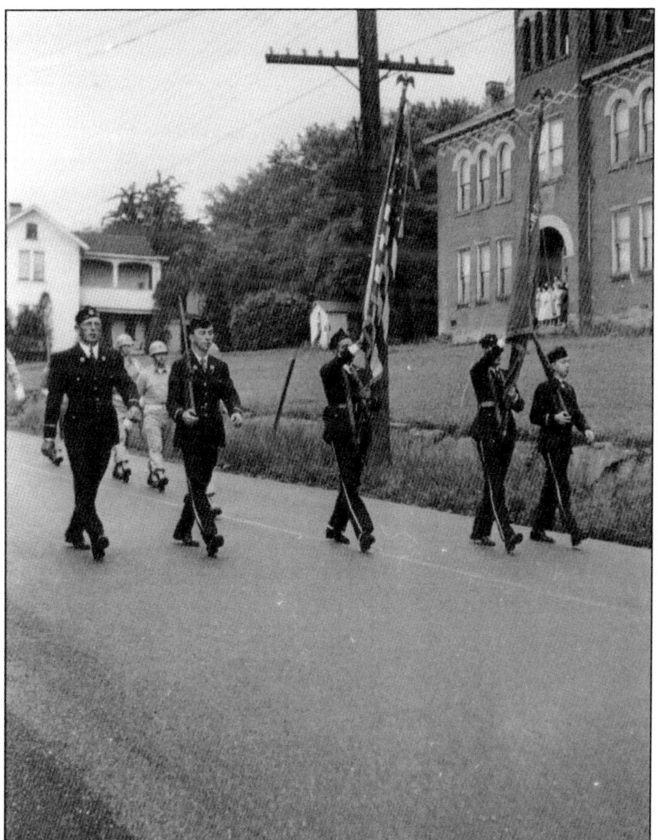

Veterans march past the Alverton Grade School on Memorial Day in 1955. The building was constructed in 1900 and served as the first high school in East Huntington Township. (Courtesy James Smith.)

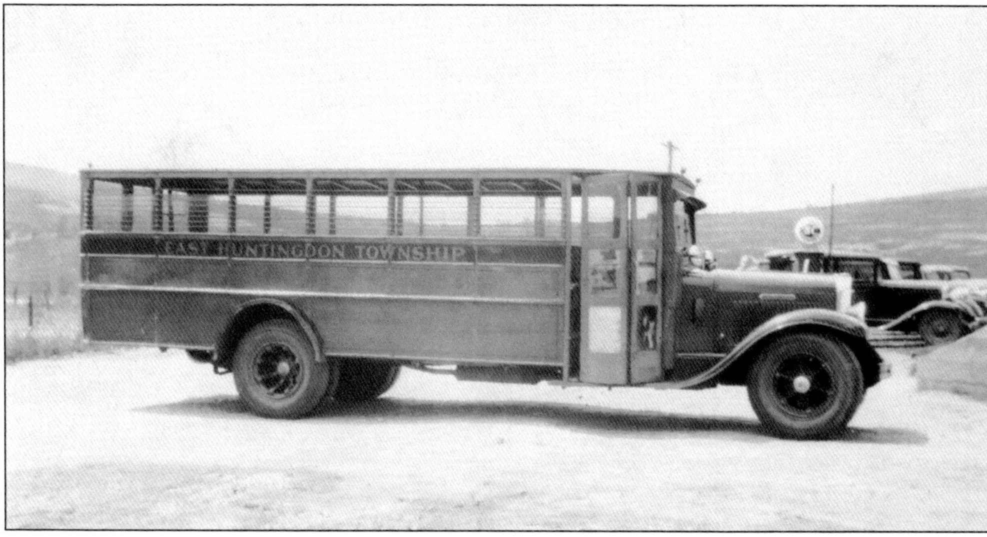

East Huntington Township occupies approximately 33 square miles; consequently, transportation was needed in order for children to attend high school and consolidated grade schools. This is one of the buses used by the township board of education in 1935. (Courtesy George Santmyer family.)

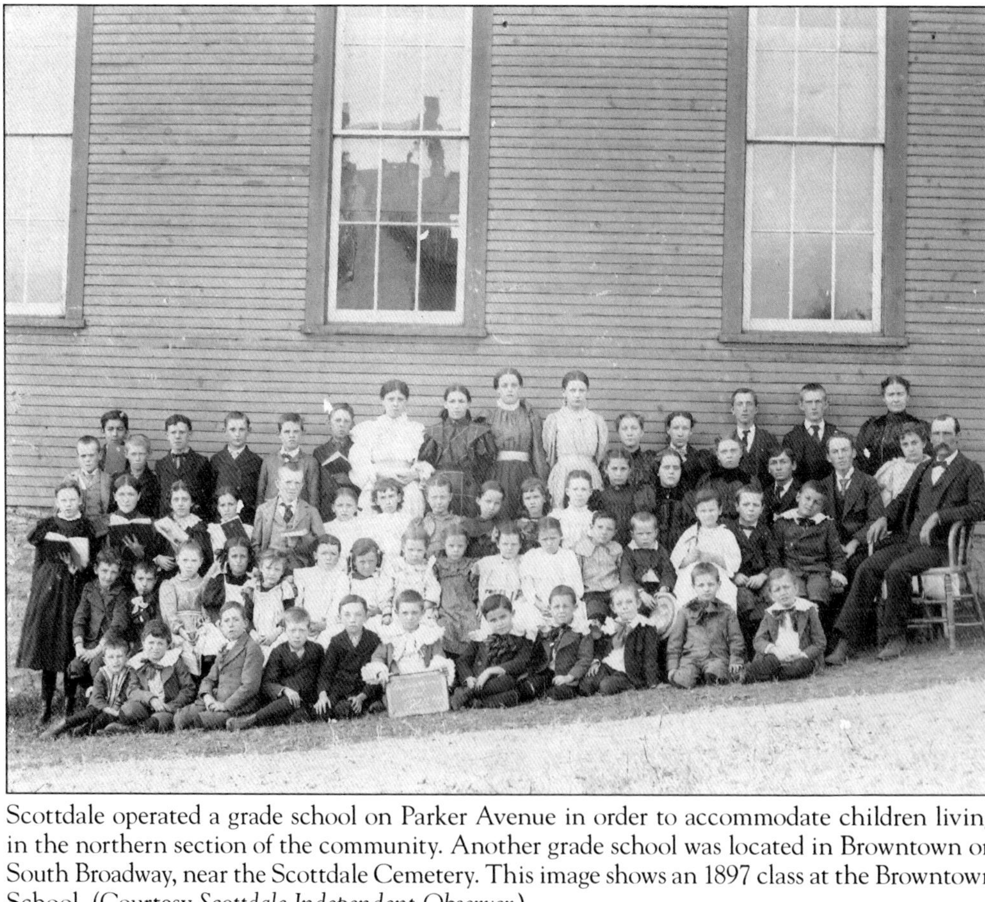

Scottdale operated a grade school on Parker Avenue in order to accommodate children living in the northern section of the community. Another grade school was located in Browntown on South Broadway, near the Scottdale Cemetery. This image shows an 1897 class at the Browntown School. (Courtesy *Scottdale Independent-Observer*.)

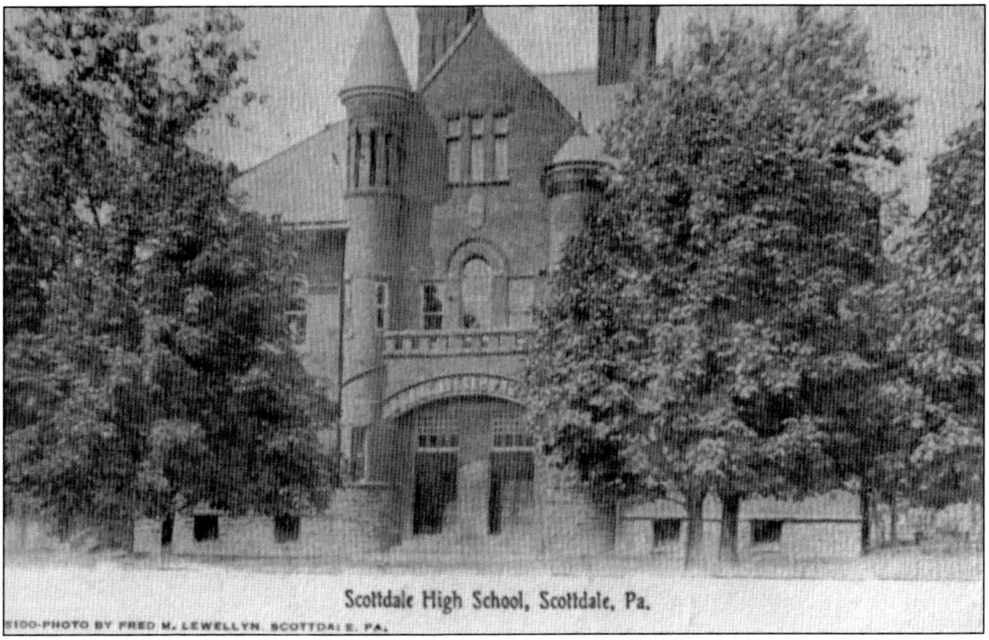

The eight-room Pittsburgh Street School was erected in 1896. The first high school classes in Scottdale were offered, on a limited basis, in this building. It replaced an older four-room school that was destroyed by fire.

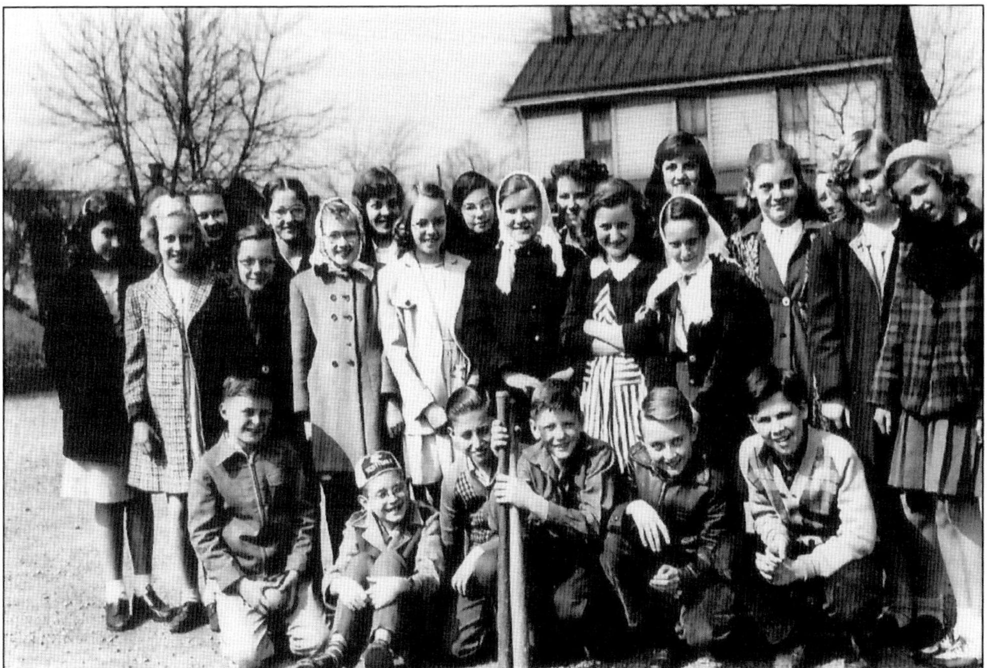

The Pittsburgh Street schoolyard was the setting for this 1945 sixth-grade class picture. (Courtesy *Scottdale Independent-Observer.*)

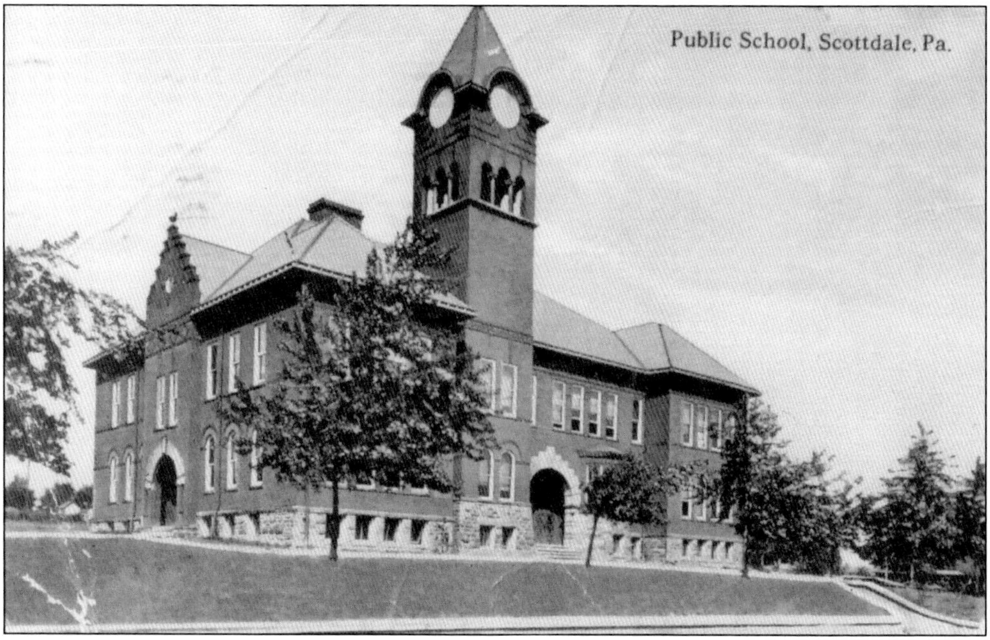

The South Chestnut Street School, erected in 1889, replaced another school building destroyed by fire in 1887. The building housed the high school until 1909. Thereafter, it functioned as a junior high school. The building was razed when the Scottdale Joint School District opened a new junior-senior high school on North Chestnut Street. The property was subsequently converted to a municipal park.

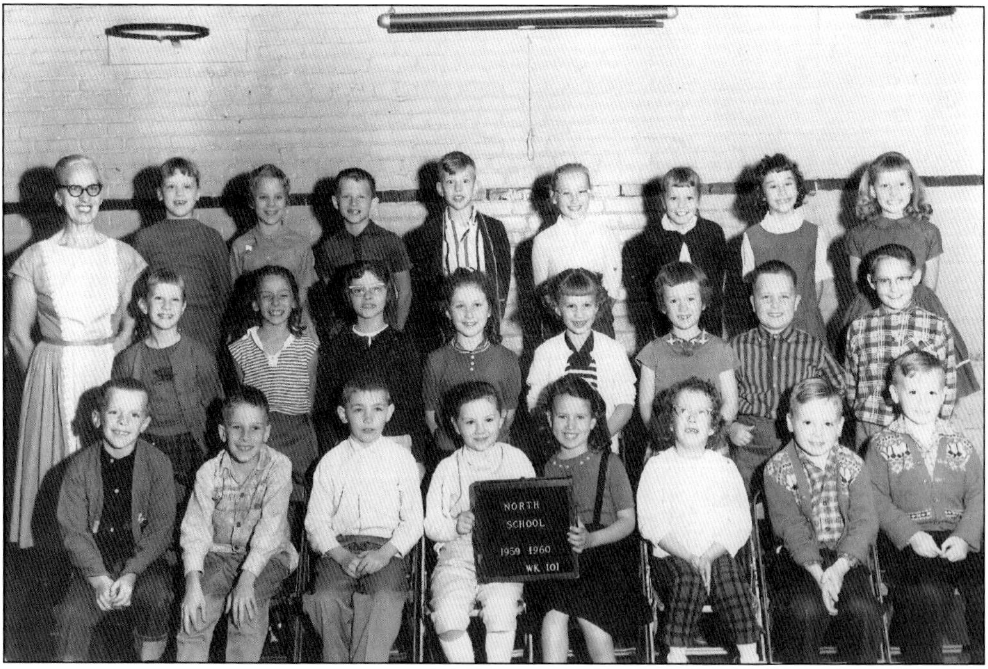

Katherine Geyer is pictured with her second-grade class at the Parker Avenue School in 1959. At the time of this publication, Geyer was 108 and the oldest resident of Scottdale. (Courtesy Joyce Moore.)

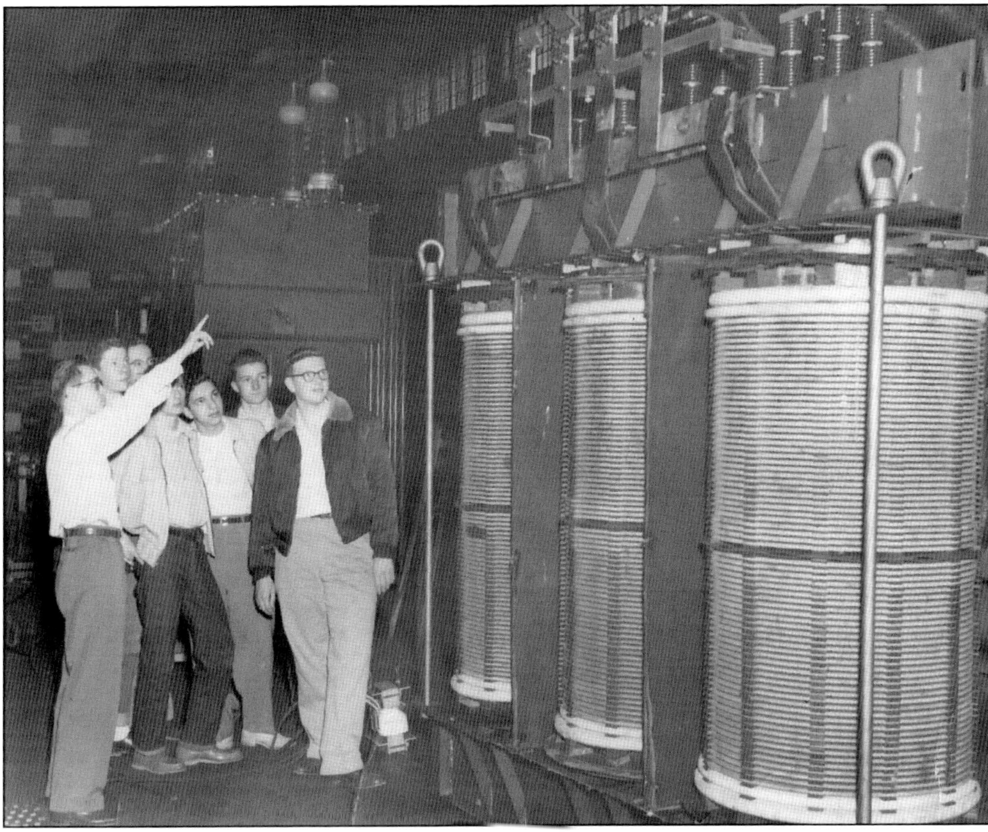

Some members of the senior class at Scottdale High School toured the Uptegraff Transformer Company on this 1953 field trip. From left to right are Donald Bownon, Anthony Chiarmonte, Francis Battle, Jacob Farrah, Gregory Bart, and Wilmer Lane. The Uptegraff employee at far left (pointing) is unidentified. (Courtesy Jacob Farrah.)

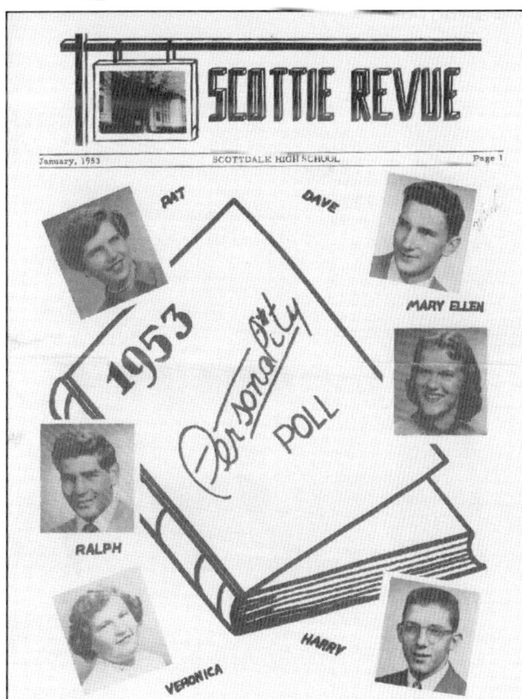

Scottdale High School students published this *Scottie Revue*, which featured the results of a personality poll. (Courtesy Jacob Farrah.)

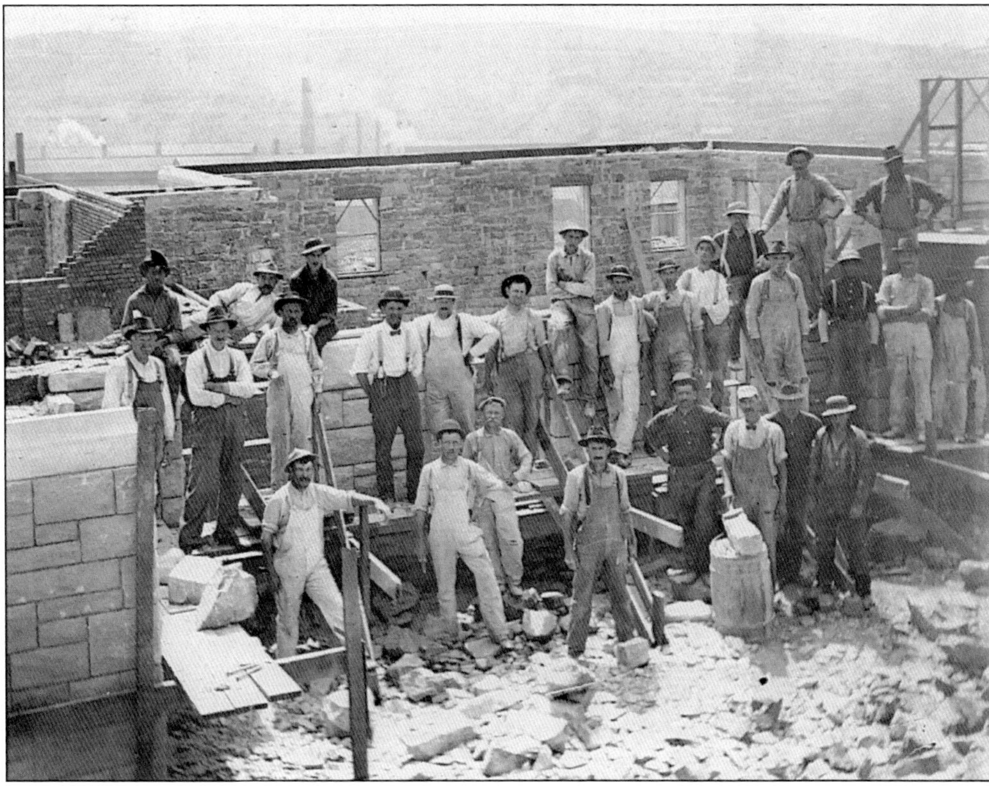

Pictured above is a scene from the construction of the high school on South Chestnut Street. It was reported that many of the stonemasons also worked for the Cochran family while building Linden Hall. Below is the completed 18-room school as it appeared soon after it opened in 1909. (Above, courtesy Bob Percy.)

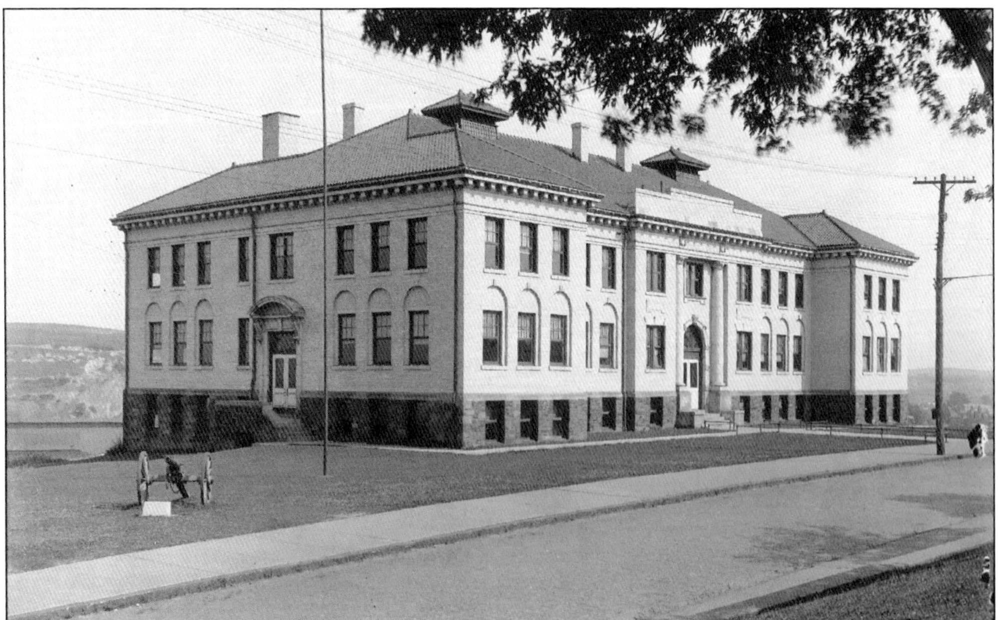

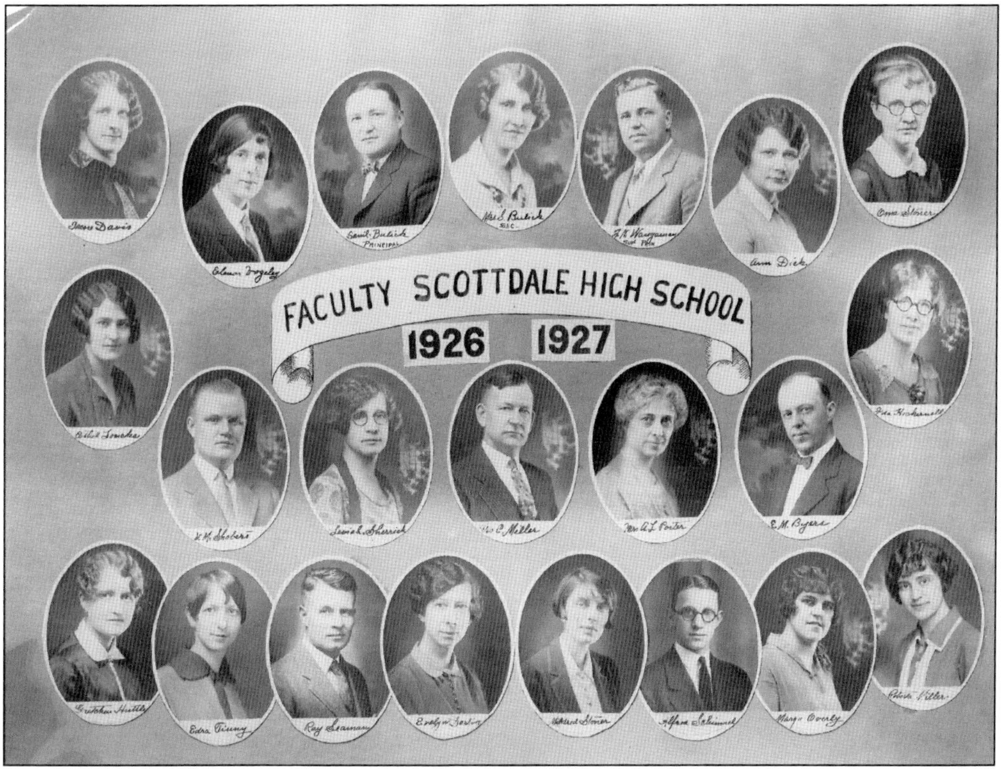

The Scottdale High School faculty appears in this 1927 photograph. (Courtesy West Overton Museums.)

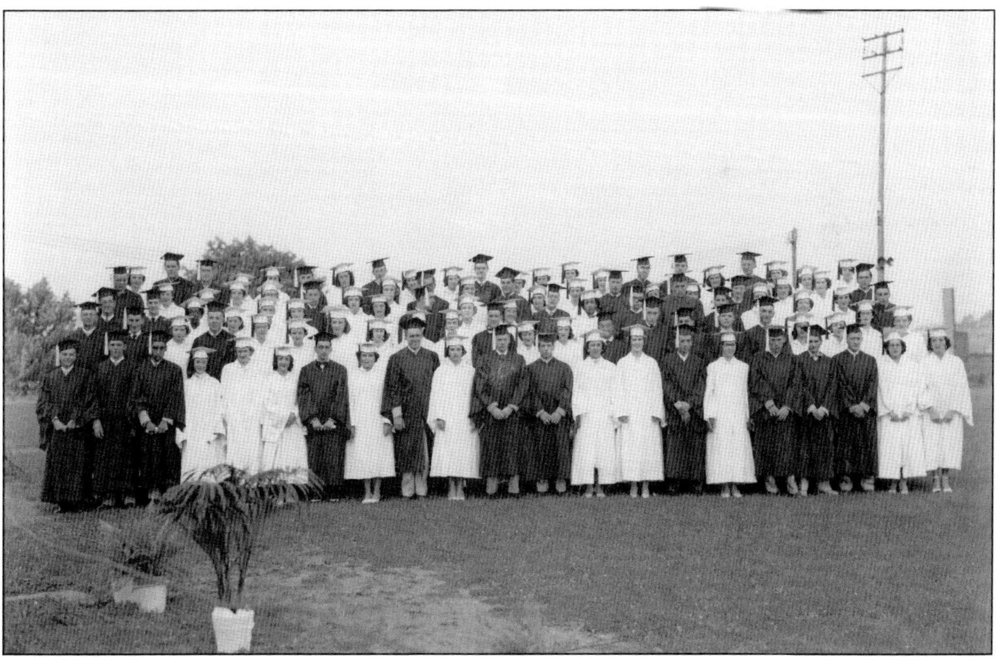

After receiving their diplomas, the 1953 graduating class assembled for a picture on the football field below the South Chestnut Street School. (Courtesy Jacob Farrah.)

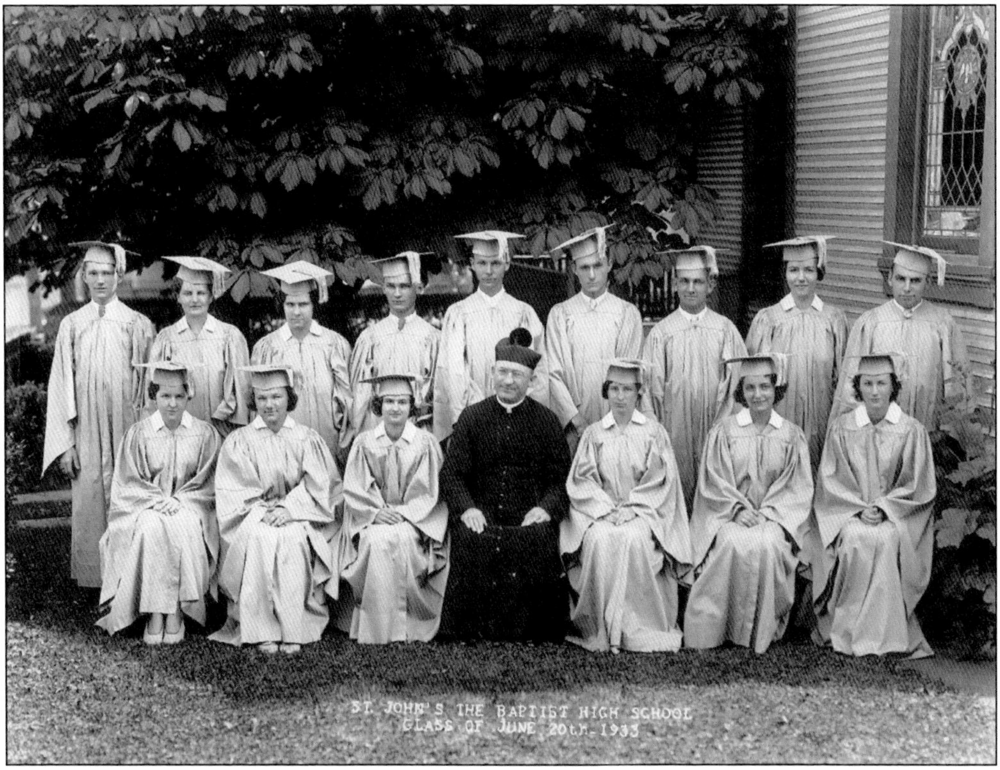

St. John's Parish operated a regional high school from 1923 to 1933. The last graduating class is pictured here. They are, from left to right, (first row) Ann Bainbridge, Melania Prutz, Clara Labiak, Rev. Patrick J. Graney, Marie Nowasky, Mary Helwig, and Kate Sherman; (second row) Larry Honeychuck, Margaret Rocheck, Theresa Thomas, Edward Eckman, William Baramak, Richard Hines, George Turk, Rose Rey, and Harry Weimer.

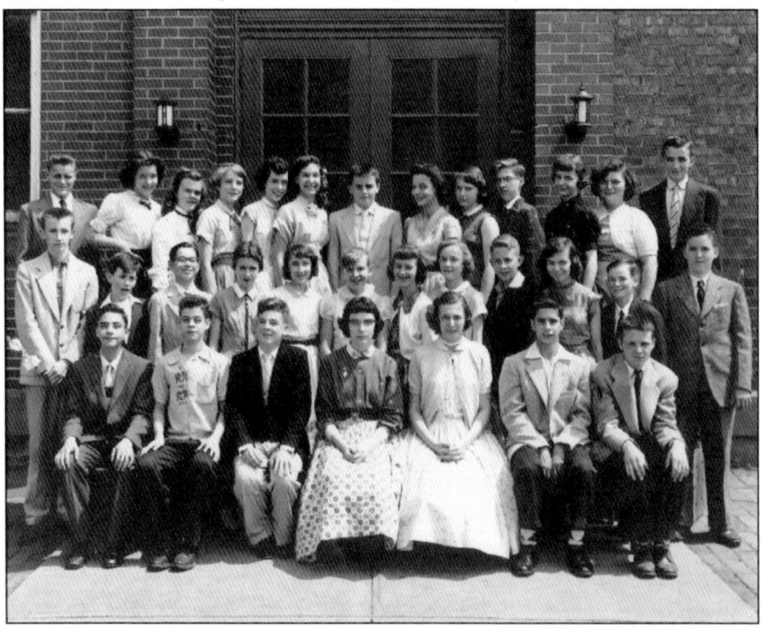

St. John's grade school graduated this class in 1956. The picture was taken on the front steps of the old three-story building. The grade school opened in 1889 and was replaced by a new structure in 1963. The school continues to serve area children. (Courtesy John Farrah family.)

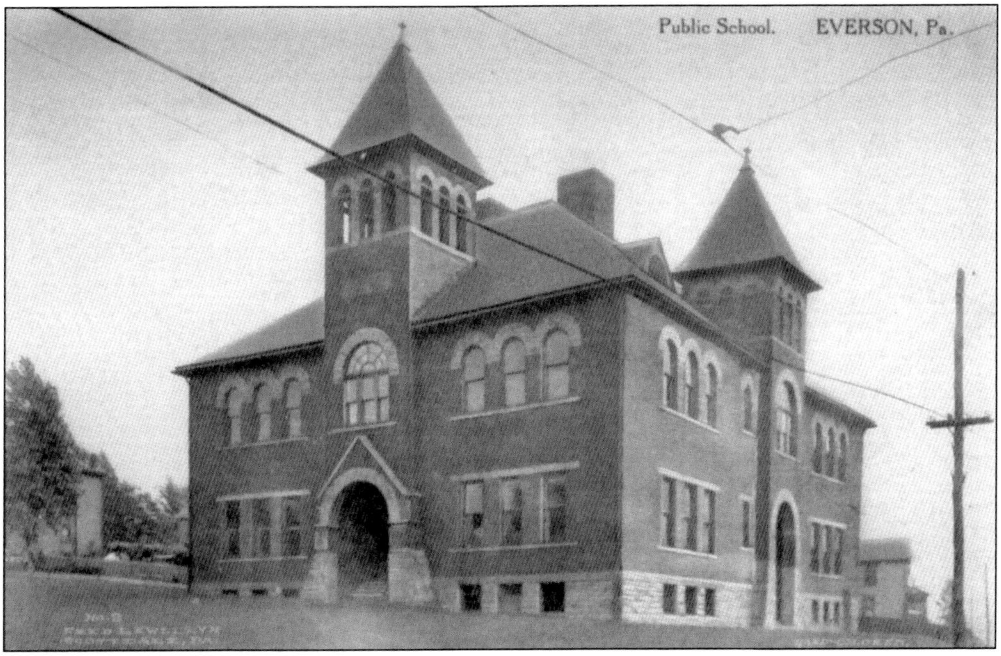

The first school in Everson was erected by the Upper Tyrone Township School Board in the late 1870s on the corner of Brown and Jones Streets. The one-room school was replaced with this building in the 1890s. The school closed after the Everson Board of Education and the township merged with Scottdale in 1953. The property was sold to the Everson Fire Company in 1962. (Courtesy Sharyn Kmieciak.)

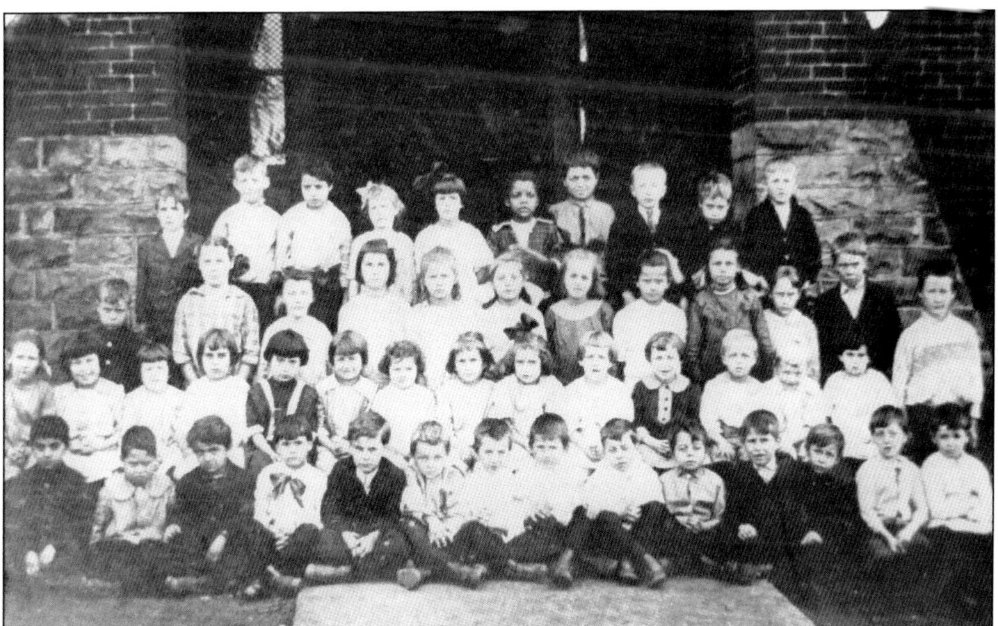

An unidentified group of students poses in front of the front door of the Everson School in 1916. (Courtesy Dr. Peggy Farrah.)

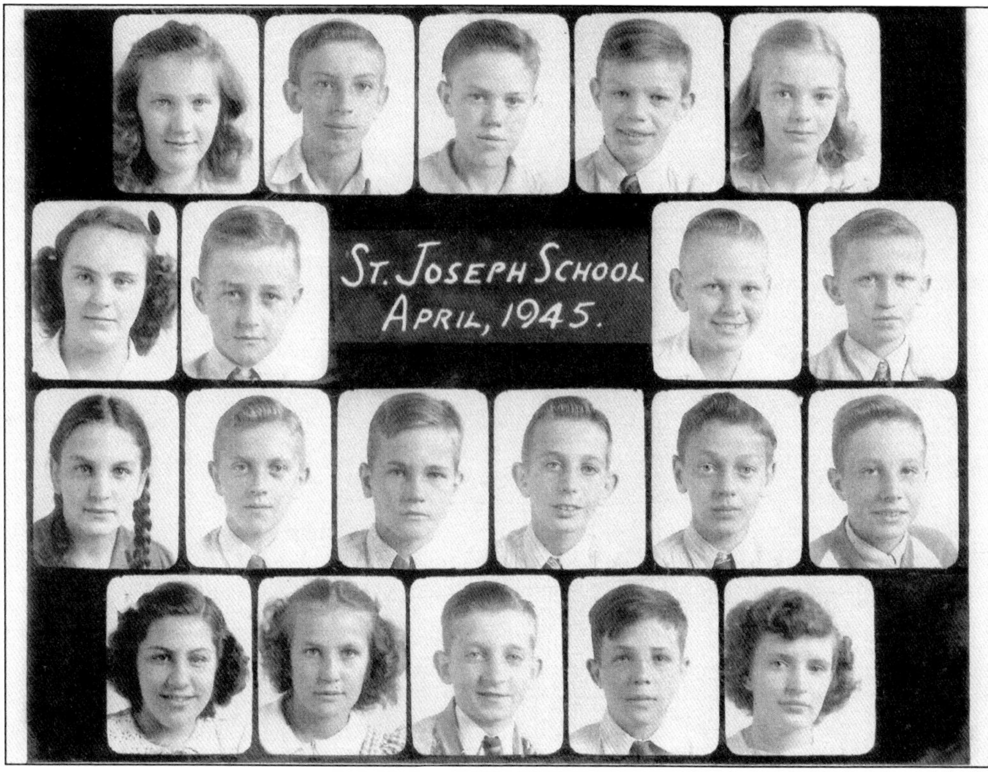

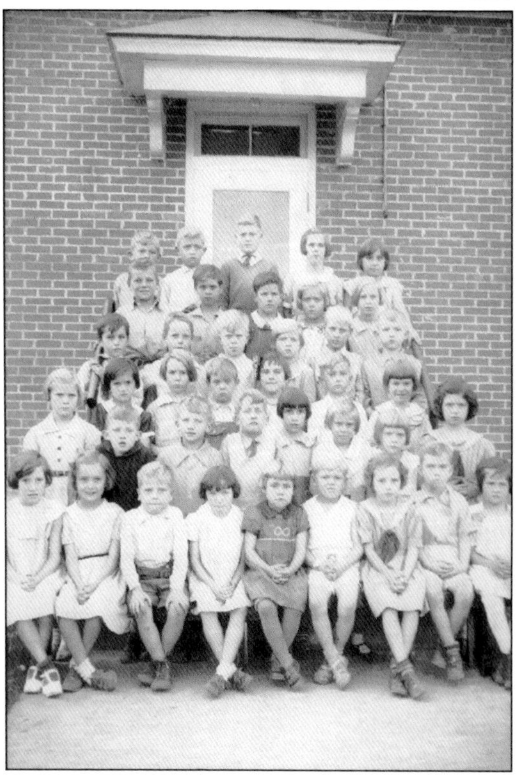

St. Joseph's Parish operated an elementary school from 1888 to 1990. Members of this seventh-grade class are, from left to right, (top row) Dorthy Ozoroski, Eugene Martinowsky, John Ostrowski, Bernard Sanzimier, and Evelyn Koshara; (second row) Felicia Kaczmarek, Raymond Polakowski, William Balgosky, and Eugene Hamrock; (third row) Veronica Martinowsky, Raymond Szwed, Joseph Levendosky, Walter Martinowsky, Vincent Opalinski, and Marion Mitrisin; (fourth row) Delores Stankiewicz, Clara Zwierzelewski, Eugene Koza, William Wesolowski, and Anastasia Nawrocki. (Courtesy Marion Mitrisin.)

These students posed in front of the South Everson Grade School in the late 1930s. This two-room building, in addition to schools in Owensdale and Kingview, was part of the Upper Tyrone Township School District before the merger with Scottdale.

This 1925 image depicts the eighth-grade class at the Kingview School. (Courtesy *Scottdale Independent-Observer*.)

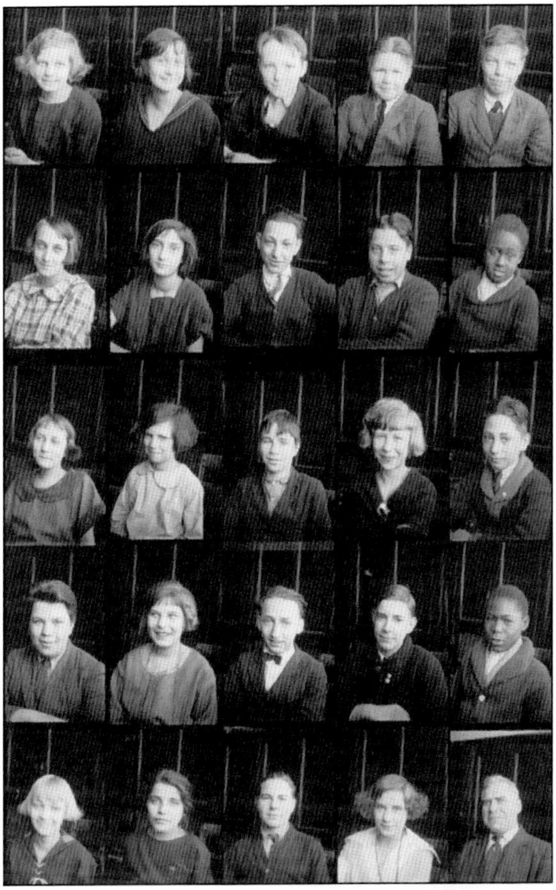

East Huntington Township opened this new high school in 1925. In addition to the standard curriculum, the school was noted throughout the region for its machine shop, which attracted students from other districts who travelled to Alverton on the streetcar. When the jointure was established in 1964, the building continued to serve as a junior high school until new facilities were constructed. The building was demolished in 2010 for a parking lot. (Courtesy Daniel Clara.)

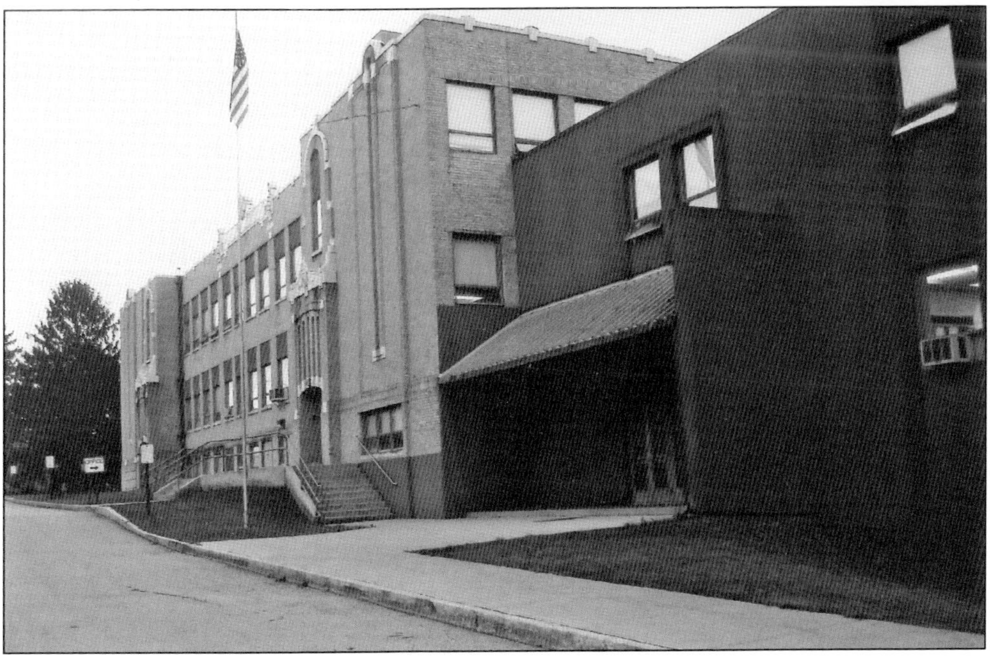

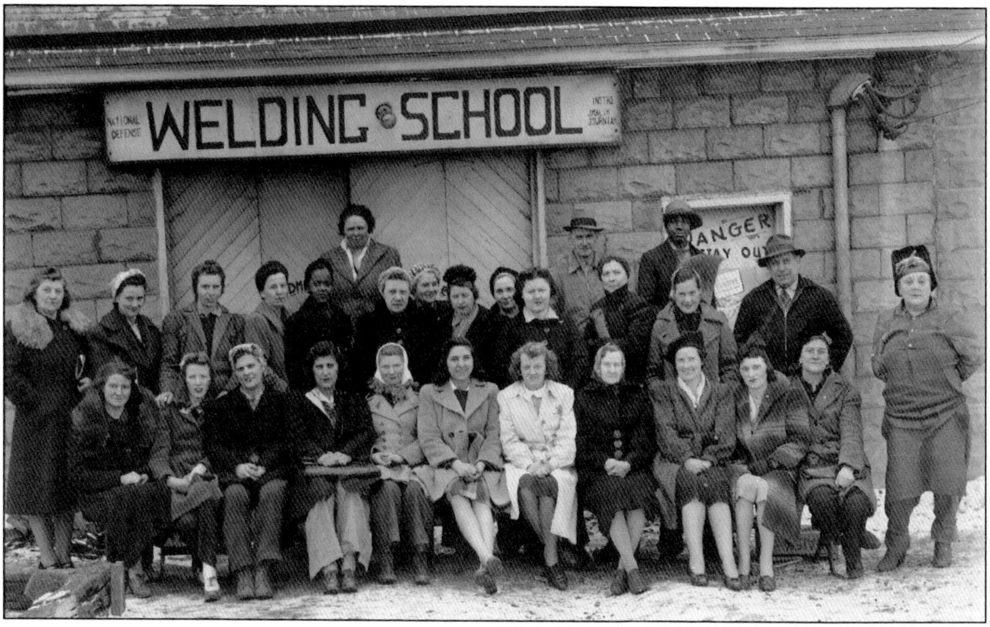

John Malik, standing in the back row next to a woman on the far right, operated a welding school at his shop in Everson during World War II. The women were training for jobs to help with the war effort. George Baker, an African American, appears to the left of Malik, directly in front of the "danger" sign. The others in the photograph are unidentified. (Courtesy *Scottdale Independent-Observer.*)

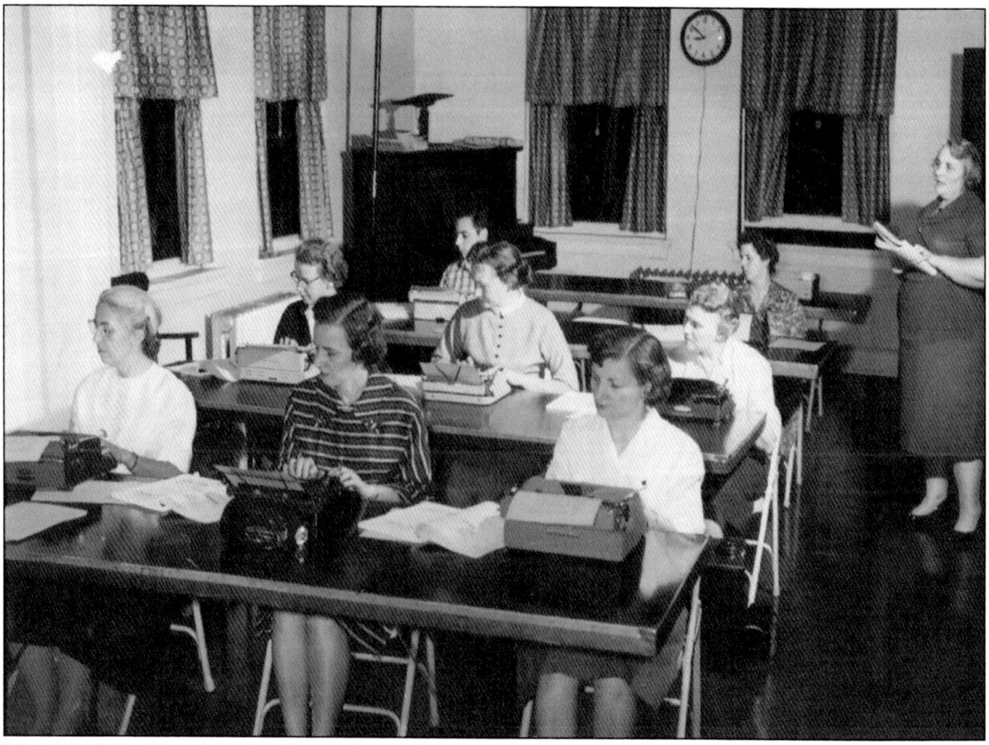

The YMCA offered night classes for adults; this is a 1950s typing class.

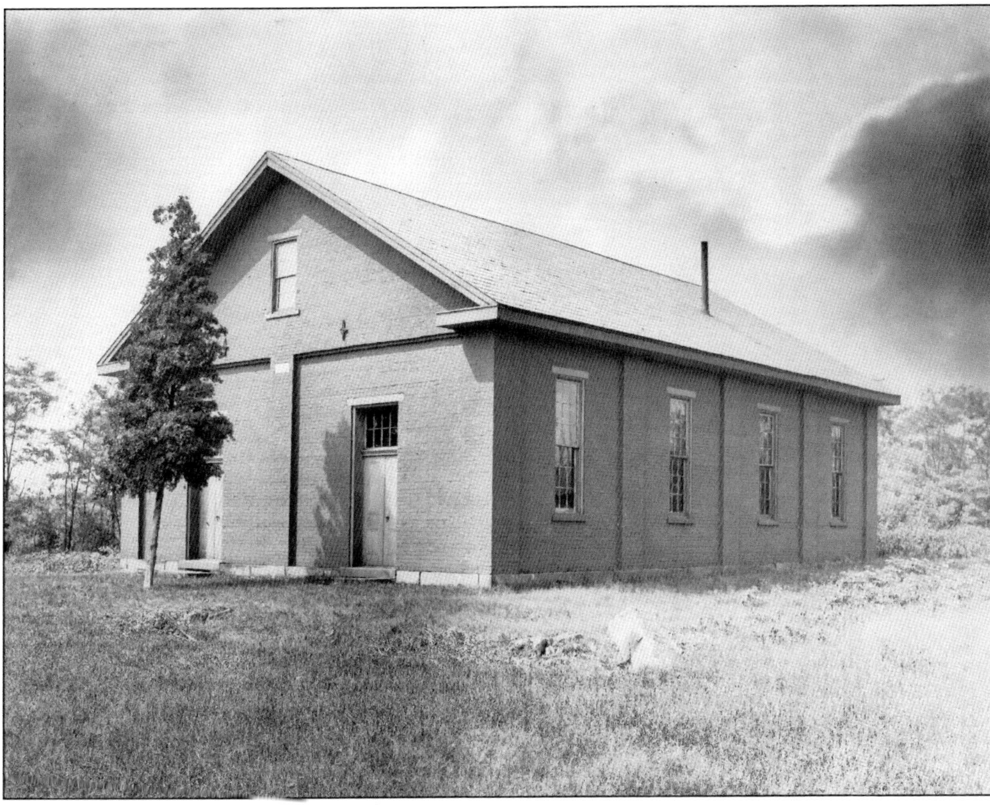

The Jacobs Creek Methodist Church was built in 1863, but the congregation was organized much earlier in 1820. (Courtesy Carol Tacconi.)

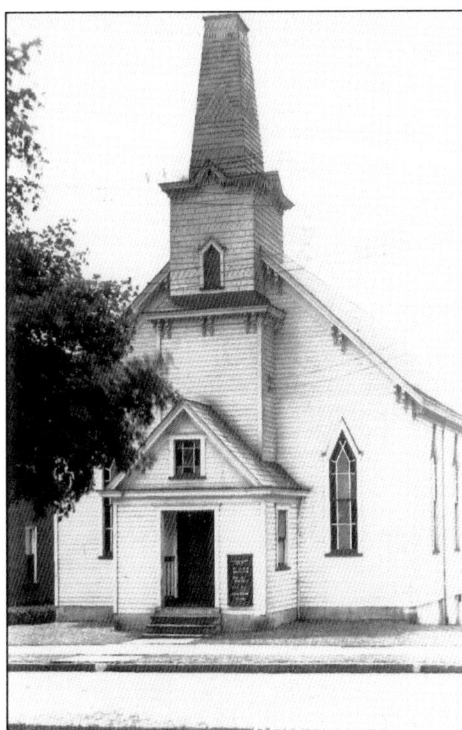

Members of the First Presbyterian Church worshiped in this building before 1900, when the congregation moved across North Chestnut Street to its current church. (Courtesy Chuck King.)

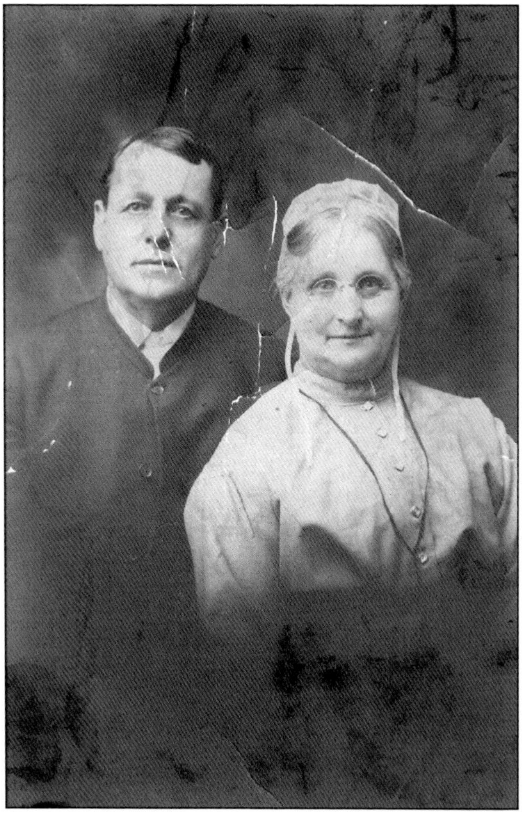

At left are Rev. Aaron Loucks and his wife, Amelia Metzler. In addition to establishing the Mennonite Publishing House, Reverend Loucks revitalized the Mennonite community in Scottdale. Below is the first meetinghouse, which was used between 1893 and 1939. (Both, courtesy Scottdale Mennonite Church.)

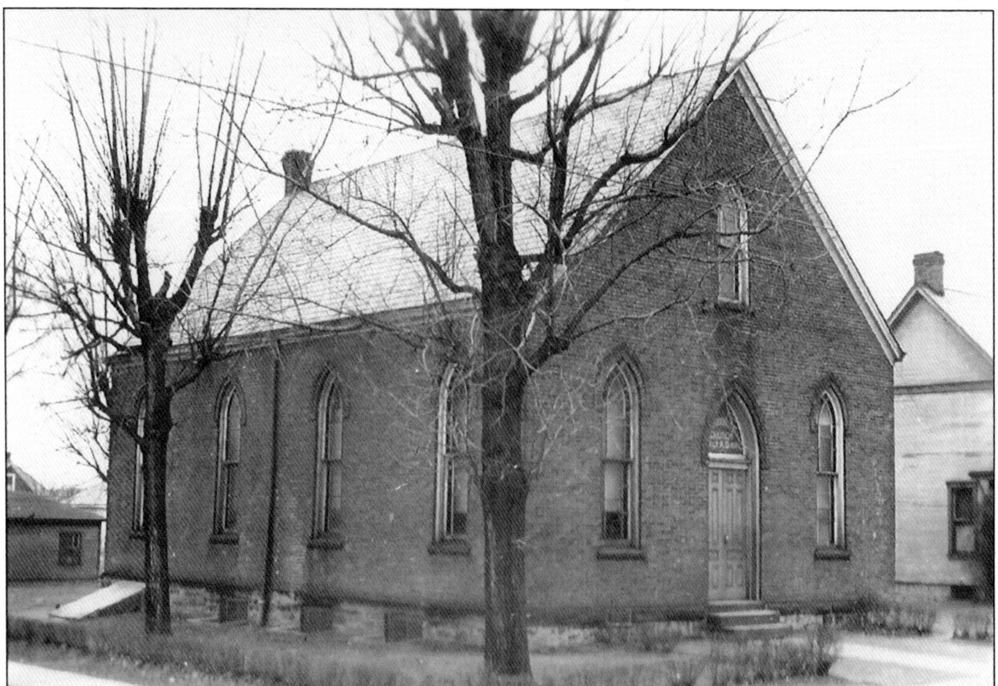

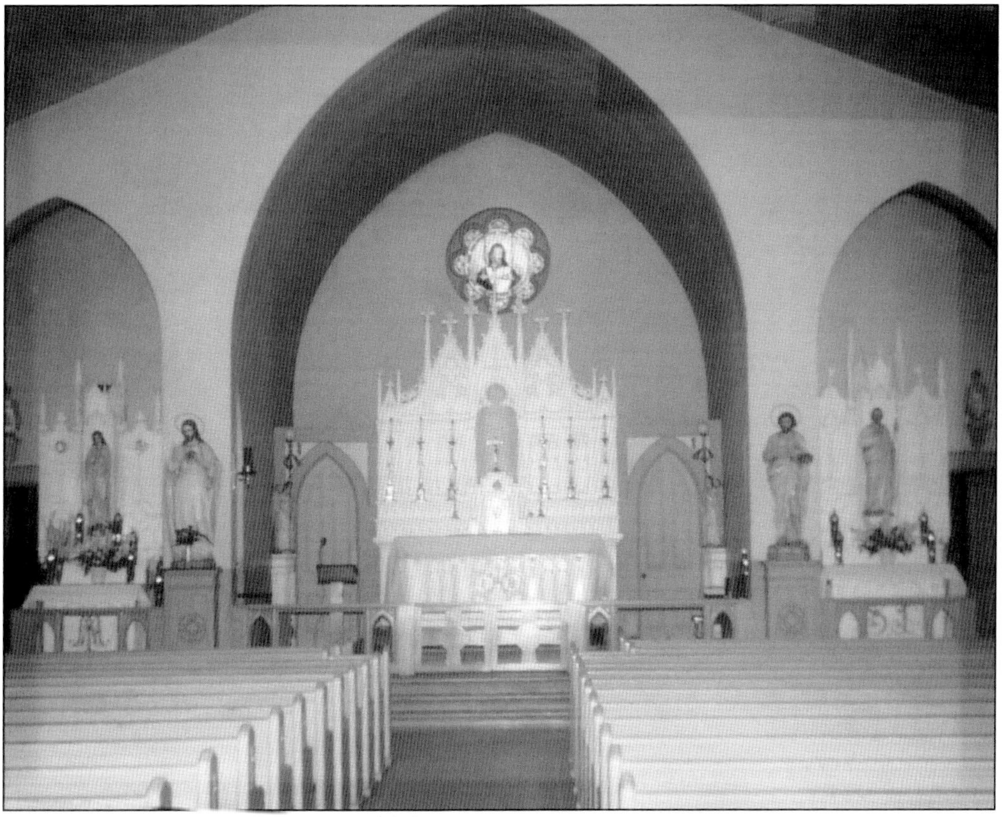

St. John the Baptist Parish was established in 1878. The old church, located next to a rectory, was dedicated in 1882. Rev. Michael Lambing was the pastor at the time of the dedication and continued to serve the parish until 1931. This is the interior of the old church just before it was razed in 1962 for the construction of a combined church and school.

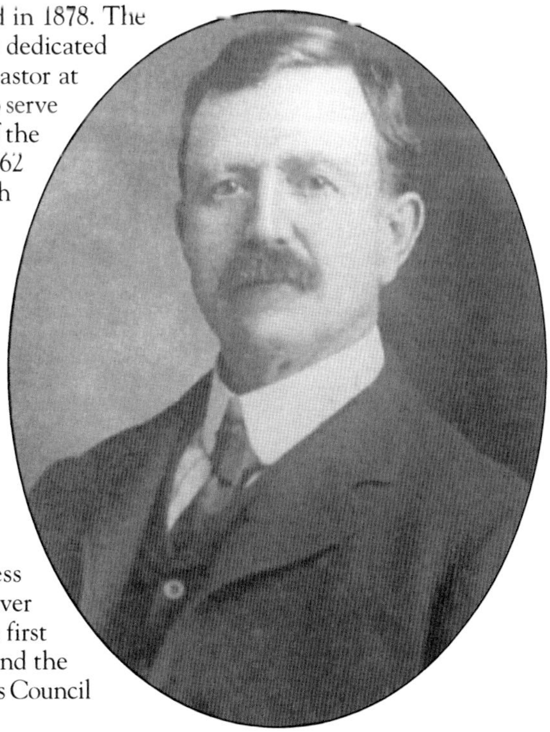

James Owens served as Scottdale burgess and was appointed postmaster by Pres. Grover Cleveland in 1886. In 1902, he became the first exalted ruler of the Scottdale Elks Lodge and the first grand knight in the Knights of Columbus Council No. 1127. (Courtesy Robert Ferguson.)

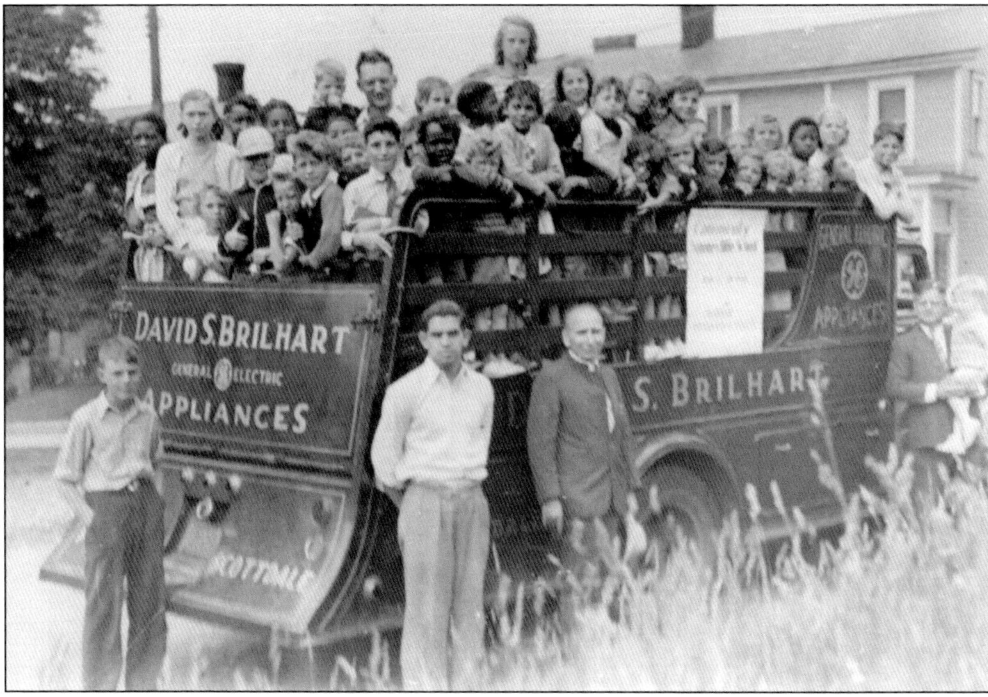

These children are enrolled in the 1940 summer Bible school that was sponsored by the Scottdale Mennonite Church. David Brilhart used one of his delivery trucks for transportation. (Courtesy Scottdale Mennonite Church.)

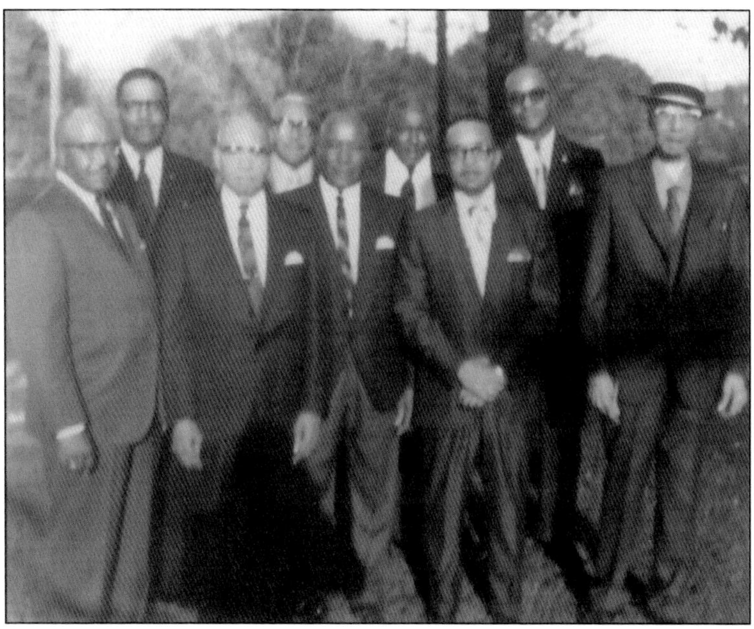

These are the trustees of the Morningstar Baptist Church around 1960. They are, from left to right, (first row) Jessie Claybrook, Clinton Garland, Frank Claybrook, James Burton, and Jess Grisby; (second row) Arthur Price, Sam Brown, James Price, and Preston Evans. (Courtesy Thelma Evans.)

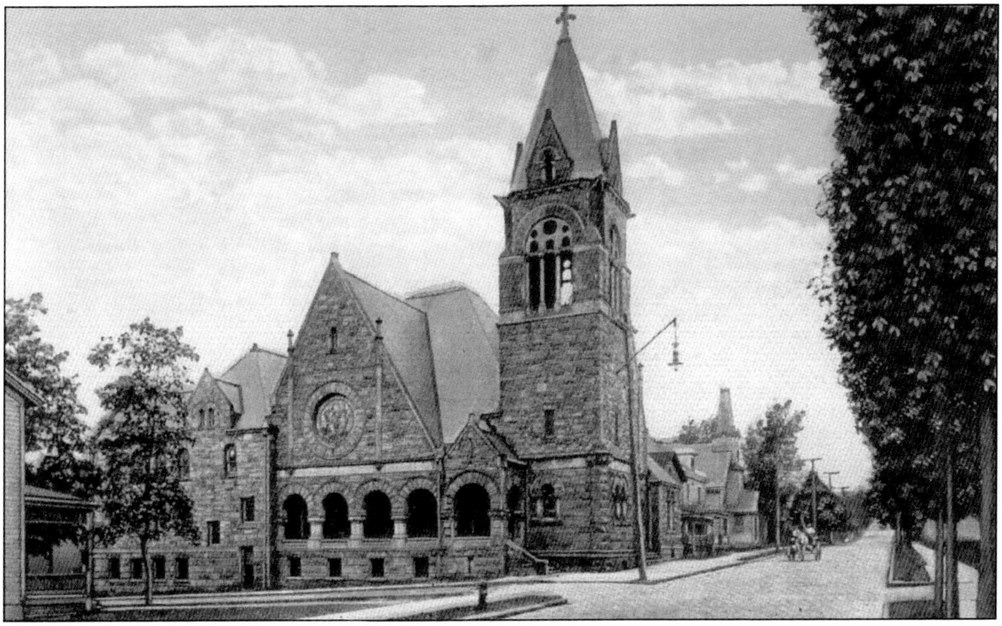

Scottdale was known for its many elegant churches. Here is the First Methodist Episcopal Church on Mulberry Street, which was constituted in 1884. The first volume of *History of Westmoreland County, Pennsylvania*, by John Boucher, printed in 1906, noted that the church was "one of the finest edifices in Westmoreland County."

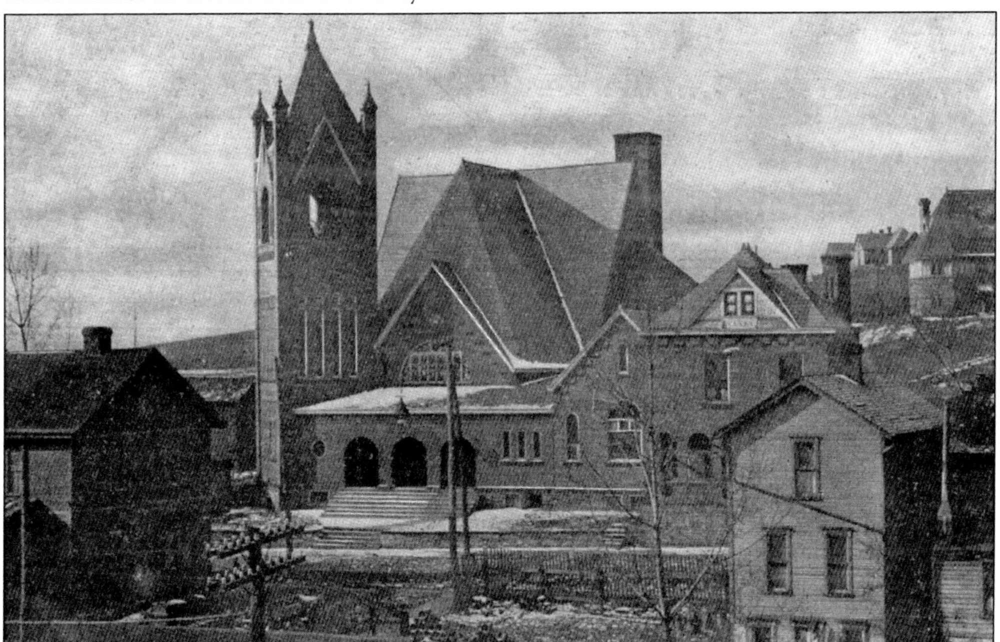

The First Evangelical United Brethren Church in Scottdale dates from 1874. Three churches occupied the same Market Street property. This redbrick building—the second church—served the congregation between 1890 and 1916. It was demolished because the congregation experienced a period of rapid growth and needed larger accommodations. The third and current church, still in use, was dedicated in September 1917.

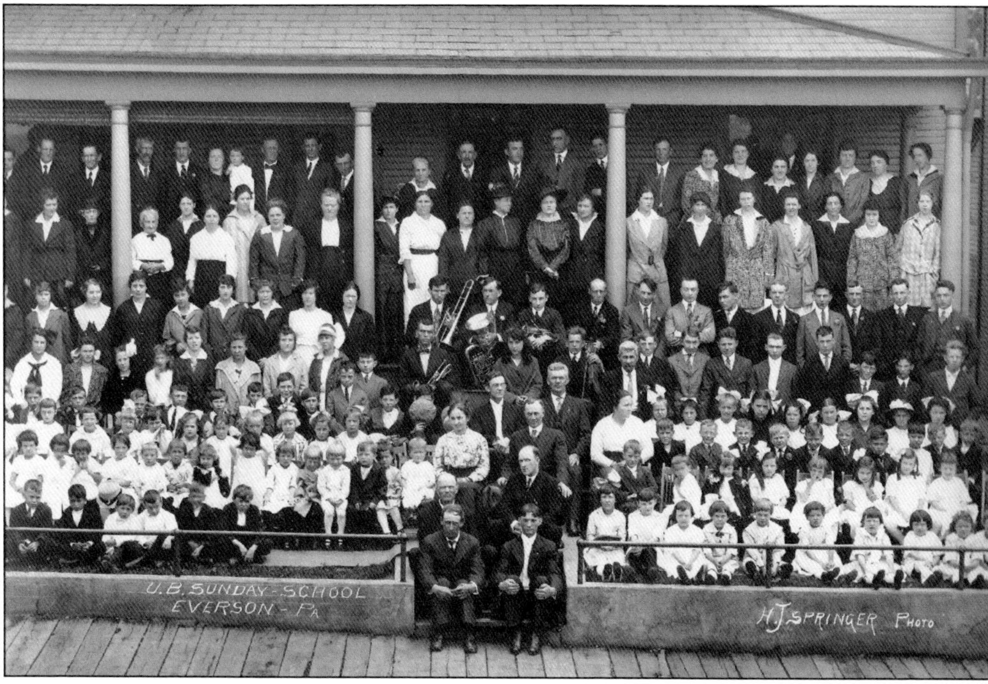

A 1900 revival meeting was the beginning of the Everson Evangelical Church. This is a section of a 1916 Sunday school class, held when the congregation was affiliated with the Church of the United Brethren in Christ. (Courtesy Chuck King.)

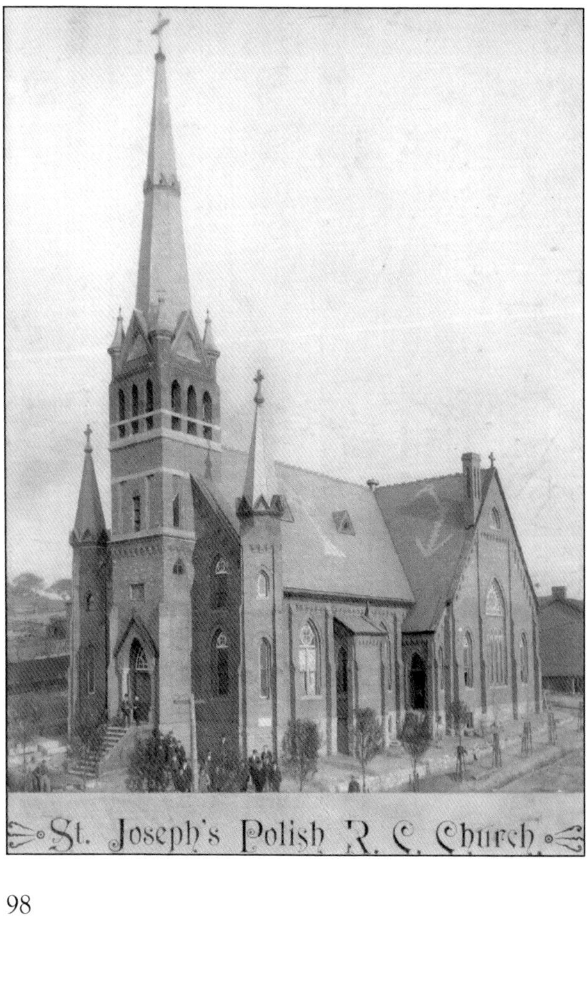

St. Joseph's was the third parish organized for Polish Catholics in the Diocese of Pittsburgh, which, at the time, included the Diocese of Greensburg. The parish was organized in 1887, and the church was completed in 1892. Although other priests served the Polish population, Rev. Alexander Szmigiel is credited with organizing St. Joseph's Parish. (Courtesy Michael Banaszak.)

In this image, members and guests celebrate the 75th anniversary of Council No. 1127, Knights of Columbus. They are, from left to right (first row) Rev. John Salko, Rev. Aloysius Borkowski, Bishop William Connaire, John Farrah (grand knight), Donald Cope, and Rev. William Gavron; (second row) Daniel Picciano, Frederick Eberharter, William Connors Jr., Francis Zaffina, Felix Prestia Jr. and Rev. Leonard Stoviak. (Courtesy John Farrah family.)

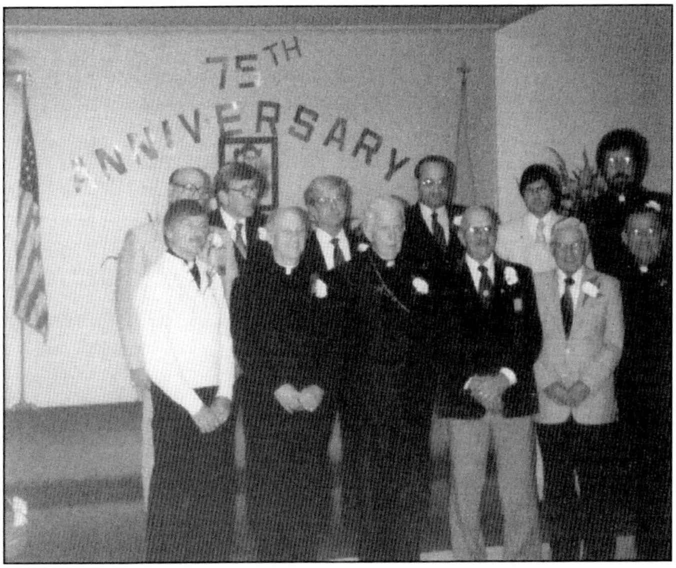

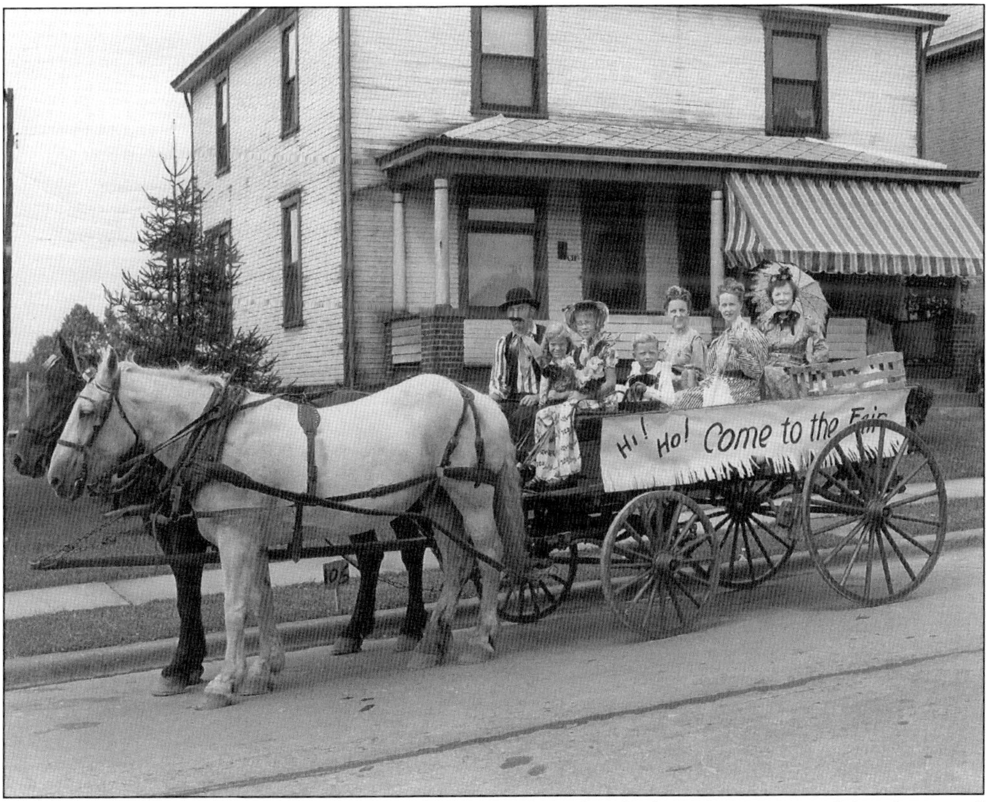

The Alpha-Y-Gradale, an organization for women affiliated with the YMCA, entered this decorated wagon in a 1949 Scottdale parade. From left to right are Arthur Porter, Marcea Maust, Carol Gray, Jack Gearhart, Keenie Gearhart, Mary Ludyared, and Clara Stauffer. (Courtesy Chuck King.)

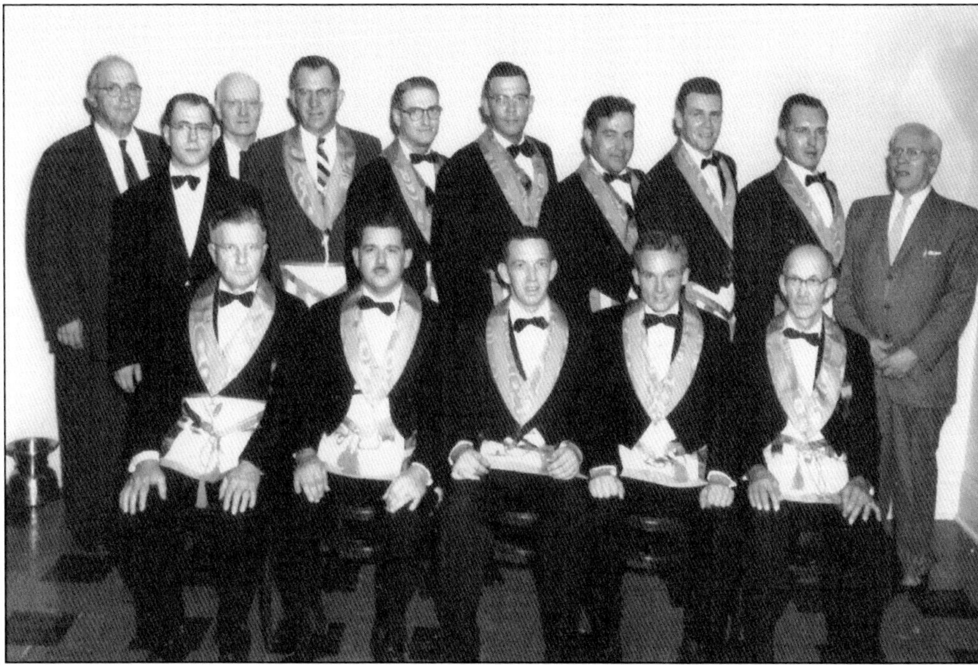

The officers and trustees of Marion Lodge No. 562 F&AM are pictured here in 1957. They are, from left to right, (first row) Roy Martz, Merle Strutz, Clayton Uber, Gilbert Seese, and Edgar Steele; (second row) Bert Shirer Jr., Earl Sturtz, Norman Snyder, Walter Kiebler, John Henderson, two unidentified, and Bert Shirer Sr.; (third row) two unidentified. (Courtesy Marion Lodge.)

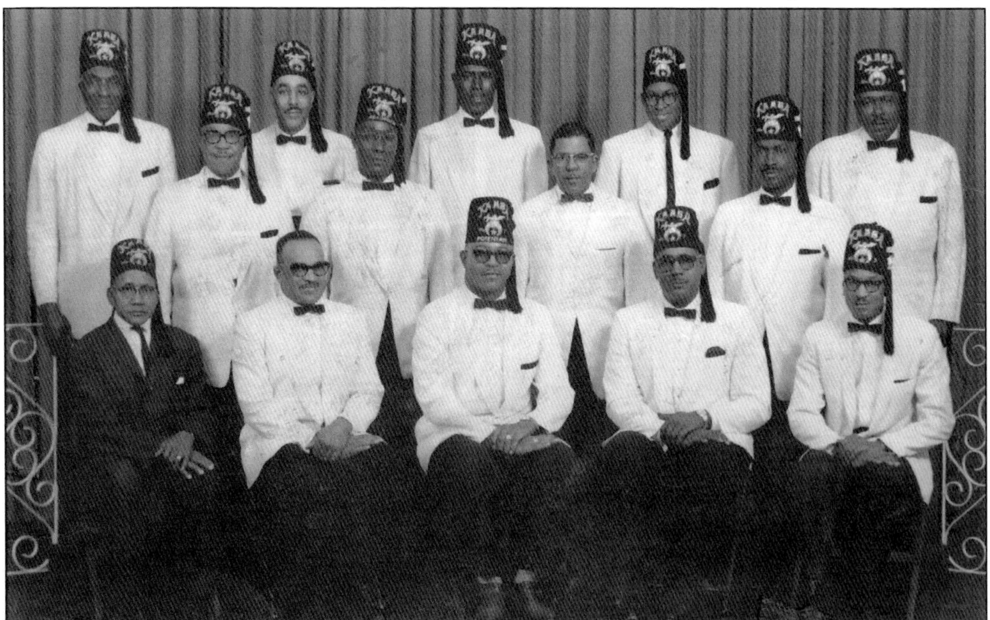

Members of Kaaba Temple Lodge pose for a group photograph in 1960. From left to right are (first row) Charles Meigs, Bud Taylor, Preston Evans (grand potentate), Arthur Price, and Clifford McAbee; (second row) Samuel Brown, John Terry, Edward King, and Marshall Groce; (third row) ? Jones, Oscar Hobsen, Lucas Meadows, Arthur Coles, and James Price. (Courtesy Thelma Evans.)

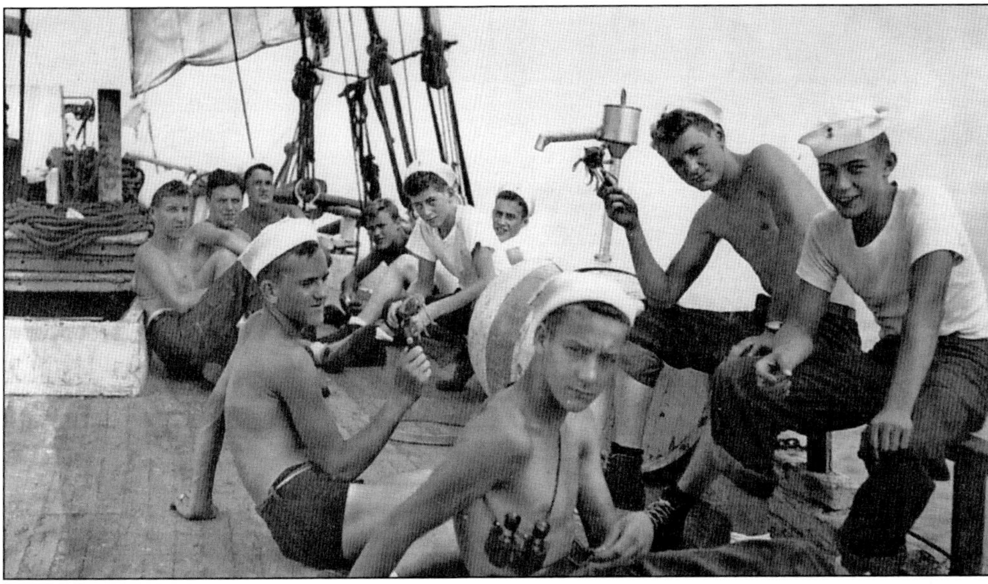

Sea Scouts are pictured here in 1946 aboard a skipjack anchored at St. Michaels, Maryland, on the Chesapeake Bay. The Scottdale YMCA sponsored the ship. (Courtesy Bob Percy.)

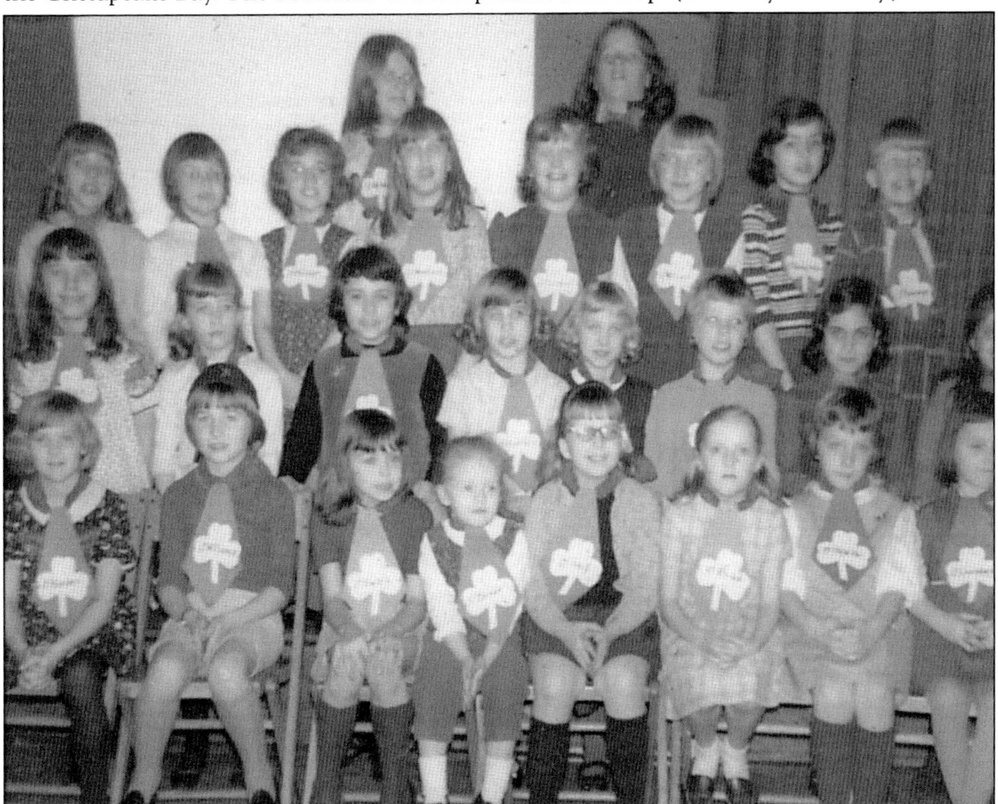

Scottdale Brownies celebrate St. Patrick's Day in 1965 by wearing traditional shamrocks; the letter O was added as a prefix to their names for the occasion. At the time of this picture, area residents supported 12 Girl Scout units with nearly 300 total participants.

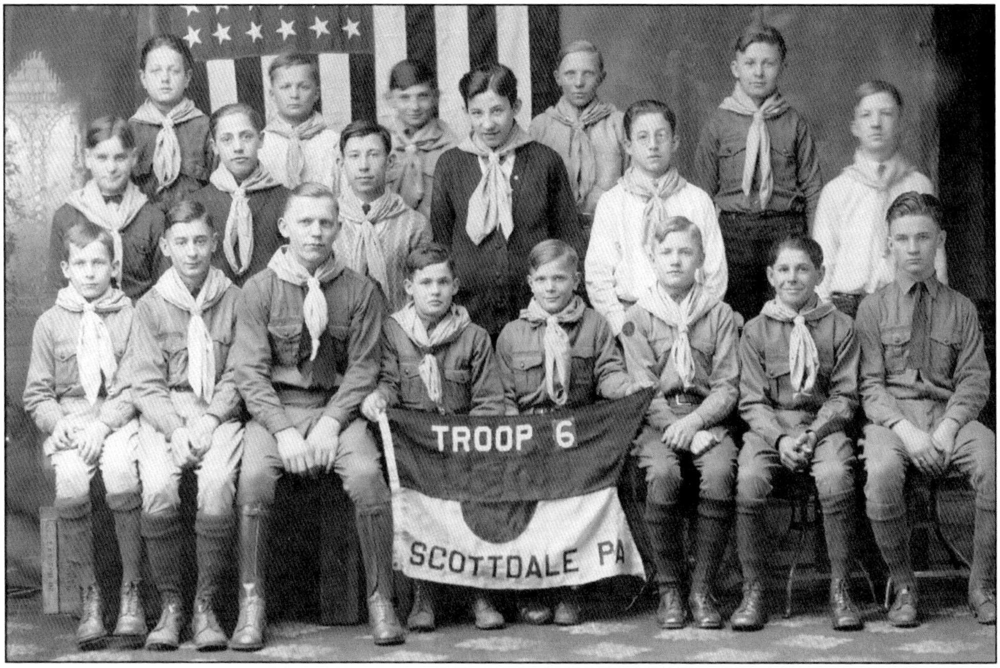

Members of Boy Scout Troop 6, sponsored by St. Joseph's Parish, pose for this 1928 photograph. They are, from left to right, (first row) Walter Radzilowski, John Koza, Scoutmaster Victor Fabiszewski, Casmir Dzinrzynski, Joseph Lewandowski, Stanley Stempniak, Joeseph Kramarski, and Edward Eckman; (second row) Edward Kesiak, Joseph Cudnik, Michael Nebesny, Casmir Obuchowicz, Henry Obuchowicz, and "Izzy" Grzywinski; (third row) Joseph Opalinski, Francis Wesolowski, Andrew Sulkowski, Bruno Kmieciak, and Joseph Urbaniak.

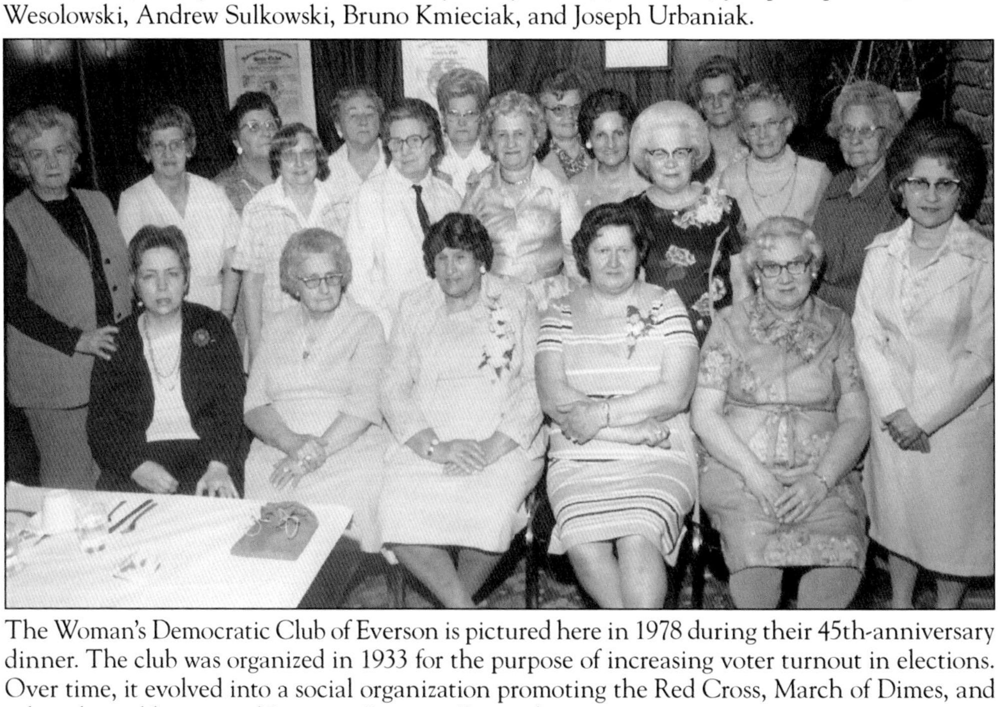

The Woman's Democratic Club of Everson is pictured here in 1978 during their 45th-anniversary dinner. The club was organized in 1933 for the purpose of increasing voter turnout in elections. Over time, it evolved into a social organization promoting the Red Cross, March of Dimes, and other charitable causes. (Courtesy Suzanne Sanner.)

Five

Celebrating and Having Fun

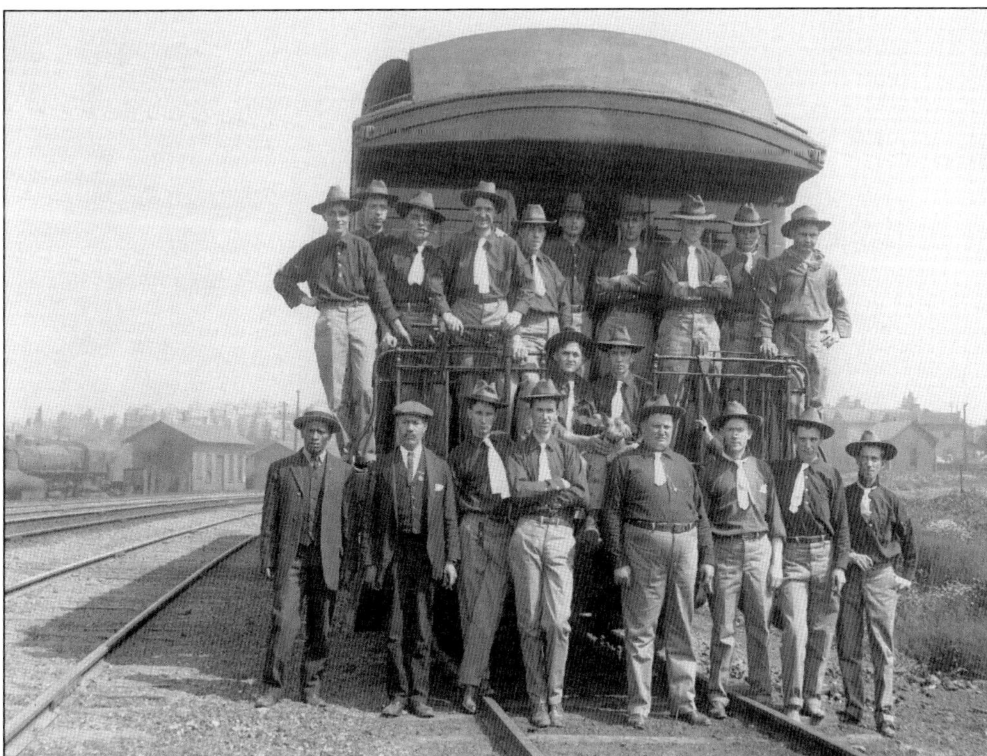

Members of the Scottdale Outdoor Club pose around 1910 on the rear car of a train that will take them on another adventure. The club traveled throughout the region for camping trips, bathing, and picnics. (Courtesy Joseph Fagan.)

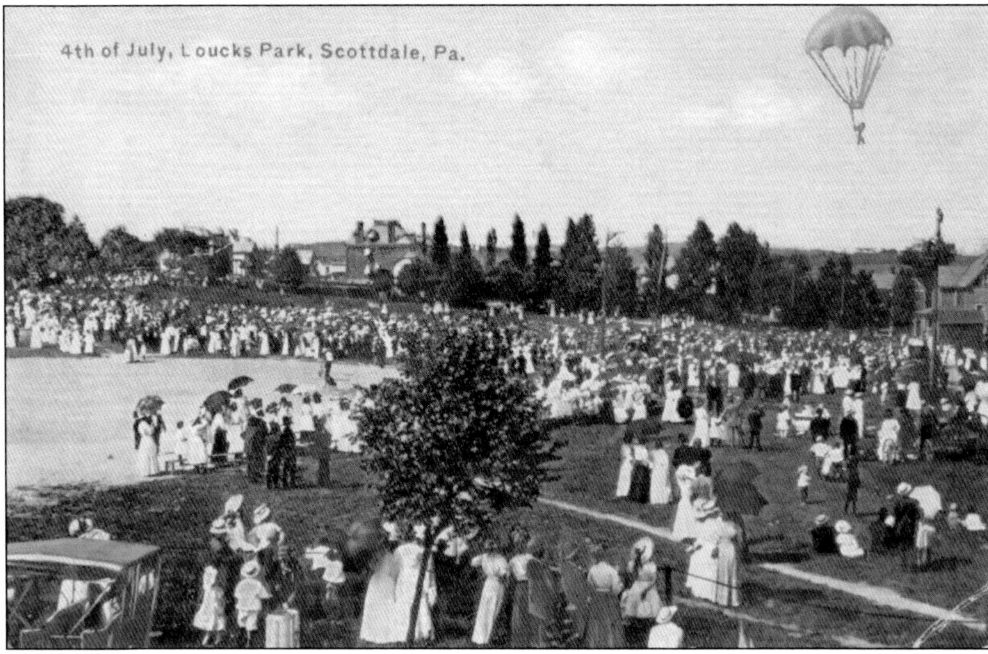

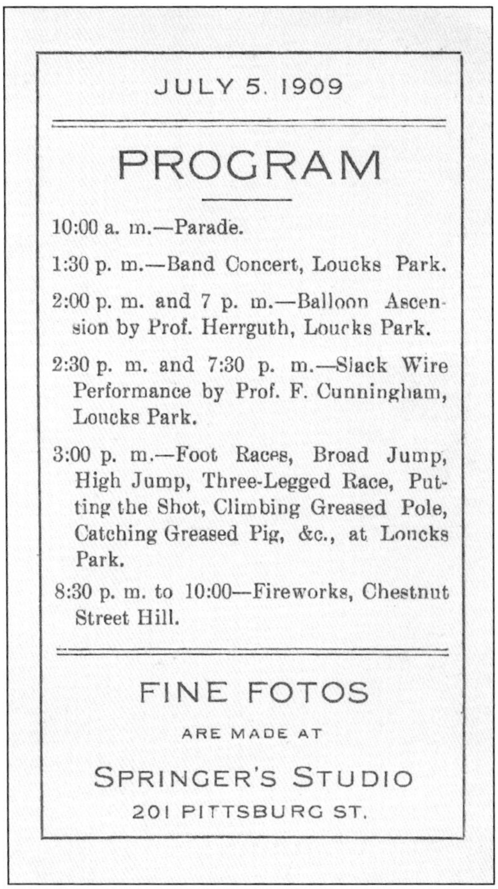

JULY 5. 1909

PROGRAM

10:00 a. m.—Parade.

1:30 p. m.—Band Concert, Loucks Park.

2:00 p. m. and 7 p. m.—Balloon Ascension by Prof. Herrguth, Lourks Park.

2:30 p. m. and 7:30 p. m.—Slack Wire Performance by Prof. F. Cunningham, Loucks Park.

3:00 p. m.—Foot Races, Broad Jump, High Jump, Three-Legged Race, Putting the Shot, Climbing Greased Pole, Catching Greased Pig, &c., at Loncks Park.

8:30 p. m. to 10:00—Fireworks, Chestnut Street Hill.

FINE FOTOS

ARE MADE AT

SPRINGER'S STUDIO

201 PITTSBURG ST.

Loucks Park is pictured above on July 4, 1909, at an event that featured a balloon ascension by Professor Herrguth. The program at left lists the professor's event, along with races and a greased pole competition. The park is still used as a location for recreational programs, community picnics, and special events.

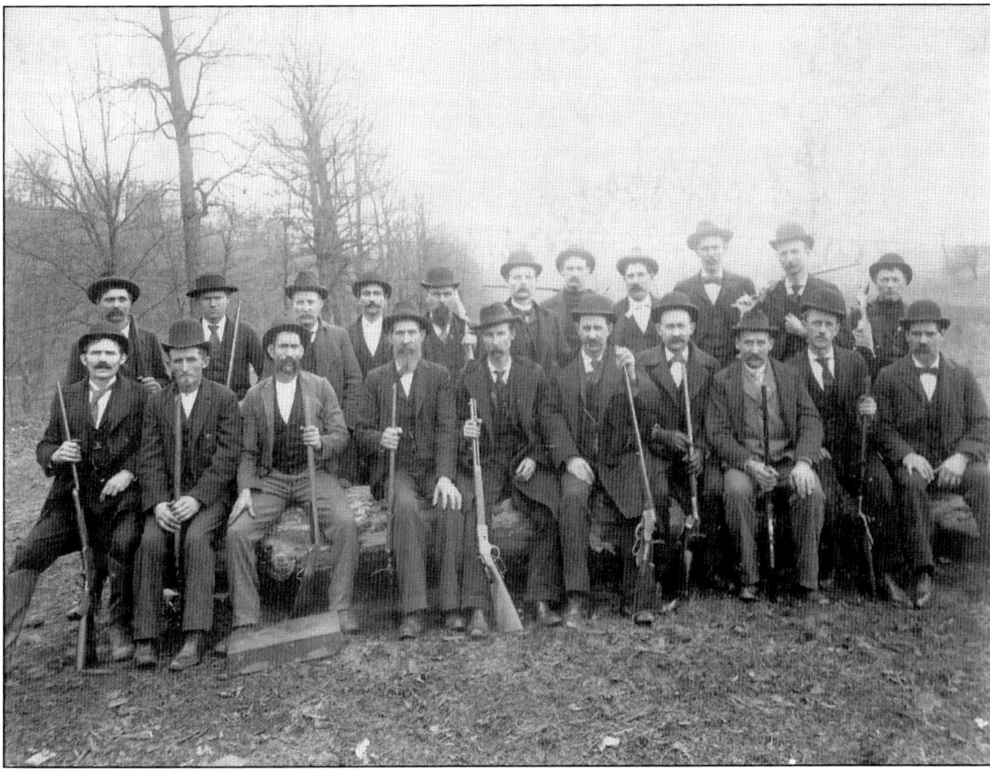

Hunting clubs were popular in Scottdale and the surrounding townships. Here is a club whose members appear ready for the start of the season around 1900. (Courtesy *Scottdale Independent-Observer.*)

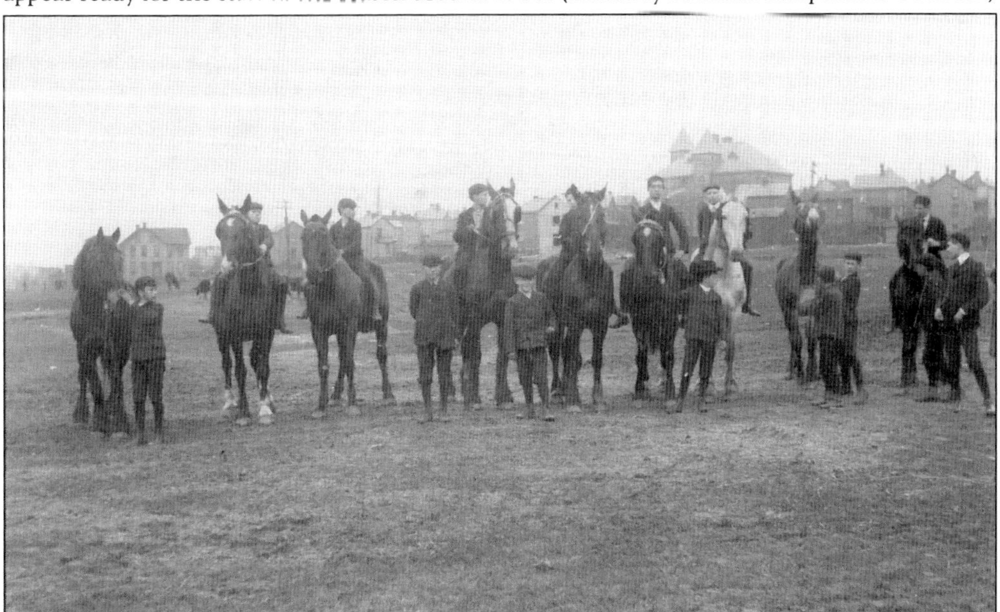

These young men enjoy horseback riding below Graff Street in Everson around 1915. Reportedly, some of the riders were subsequently fined in Scottdale for exceeding the speed limit on Broadway. (Courtesy Michael Banaszak.)

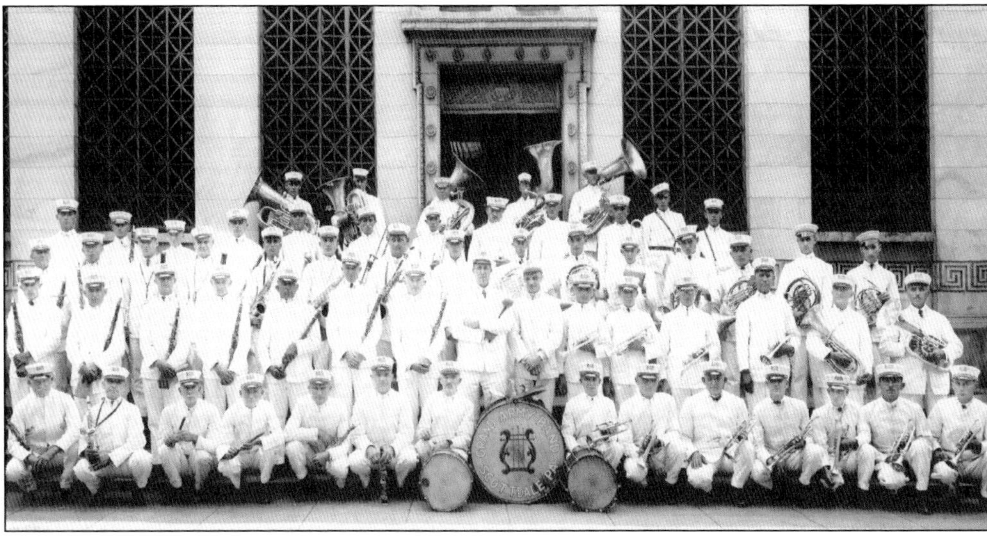

The Grand Army Band was organized in 1893 as the Scottdale Cornet Band. For 57 years, it led Memorial Day parades and entertained crowds from the grandstand at Loucks Park. (Courtesy West Overton Museums.)

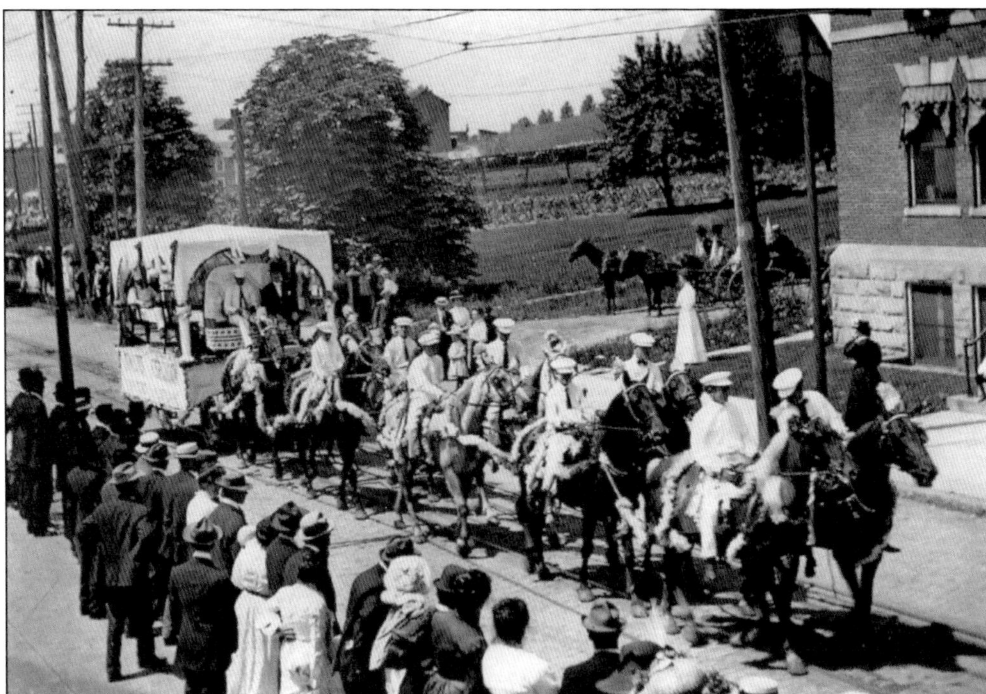

On July 4, 1908, a wagon team decorated by the Ferguson Furniture Store passes the Jacob S. Loucks Farm and the Frick corporate offices on South Broadway. (Courtesy Robert Ferguson.)

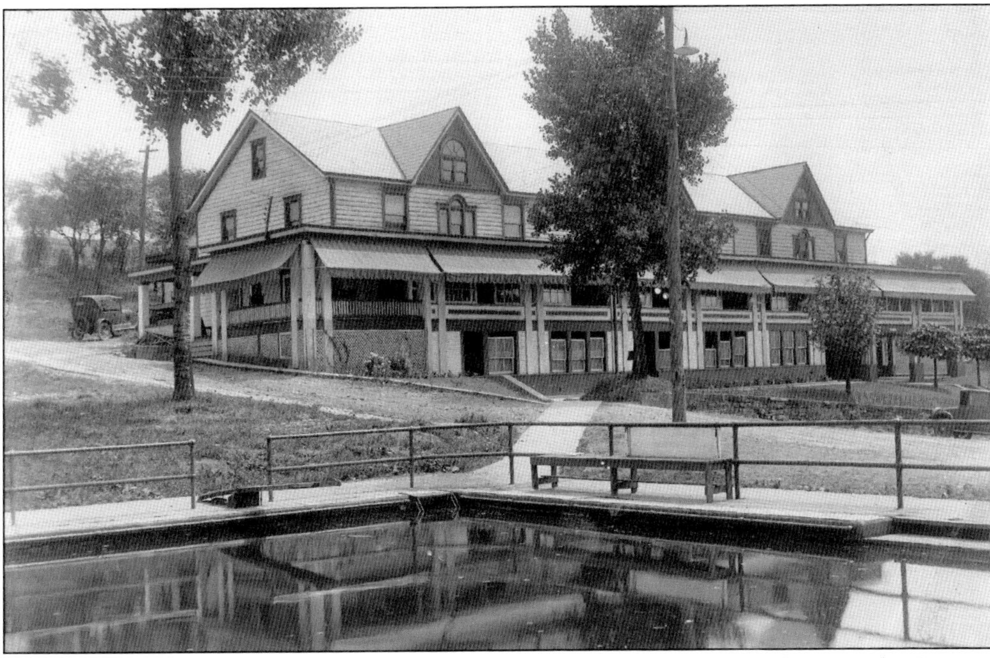

The Pleasant Valley Country Club, pictured around 1929, was built on the Detwiler Farm in 1922. It featured tennis courts, an outdoor swimming pool, and, in the beginning, a nine-hole golf course. The club hosted proms, reunions, and anniversaries and served as a meeting place for many organizations. (Courtesy Carol Tacconi.)

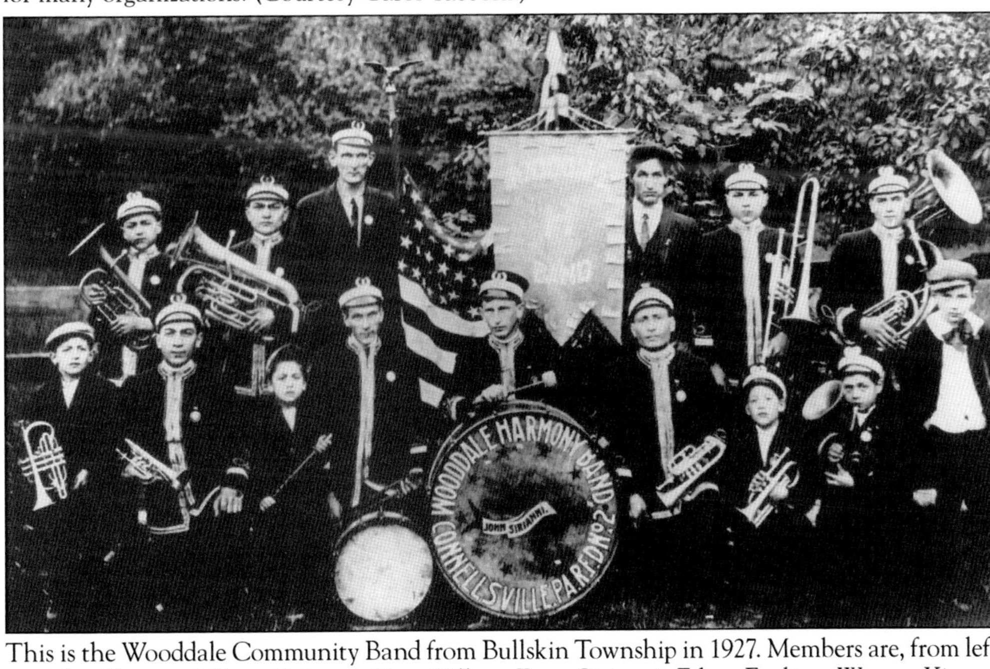

This is the Wooddale Community Band from Bullskin Township in 1927. Members are, from left to right, (first row) Fiore Sirianni, Tom Gillott, Ettor Sirianni, Edgar Exeline, Warren Kineer, John Sirianni (band leader), Augustine Sirianni, Frank Gillott, Jr. and Earl Wiltrout; (second row) Flourine Gillott, Tony Gillott, Jess Wiltrout, Henry Nicholson, Herman Gillott, and Joseph Gillott. (Courtesy Edward Cope.)

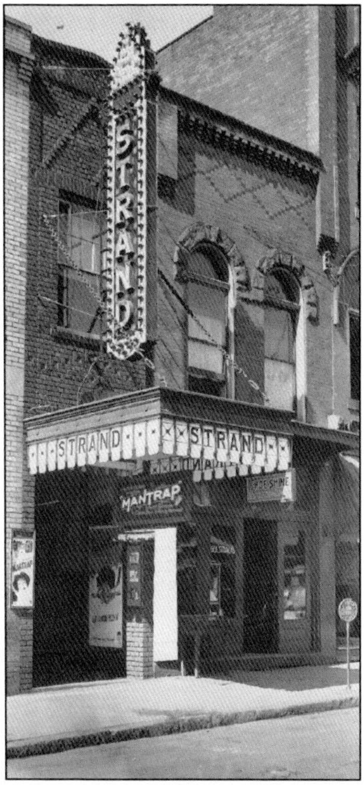

The Geyer House, dating from 1900, became the Strand Theater in 1924. It hosted events ranging from public lectures to vaudeville acts and movies. Many young residents fondly remember going to the Stand for the Saturday matinee. Today, the theater is home to Scottdale Showtime, Inc., a nonprofit organization that restored the interior and initiated a production schedule of plays and musicals. The snack bar in the lobby is pictured below around 1953; the smell of popcorn was hard to resist and even attracted customers who were not going to the movies. (Both, courtesy *Scottdale Independent-Observer.*)

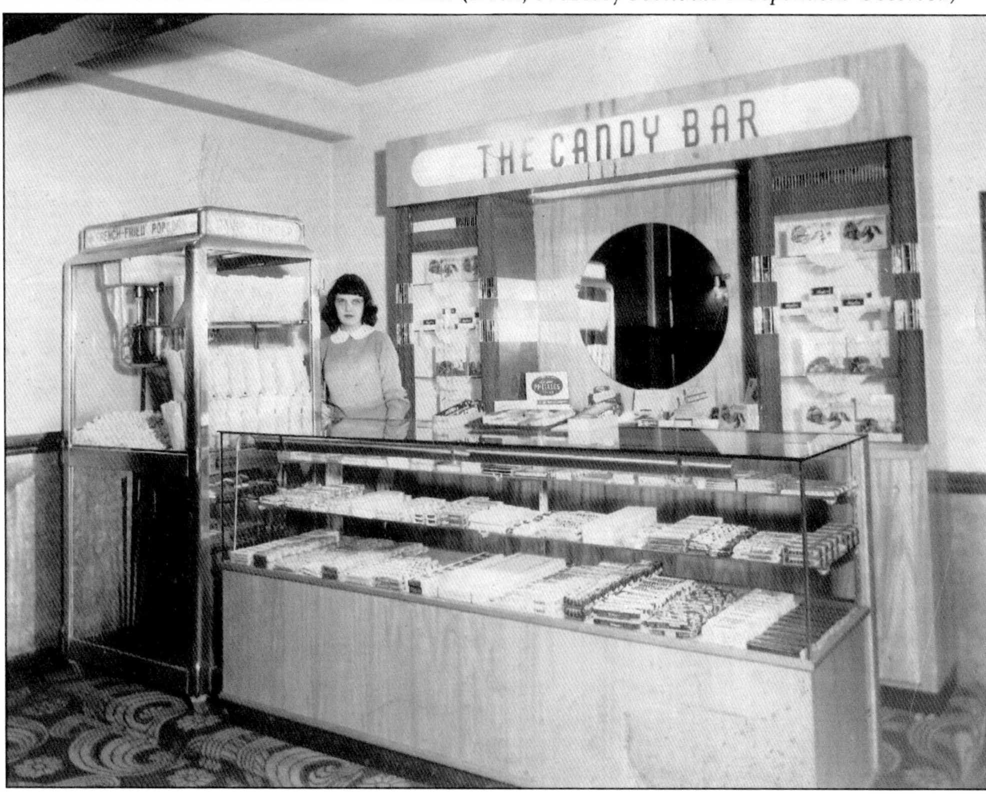

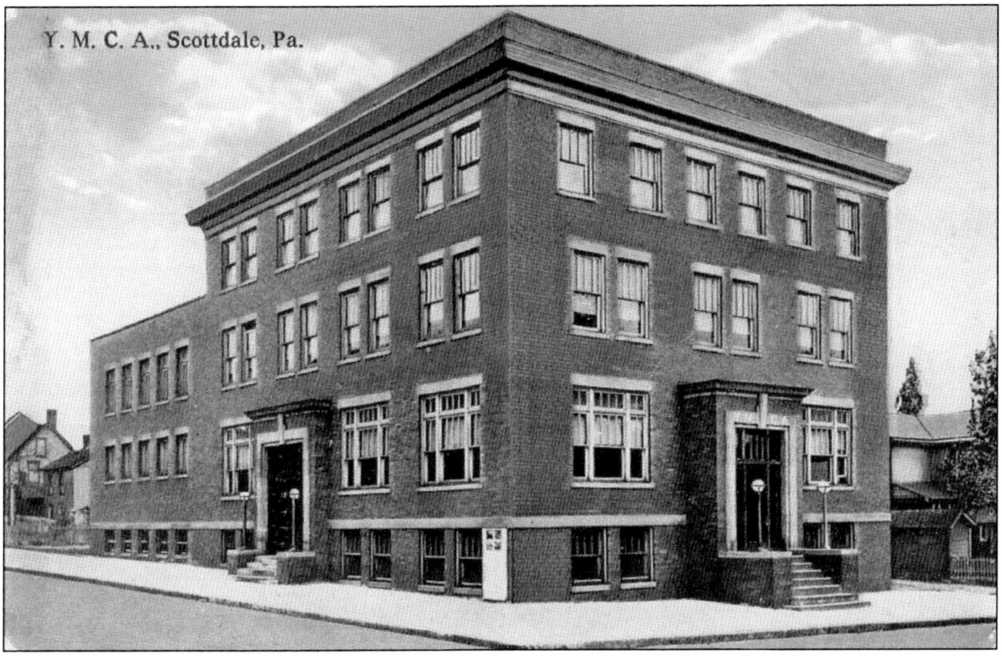

The Scottdale YMCA opened on Spring Street in 1913. In addition to physical activities, it sponsored Scout troops and served as a meeting place for many community organizations.

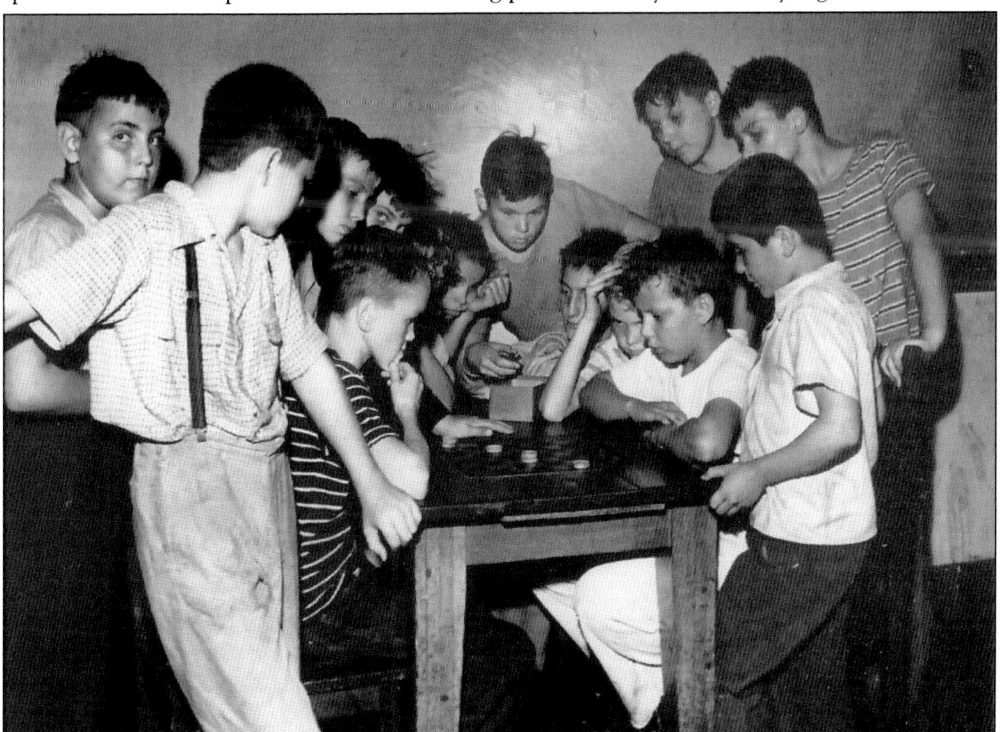

The YMCA was the place to go after school and on Saturday. This 1950s checkers game apparently attracted a crowd trying to anticipate the next move. (Courtesy *Scottdale Independent-Observer.*)

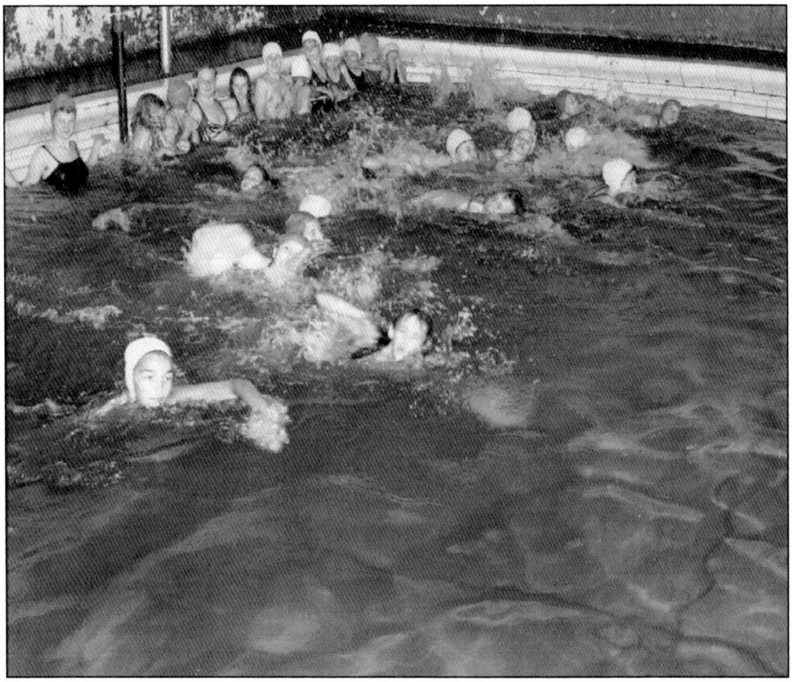

Most young people learned to swim at the YMCA. This is a c. 1950 girls' swimming class in the old pool. Beginners were limited to the three-foot section, which was separated from the deep end by a rope. The pool was also used for Red Cross lifesaving classes.

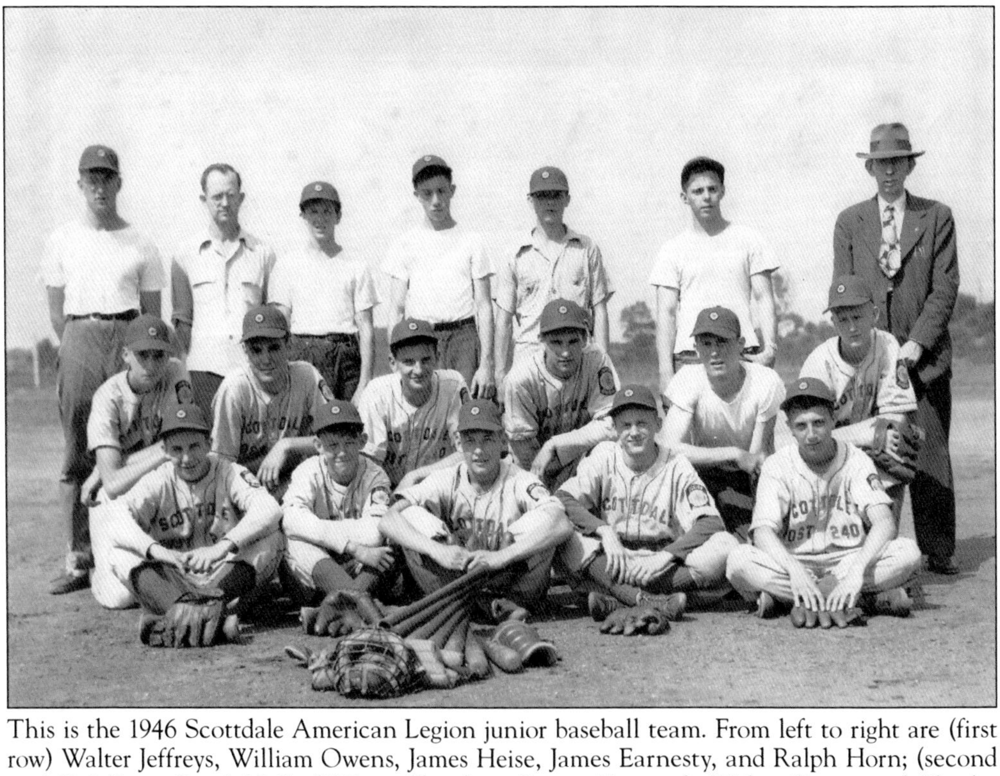

This is the 1946 Scottdale American Legion junior baseball team. From left to right are (first row) Walter Jeffreys, William Owens, James Heise, James Earnesty, and Ralph Horn; (second row) Bob Percy, Frank Nelly, William Slaughter, Steven Zemanek, Walter Green, and Charles Dunlevy; (third row) Lee Dunlevy, Edward Dunlevy, Lee Sherman, Robert Rollinson, Ronald Nicklow, Jim Eicher, and George Freeman. (Courtesy Bob Percy.)

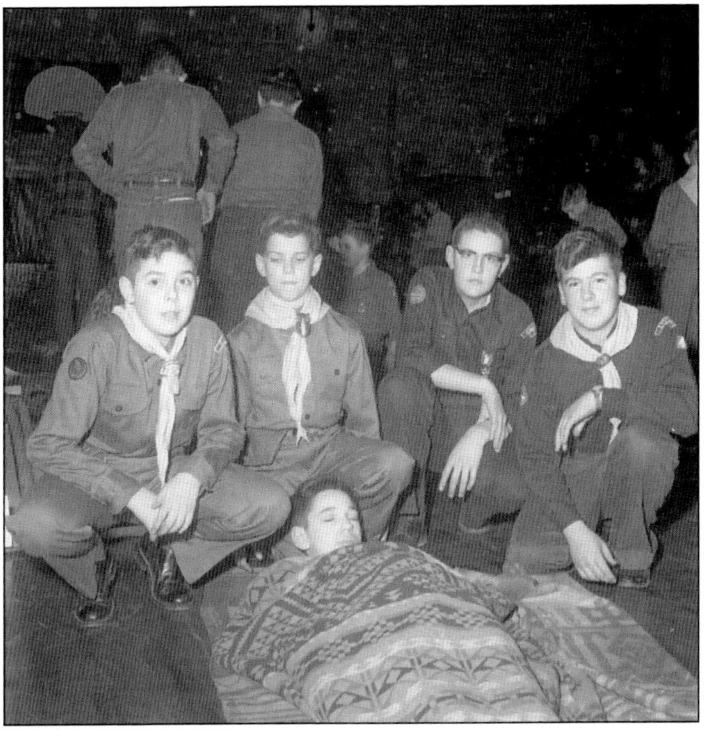

The Scottdale Armory was a venue for many community events, including this 1957 first-aid meet sponsored by the Braddock Trails District, Boy Scouts of America. Here, a patrol from Troop 4 in Everson waits for the judge's evaluation of its performance in responding to a medical emergency. From left to right are Denny Leighty, unidentified, William Boyce, and Timothy O'Hanlon. The "patient," covered in a blanket, is James Scardina. (Courtesy James Smith.)

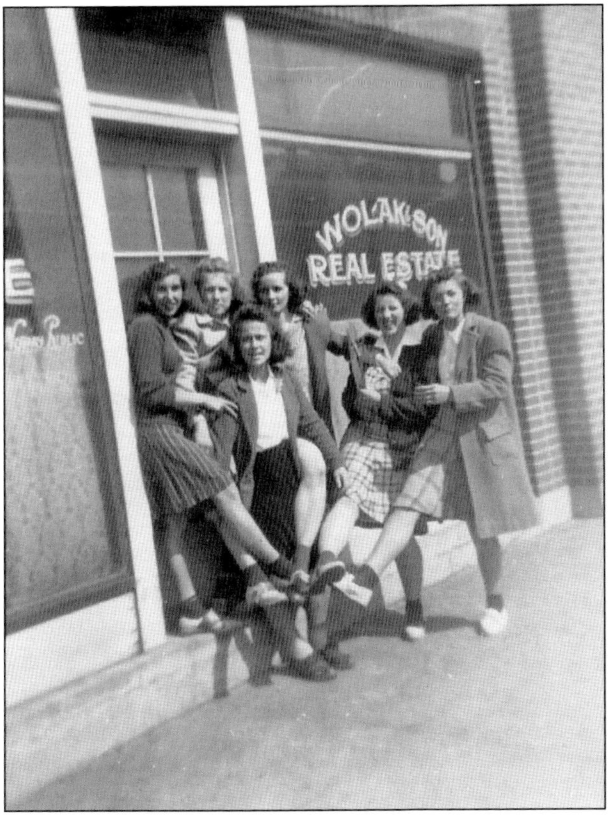

These young ladies pose around 1950 in front of the Wolak Real Estate Office, which occupied the first floor of the Everson Polish Club. They are, from left to right, Adele Dayoob, Ann Kovalcik, Gladys Kovalcik, Anatasia Lesniak, and Eileen Mahokey. Irene Luczka appears in front of Ann and Gladys Kovalcik. (Courtesy Michael Banaszak.)

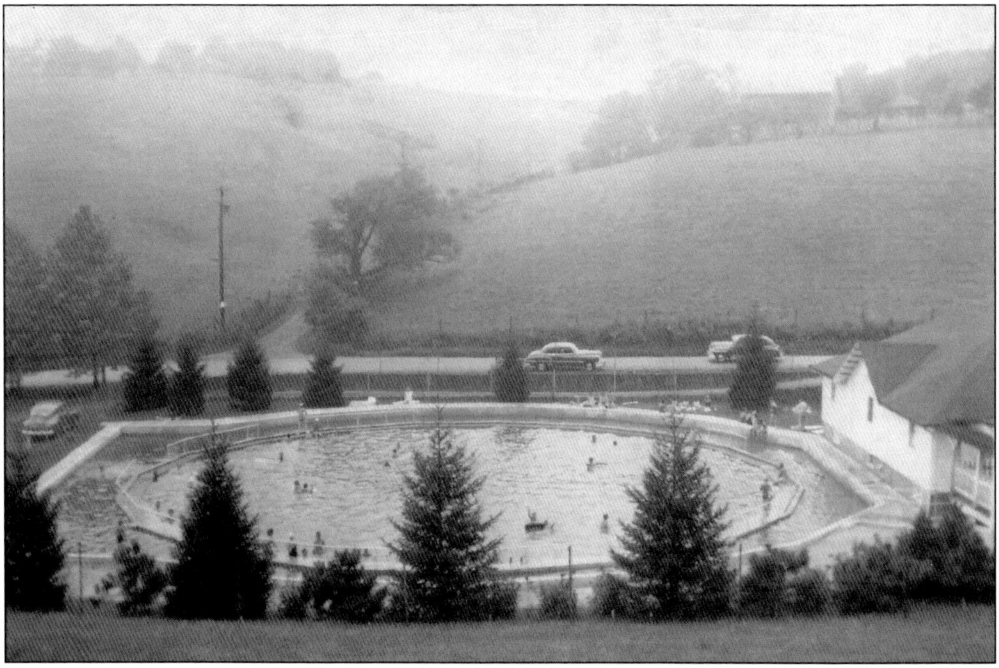

George Briercheck opened Lake Forest Park in the early 1930s. In addition to providing an area for swimming and boating, it was a favorite spot for family picnics and, during the winter, ice-skating. This is a view of the pool and the bathhouse from the picnic grove on the hill. (Courtesy Eva Reed.)

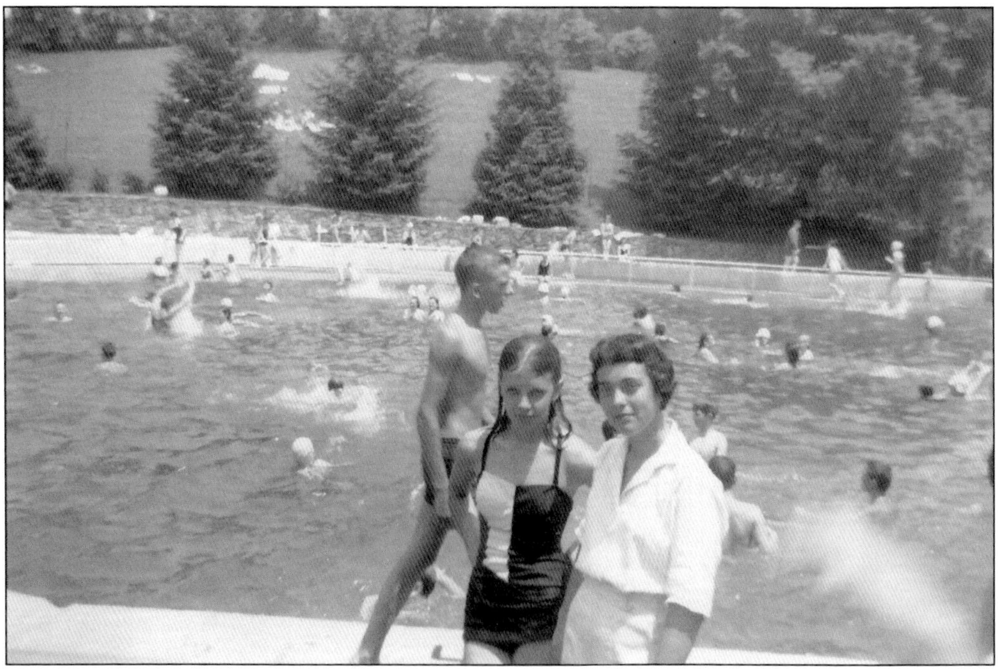

Darlene Patterson (left) and Marjorie Marasco (right) pose in front of the pool during the 1959 summer season. The hillside in the background was popular for sunbathing. (Courtesy Carol Tacconi.)

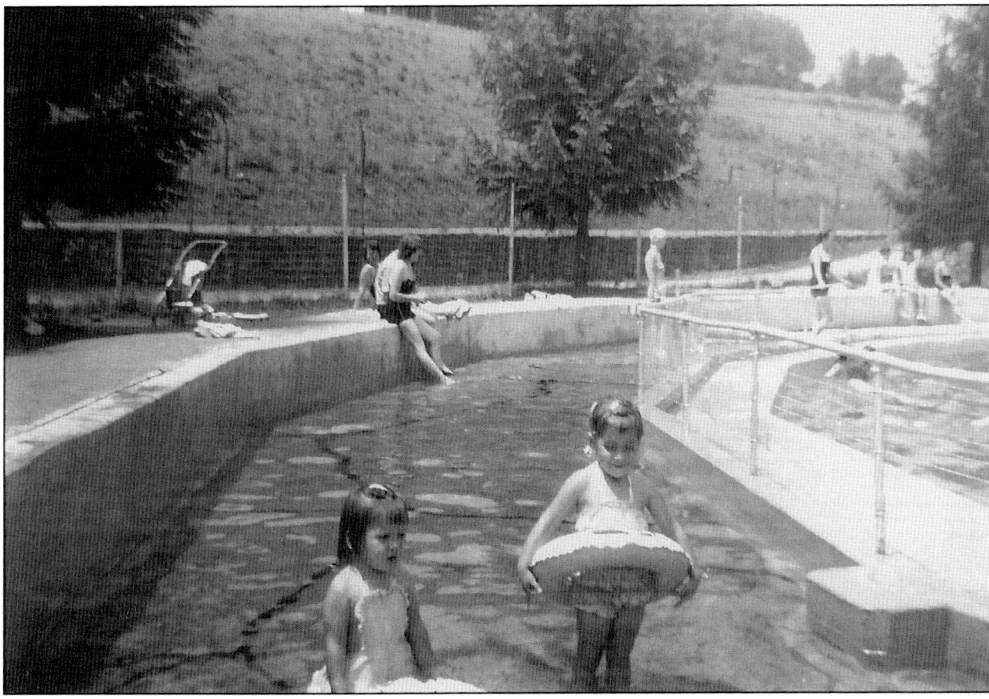

Maureen Houck, in the tube, and Mary Beth Houck get their feet wet in the kids' pool at Lake Forest Park in 1959. (Courtesy Carol Tacconi.)

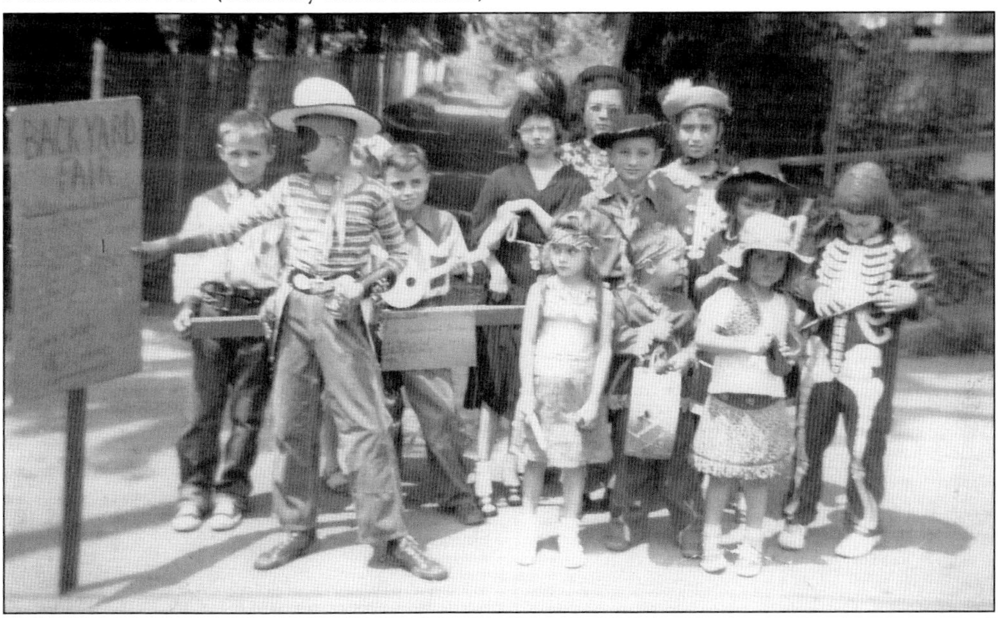

In addition to other youth organizations, some neighborhoods encouraged children to plan special events and activities. Pictured here are Everson children dressed in costumes during a parade advertising their 1948 backyard fair, which featured games and prizes. They are, from left to right, (first row) Edward Bambery, Jean Farrah, Gerald Gaal, and Rosemarie and James Delbuci; (second row) Paul Eckman, Daniel Farrah, Mary Jane Tartle, Kenneth Collins, and Marjorie Eckman; (third row) unidentified, Mary Lou Gaal, and Robert Farrah.

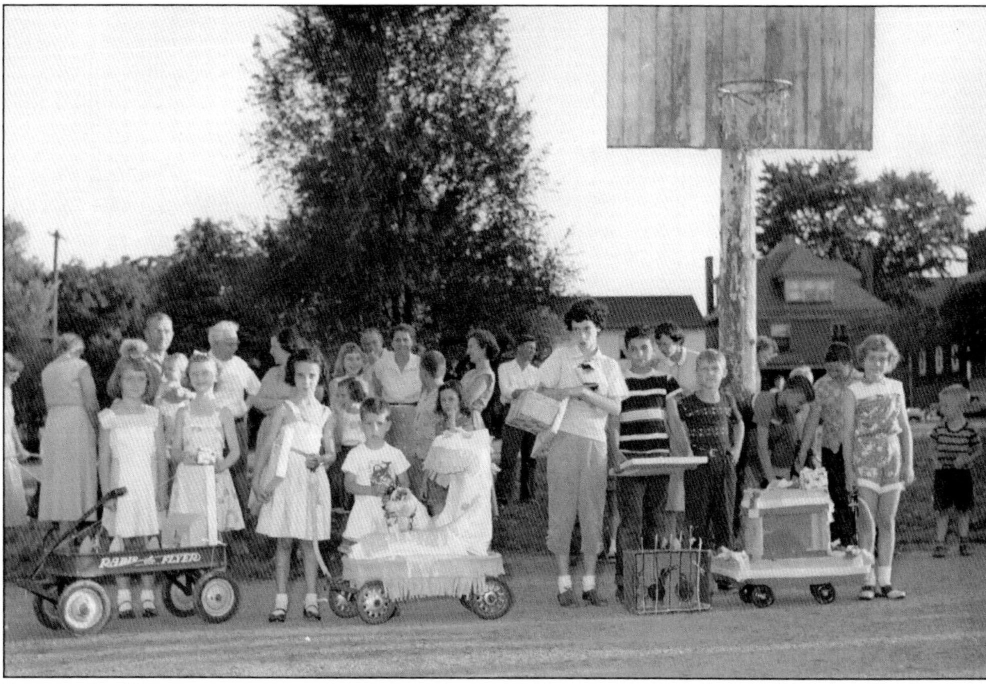

During the 75th-anniversary celebration of Scottdale's incorporation, organizers scheduled a pet parade for children. Pictured above are some of the children waiting for judges to review their entries. Peggy Robbins Wingert, holding her cat, is the fifth person from the right. The other competitors and spectators are unidentified. Below are the winners in the feline competition holding their pets and prizes. (Both, courtesy *Scottdale Independent-Observer.*)

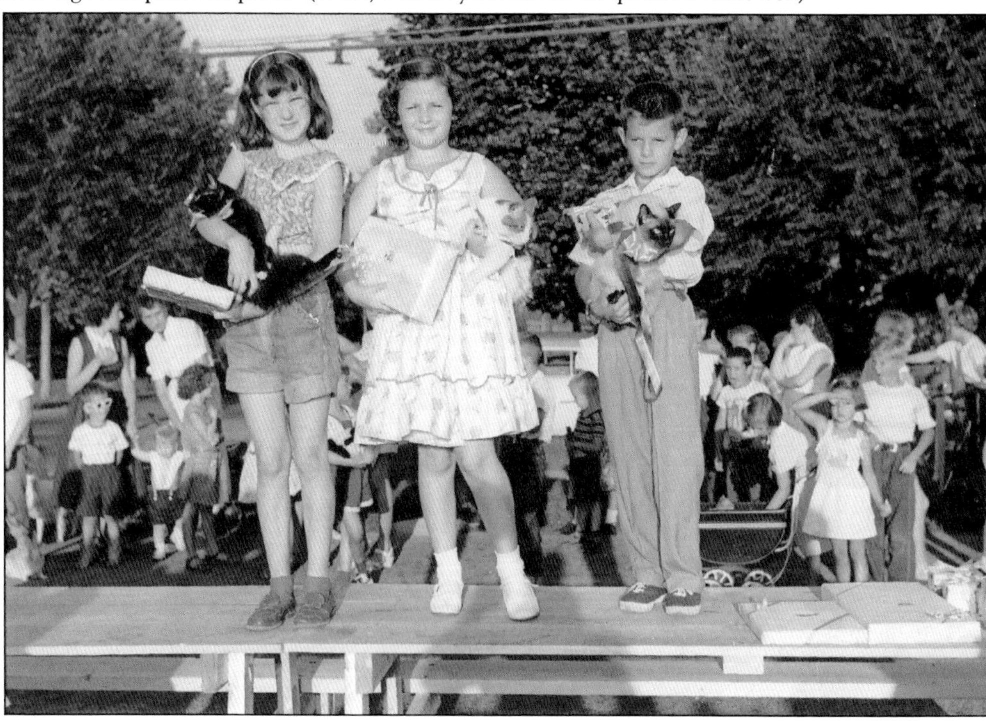

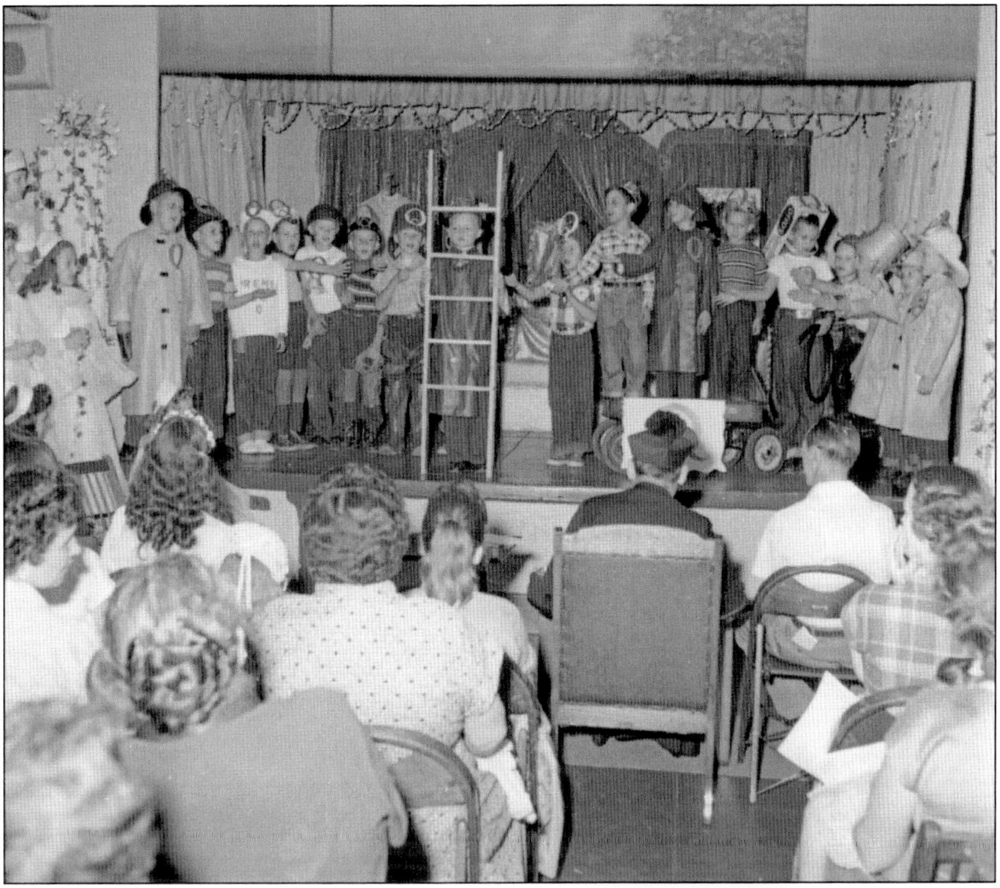

Grade-school students performed many plays each year for parents and other children. Pictured here in 1955 is a performance during the Christmas season at St. Joseph's School. The pastor, Rev. Anthony Politowski (seated in the middle of the front row), has the best view. (Courtesy James Smith.)

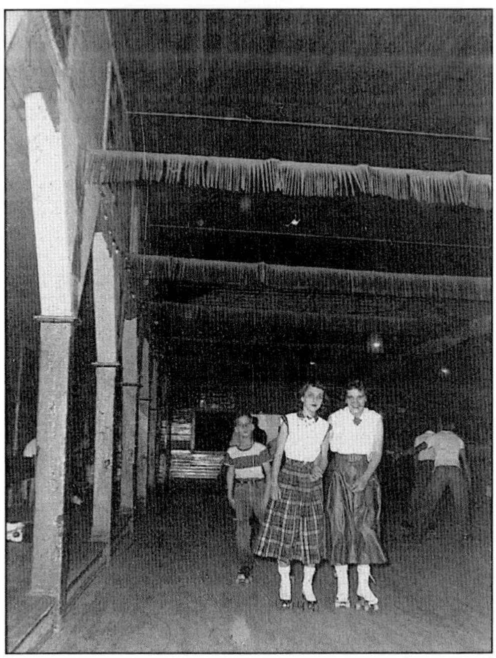

Steiner's Skating Rink on Third Avenue, pictured around 1950, was a popular destination on Saturday afternoons. The music was loud and the inside was dark. Skate boys patrolled the rink in order to help those who needed more practice on wheels.

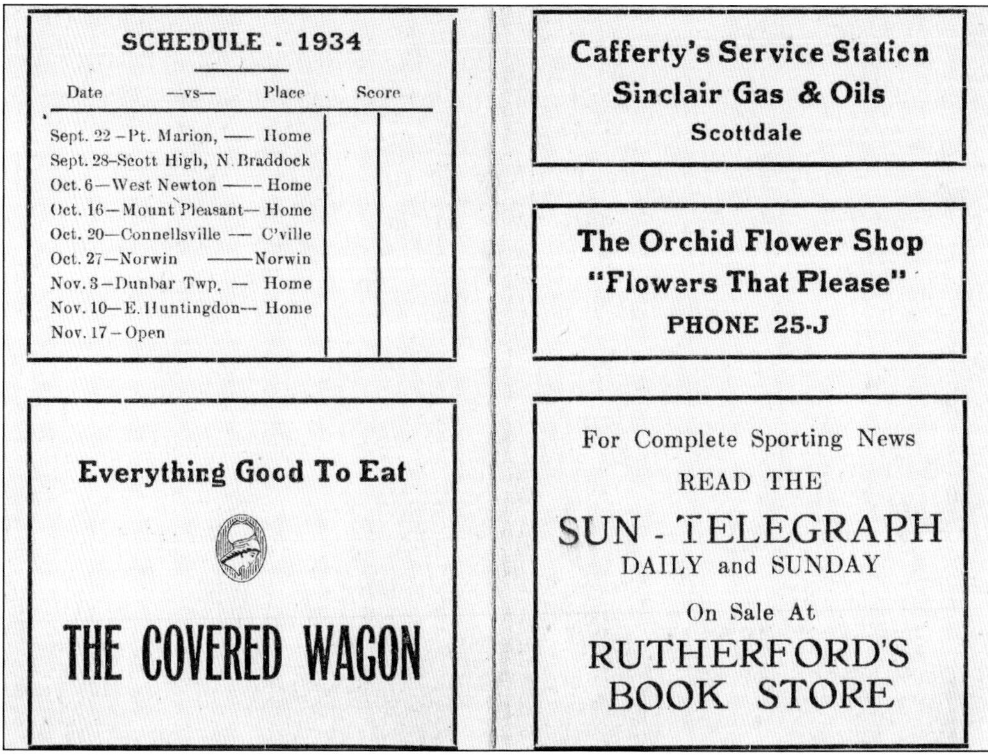

SCHEDULE - 1934

Date —vs— Place	Score
Sept. 22 – Pt. Marion, —— Home	
Sept. 28–Scott High, N. Braddock	
Oct. 6—West Newton —— Home	
Oct. 16—Mount Pleasant— Home	
Oct. 20—Connellsville — C'ville	
Oct. 27—Norwin ——Norwin	
Nov. 3—Dunbar Twp. — Home	
Nov. 10—E. Huntingdon— Home	
Nov. 17 – Open	

Cafferty's Service Station
Sinclair Gas & Oils
Scottdale

The Orchid Flower Shop
"Flowers That Please"
PHONE 25-J

Everything Good To Eat

THE COVERED WAGON

For Complete Sporting News
READ THE
SUN - TELEGRAPH
DAILY and SUNDAY
On Sale At
RUTHERFORD'S
BOOK STORE

The football schedule for Scottdale High School was always very competitive, especially when it played the teams listed on this program. (Courtesy Sharyn Kmieciak.)

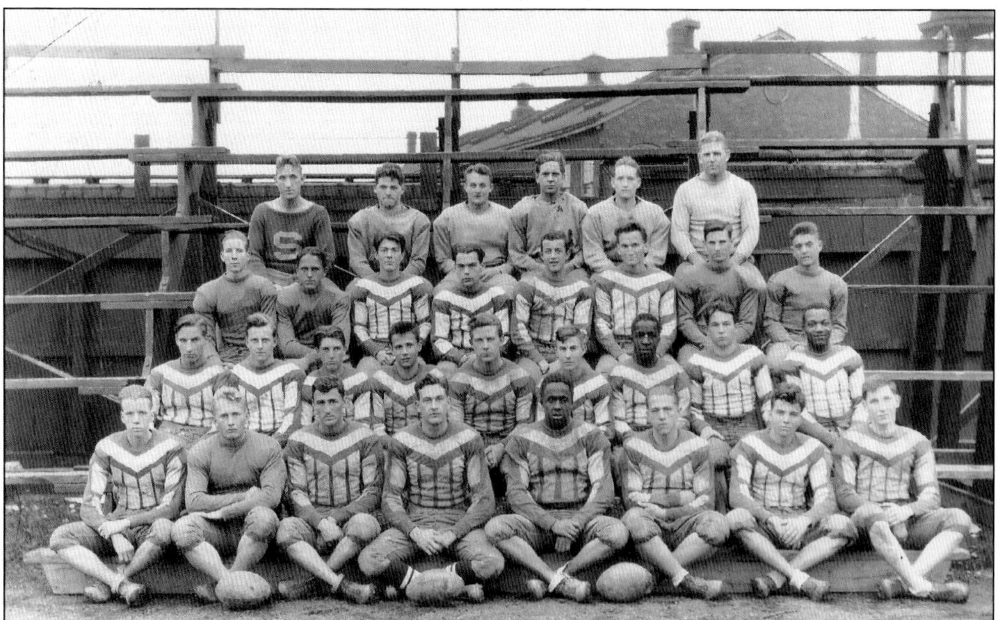

Members of the 1933 football squad are pictured here at Athletic Park, where games were played before 1935. The park was located on the south side of Scottdale Street between Crescent and Franklin Streets. (Courtesy Chuck King.)

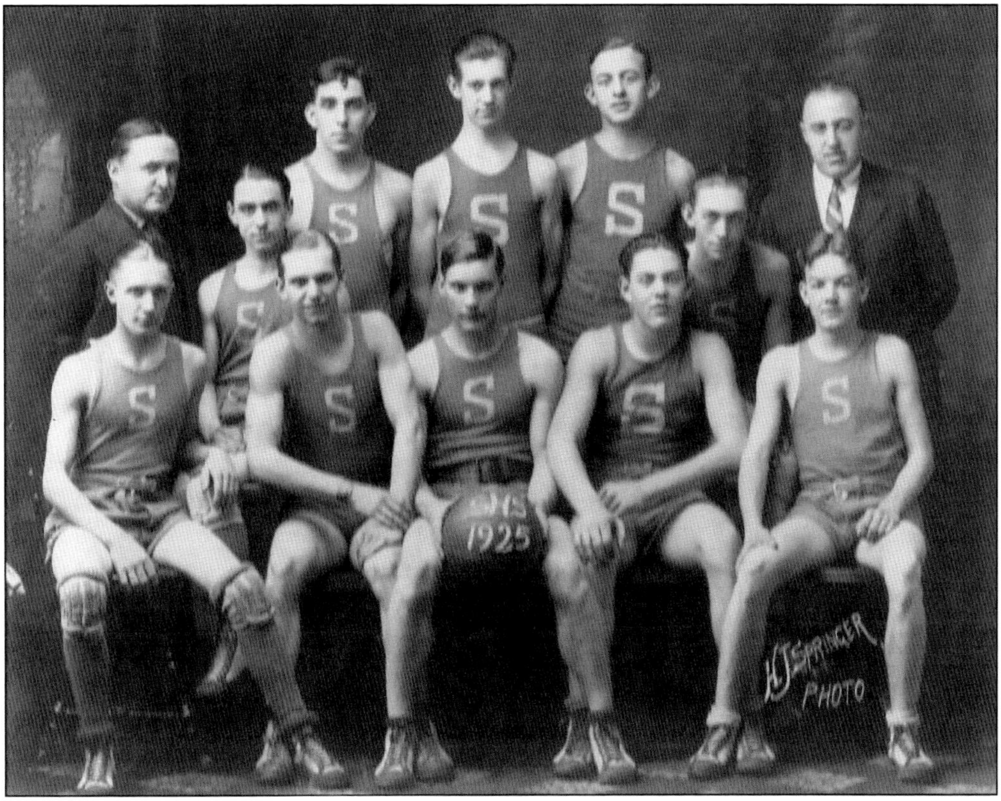

Two Scottdale basketball teams are pictured in 1925 (above) and 1927 (below). The 1925 men's team won 17 out of 19 games and played in the Westmoreland County finals at Vandergrift. (Above, courtesy Bob Percy; below, courtesy West Overton Museums.)

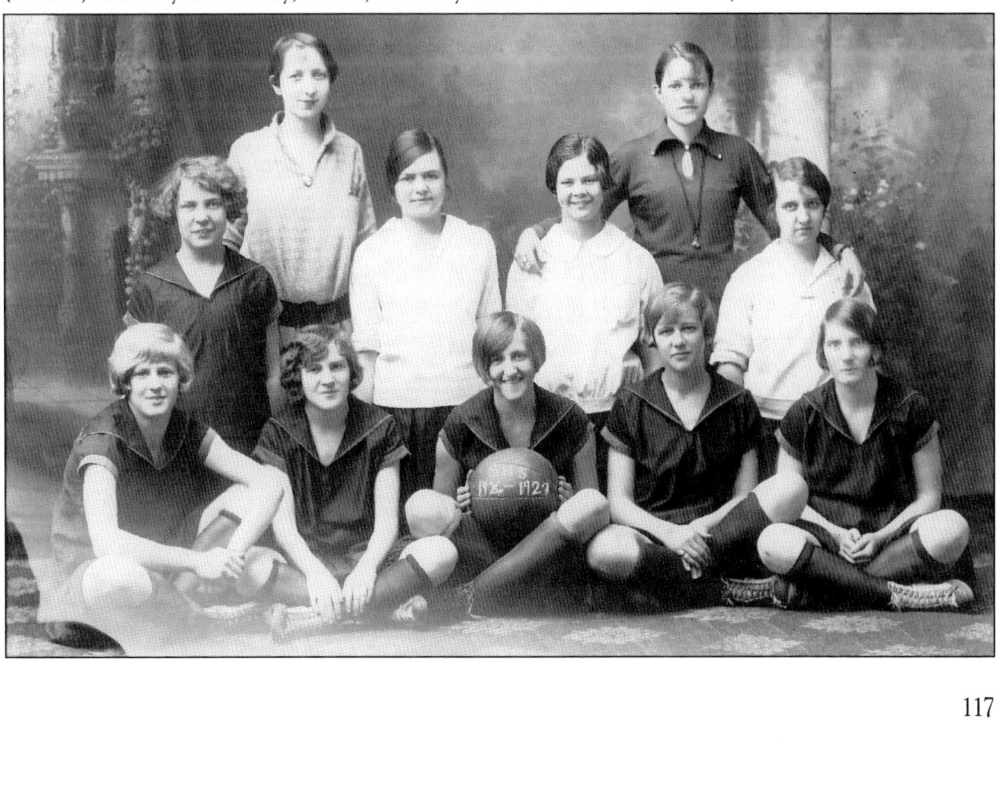

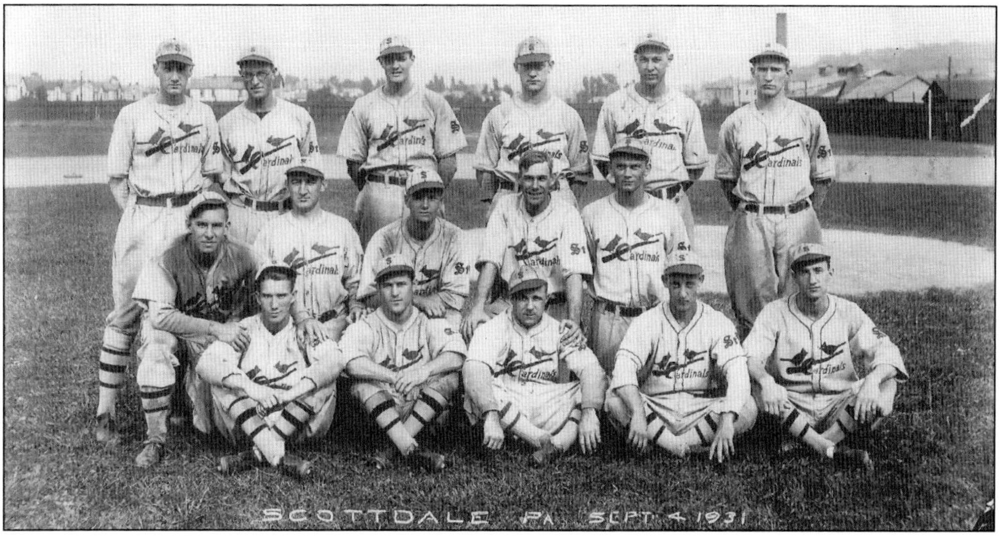

The 1931 Cardinals of the Middle Atlantic League pose in Athletic Park for a photograph at the end of their last season in Scottdale. From left to right are (first row) Michael Ryba, Armand Seghetti, two unidentified, and James Winford; (second row) James Boucher, Bert Bruckman, and three unidentified; (third row) unidentified, Merle Anderson, William Lee, Adolf Lange, unidentified, and Clay Hopper.

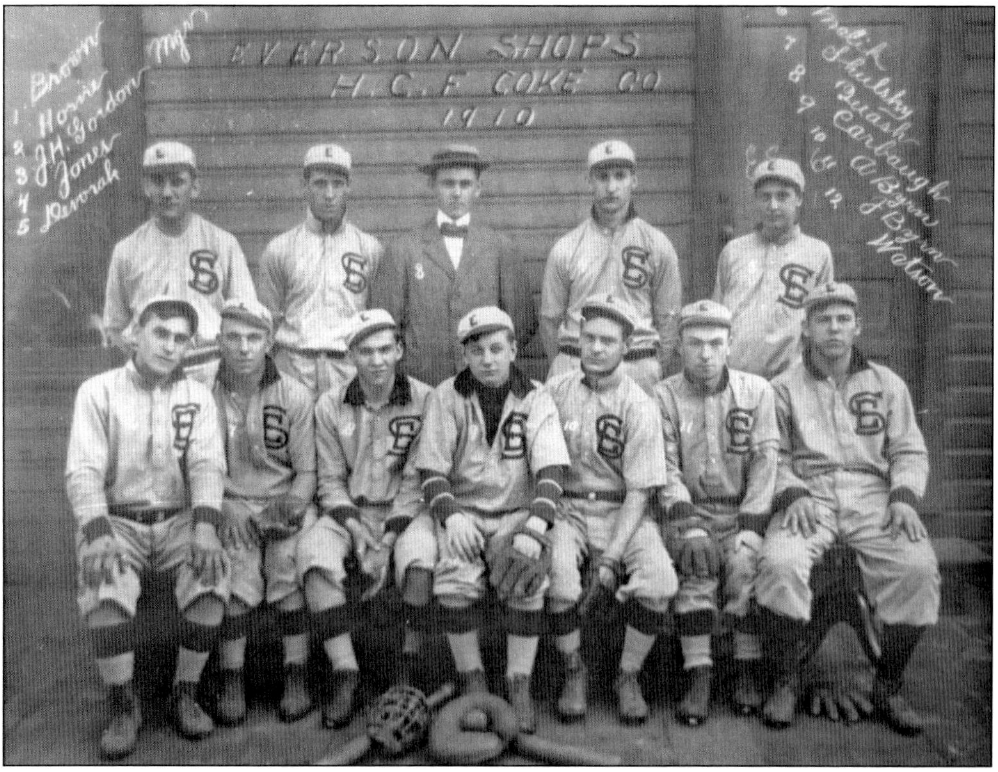

Coal and steel companies sponsored baseball teams that attracted huge crowds throughout the coke region. This 1910 image shows the team from the Everson Car Shops, sponsored by the H.C. Frick Coke Company. (Courtesy Dora Curry.)

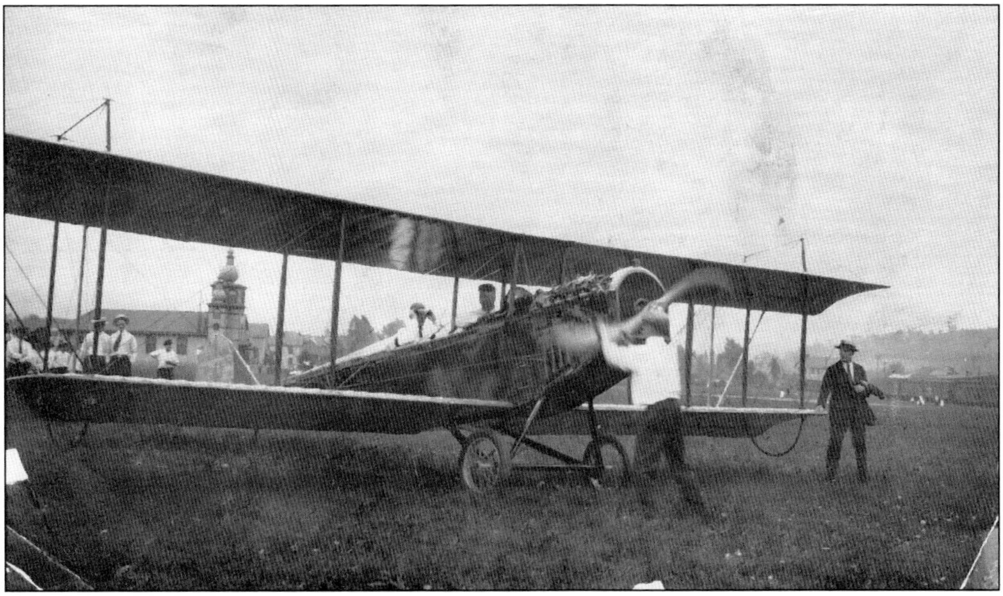

Scottdale was home to many aviation pioneers. This aircraft is being prepared for takeoff in Swedetown around 1925. Carl Strickler is the pilot, Jerry Elder is spinning the propeller, and Charles Coughenour follows near the wing. The three men purchased the plane in order to participate in air shows and races, which were popular at the time. The first St. John's Byzantine Catholic Church appears in the background. (Courtesy Jonathan Fox.)

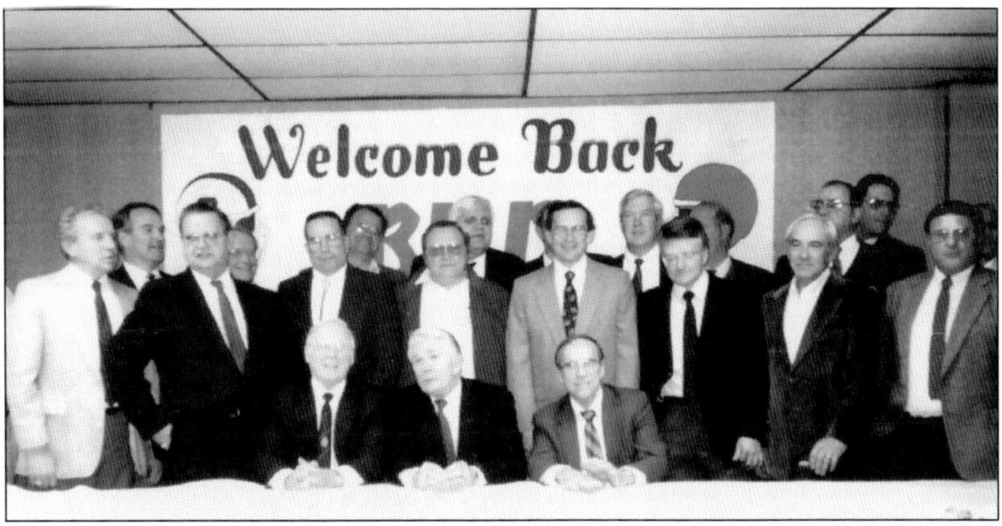

The 1956 Scottdale football team gathers to honor its former coach, Leon "Bud" Carson. Pictured are, from left to right, (first row) Vernon Behanna, Leon Carson, and Harry Mehalich; (second row) Edward Kaper, James Robbins, John Keffer, Harry Roczycki, Michael Mehalich, William Waters, Jerry Eicher, and Joseph Ivan; (third row) Donald Kimball, Charles Hebenthaw, James Vies, William Byble, unidentified, James Ruth, unidentified, Marcus Laurer, Anthony Comforti, and unidentified. (Courtesy Jerry Eicher.)

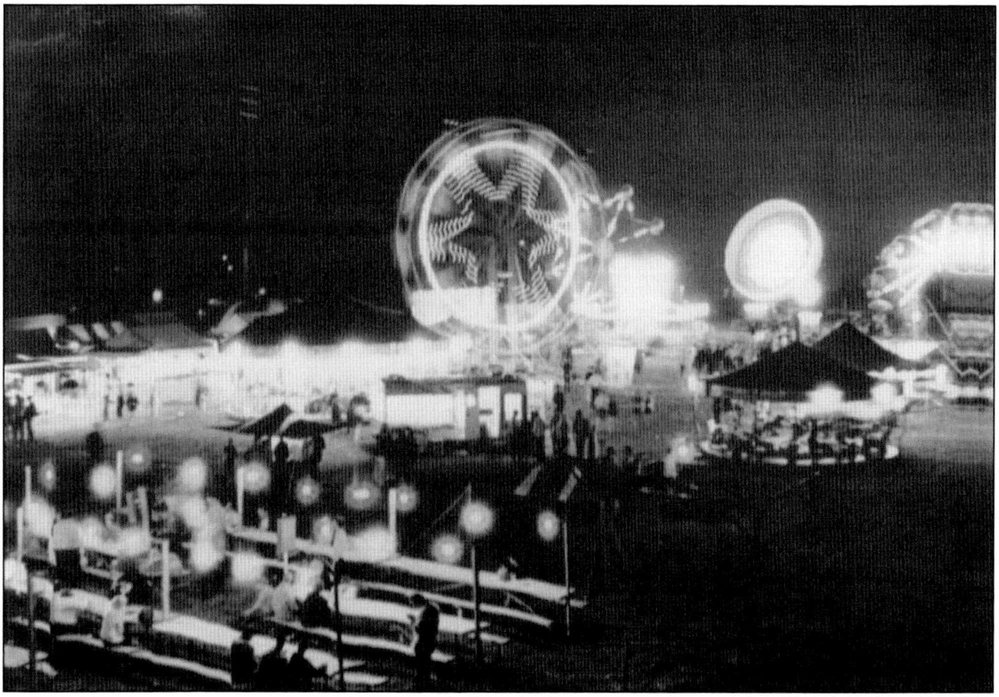

A highlight of summer was the annual firemen's fair and parade. This Scottdale fair was held around 1955 on the old football field. (Courtesy Scottdale Fire Department.)

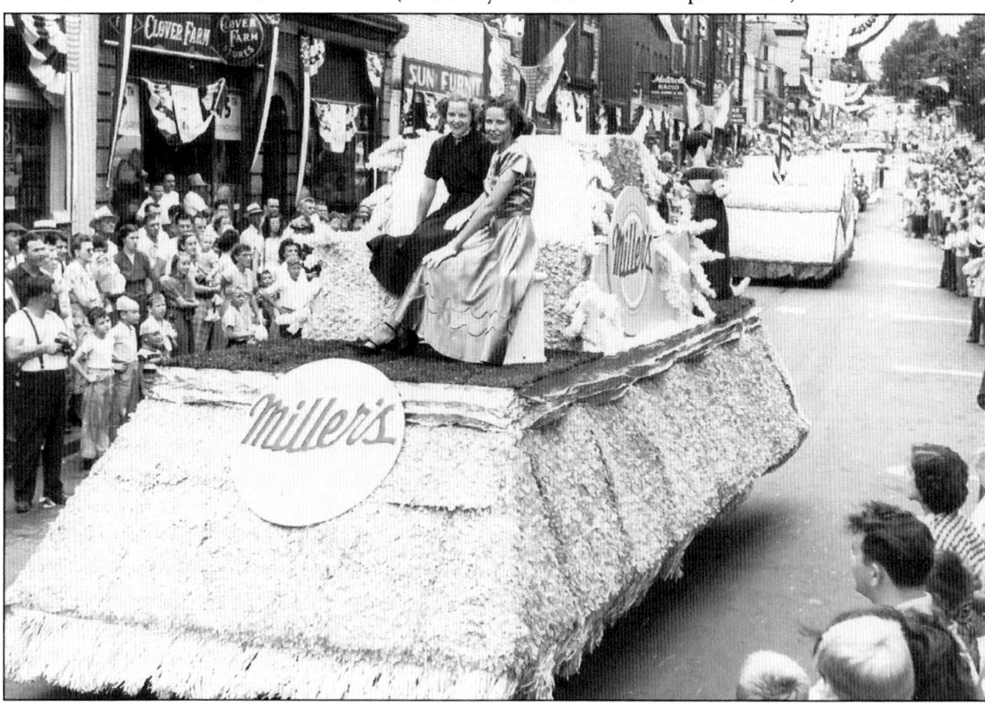

Miller's Department Store was an established business on Pittsburgh Street for nearly 90 years. The store entered this attractive float in Scottdale's 75th-anniversary parade. Elizabeth Weaver (left) and Ruth Andrish are waving to the crowd. (Courtesy Chuck King.)

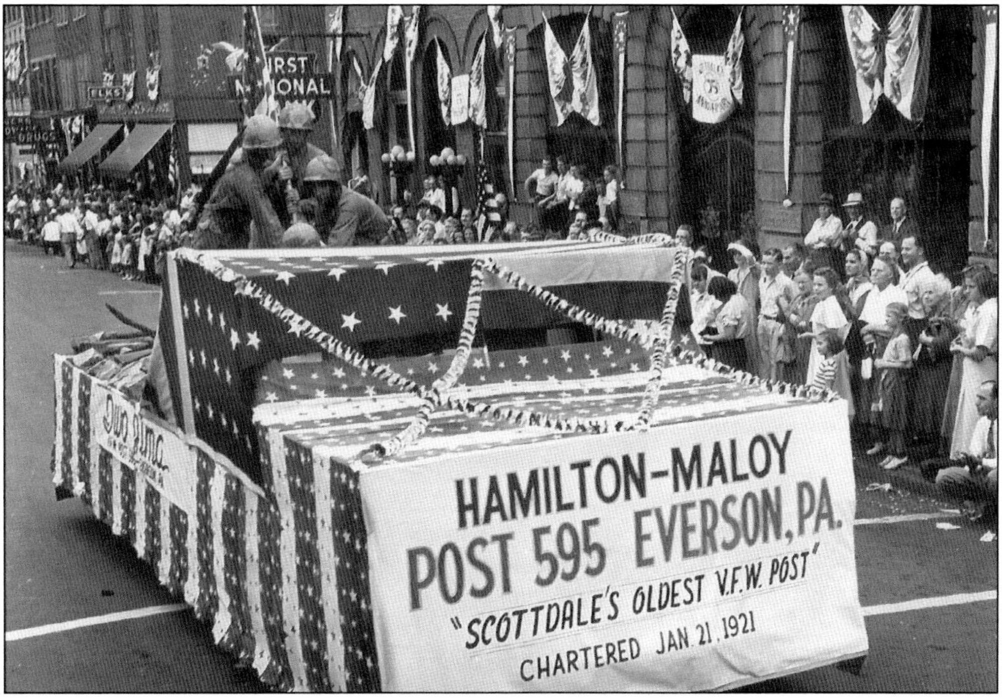

The Everson Veterans of Foreign Wars created this entry for the 75th-anniversary parade, which featured the US Marines raising the flag on the summit of Mount Suribachi. (Courtesy Chuck King.)

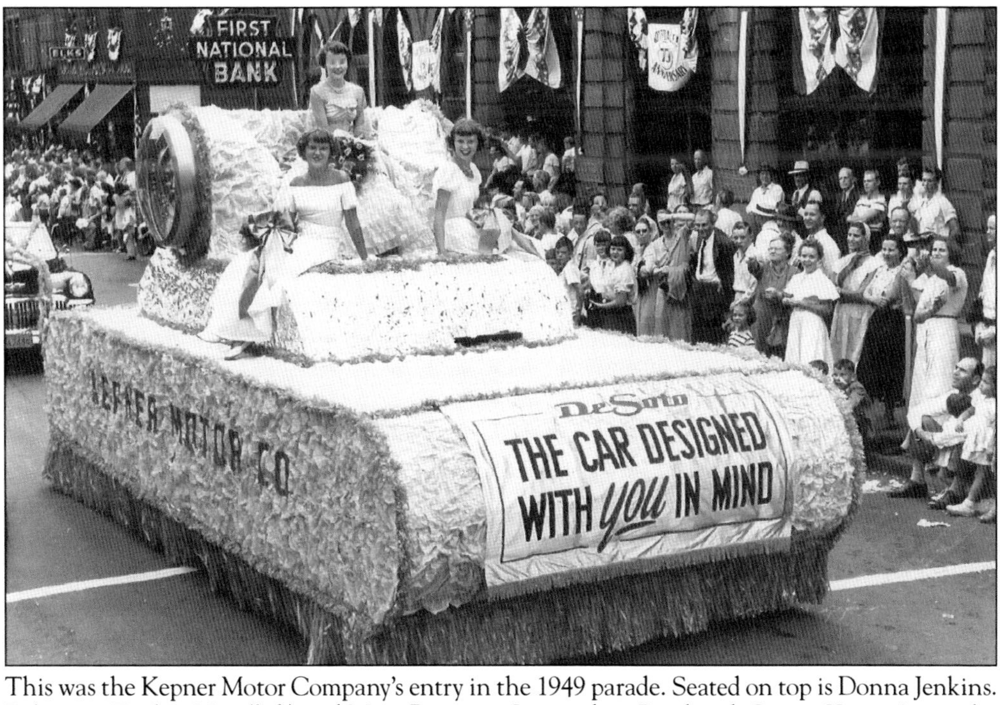

This was the Kepner Motor Company's entry in the 1949 parade. Seated on top is Donna Jenkins. Below are Tinkey Nist (left) and Mary Brennen. Located on Pittsburgh Street, Kepner's was the dealership for Plymouth and DeSoto automobiles. (Courtesy Chuck King.)

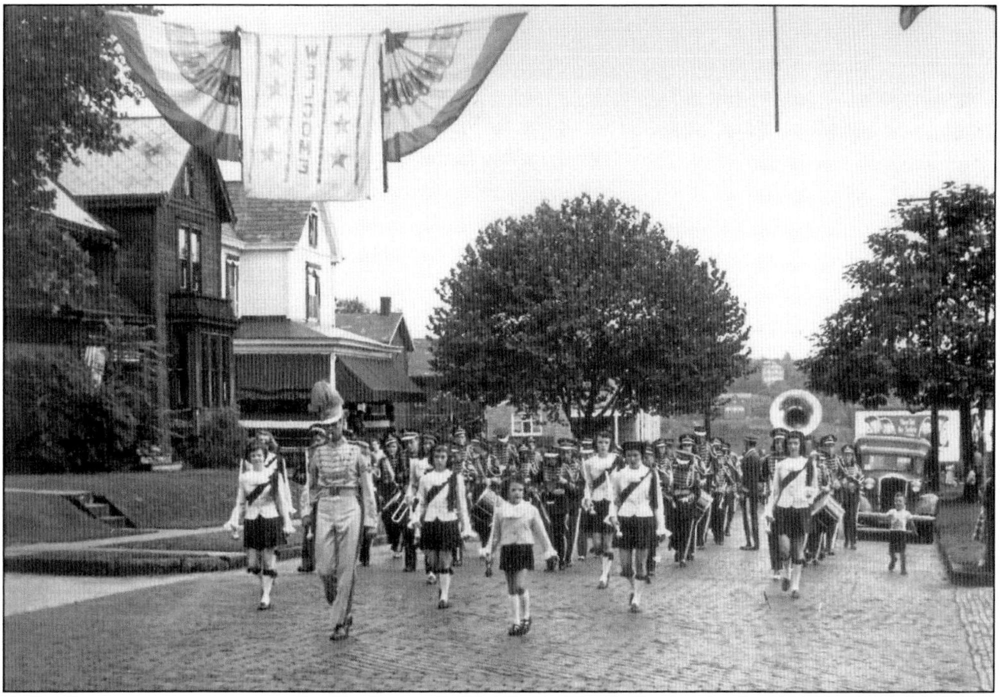

The Scottdale High School Band is pictured on Mulberry Street during a parade in 1950. David Acres is the drum major. (Courtesy Scottdale Bank and Trust Company.)

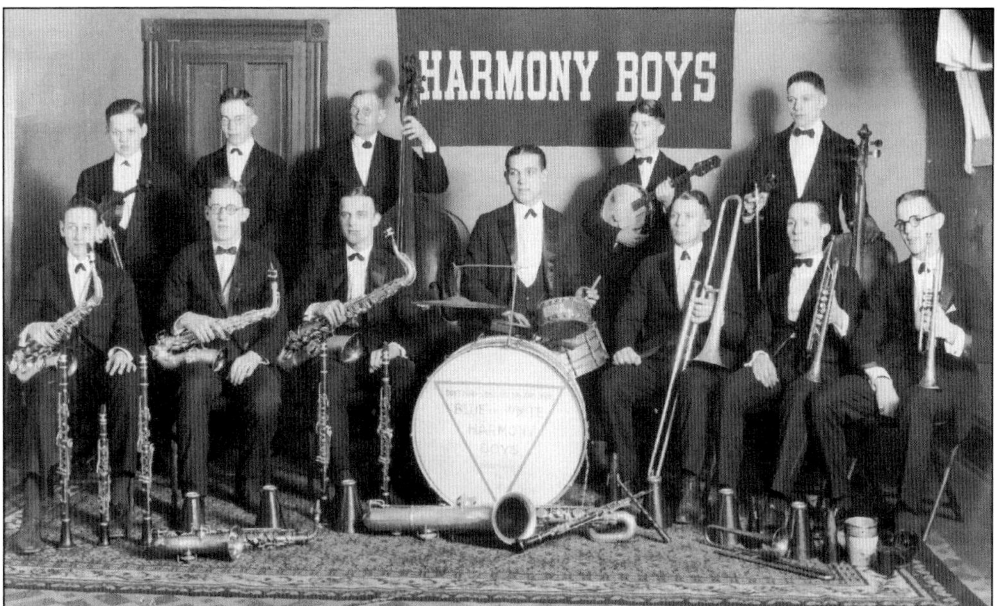

Above are the Harmony Boys from Scottdale. In addition to performing at local venues, they played at colleges and universities. Herbert Morrison (standing second from right) was a band member. In later years, as a newspaper reporter, he covered the *Hindenburg* airship disaster in 1937, and his broadcast became legendary in the radio industry. Morrison was the first news director at WTAE-TV in Pittsburgh. (Courtesy Marilyn Gaut.)

Residents gather at the American Hardware Store to demonstrate their support for a fundraiser to benefit the YMCA. Pictured here are, from left to right, (first row) Donald Zimmerman, James Stoner, and Eugene Shelby; (second row) Harold Pearse, William Bair, and Richard Frost. The fundraiser was a hole-in-one tournament to be held at Loucks Park. (Courtesy *Scottdale Independent-Observer.*)

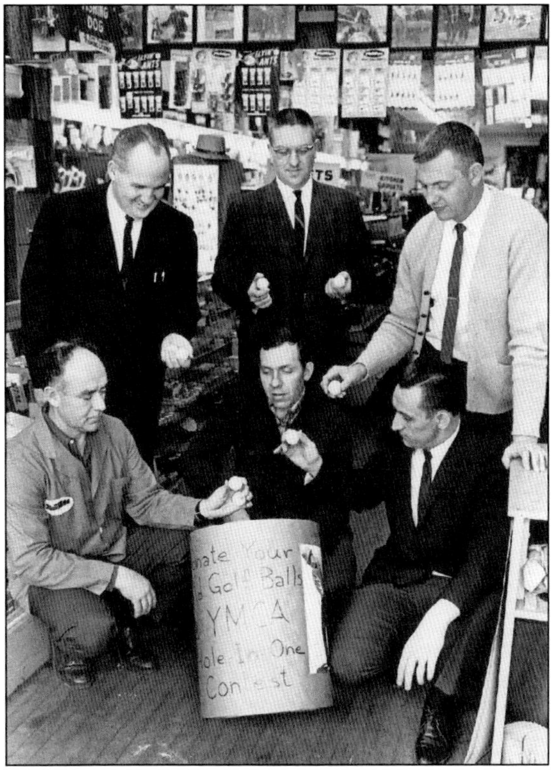

Here is a view of the new Scottdale Public Library, which occupies the former site of the YMCA. It opened in 2008 and contains a special children's room dedicated to Beth Ann Johnson, who lost her life over Lockerbie, Scotland.

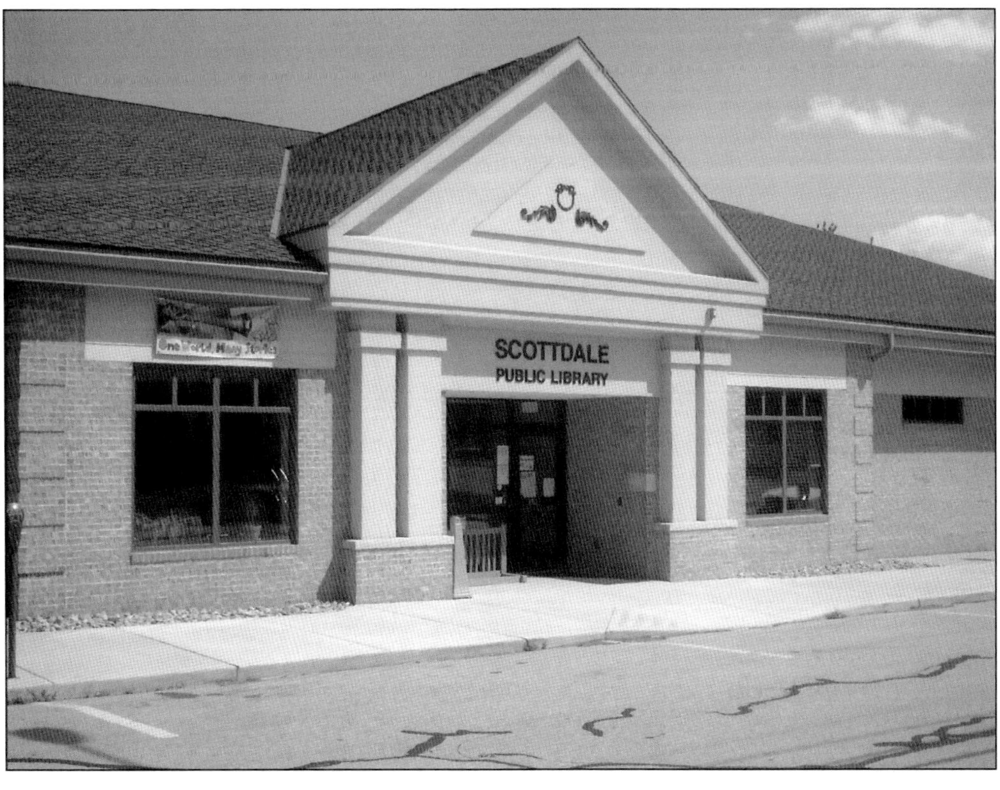

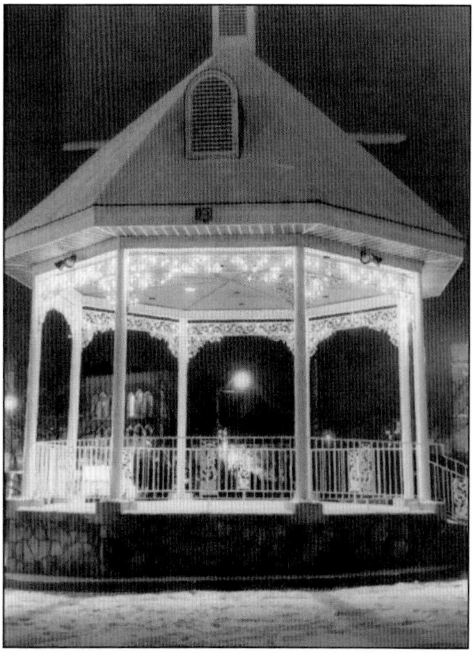

The gazebo is located on property once occupied by the Arcade Theatre. The corner continues to serve as an entertainment venue, hosting summer concerts and other activities. It was dedicated in 1978 to the memory of Joseph Martinsek, who was a charter member of the Lions Club and was active in many Scottdale organizations. (Courtesy *Scottdale Independent-Observer.*)

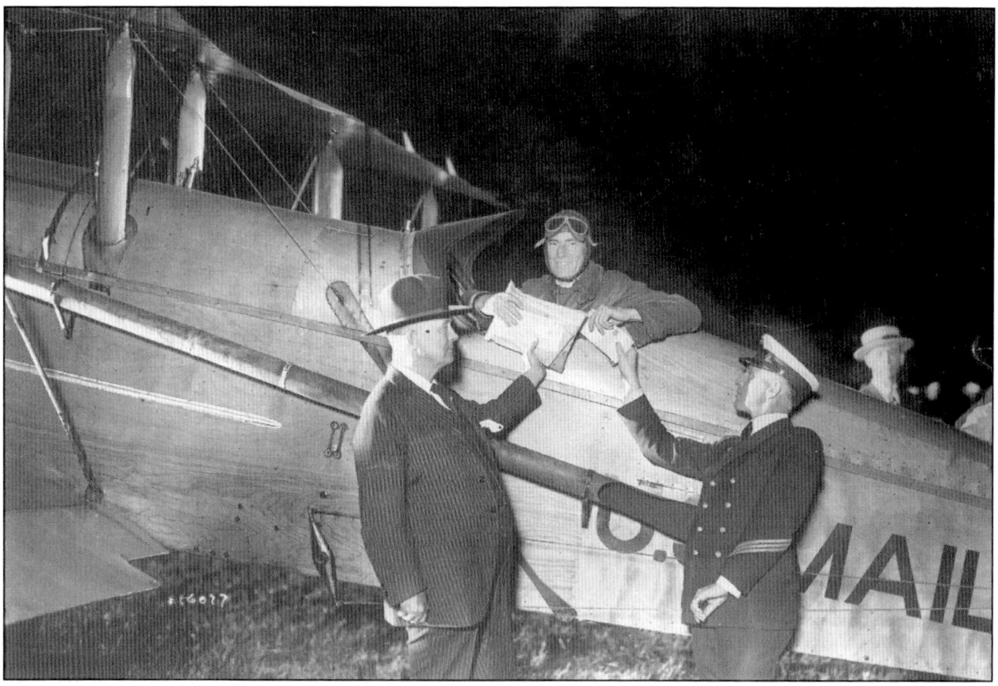

In 1970, Scottdale dedicated another monument near the gazebo to James De Witt Hill, who is pictured here around 1924 when he was a pilot for the US Air Mail Service. He and several others inaugurated night flights between Chicago and New York. Hill was born in Scottdale. He trained pilots during World War I, tested planes for several airplane manufacturers, and competed in air shows. His close friend Charlie Carroll, also from Scottdale, named the Latrobe Airport in his honor. In 1927, Hill and two associates disappeared over the Atlantic in an attempt to fly nonstop from Maine to Rome.

Six

Representing a Hometown

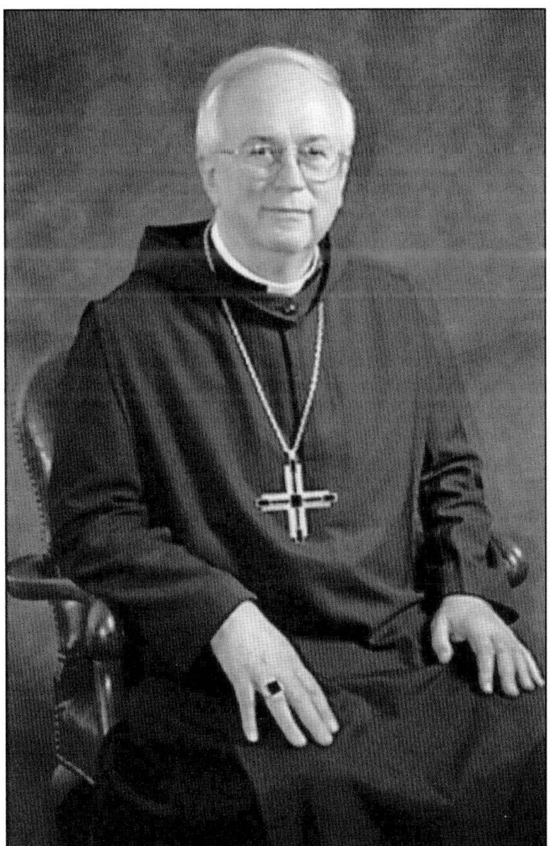

Douglas R. Nowicki was born in Everson and attended St. Joseph's School. In 1991, he was elected the 11th archabbot of the St. Vincent Benedictine Archabbey, where he also serves as chancellor of the college and seminary. Before his election, Right Reverend Nowicki was secretary of education for the Diocese of Pittsburgh, a staff member at Children's Hospital of Pittsburgh, and a longtime consultant for *Mister Rogers' Neighborhood.* (Courtesy St. Vincent College.)

Barbara Smith is from Everson and is a trailblazer for African Americans through her successes as a fashion model, restaurateur, host of the television show *B Smith with Style*, author, and entertainer. She appeared on five covers of *Essence* magazine and was the first African American model to grace the cover of *Mademoiselle*. In 2001, she launched her own line of merchandise, and in 2009, she was honored by Black Entertainment Television (BET) for entrepreneurship. (Courtesy The Rosen Group.)

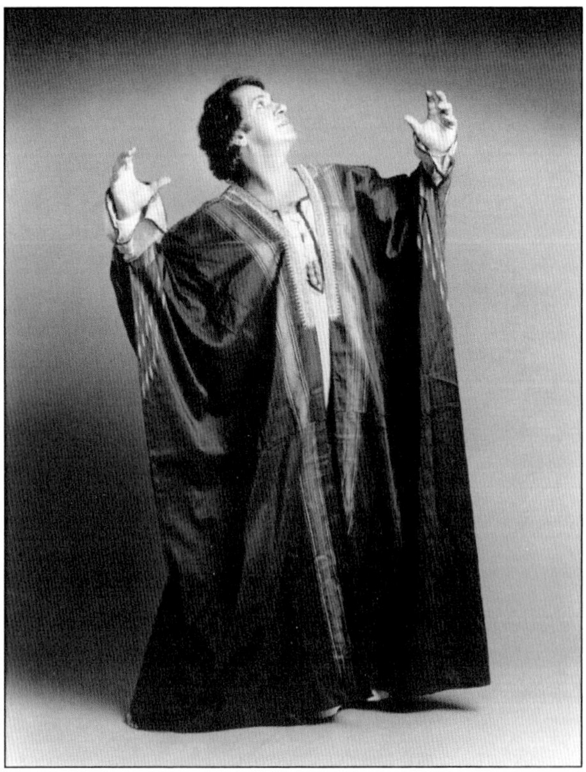

Robert Ibrahim Farrah was born in Everson and became interested in traditional Near East dancing and culture. After moving to New York, he taught master dance classes at Carnegie Hall and other studios, including his own School of Near East Dance. He established the Ibrahim Farrah Near East Dance Group, which performed throughout the world. Farrah also created *Arabesqué* magazine—another expression of his passion for dance. (Courtesy Phyllis Saretta.)

At Southmoreland High School, Russell Grimm earned nine varsity letters. As a student at the University of Pittsburgh, he was an All-American center and was drafted by the Washington Redskins. He was a Redskin for 11 seasons and played in four Super Bowls, three of which the Redskins won. He was a coach for the Redskins and the Pittsburgh Steelers and is currently assistant head coach for the Arizona Cardinals. (Courtesy *Scottdale Independent-Observer.*)

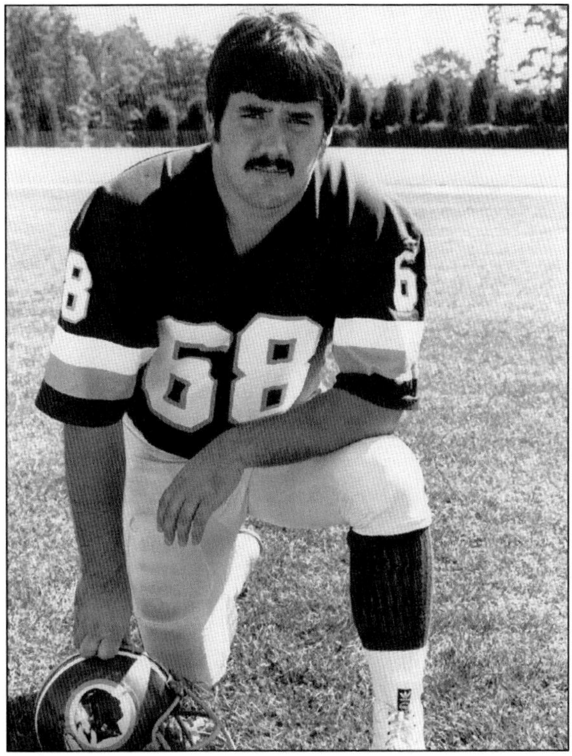

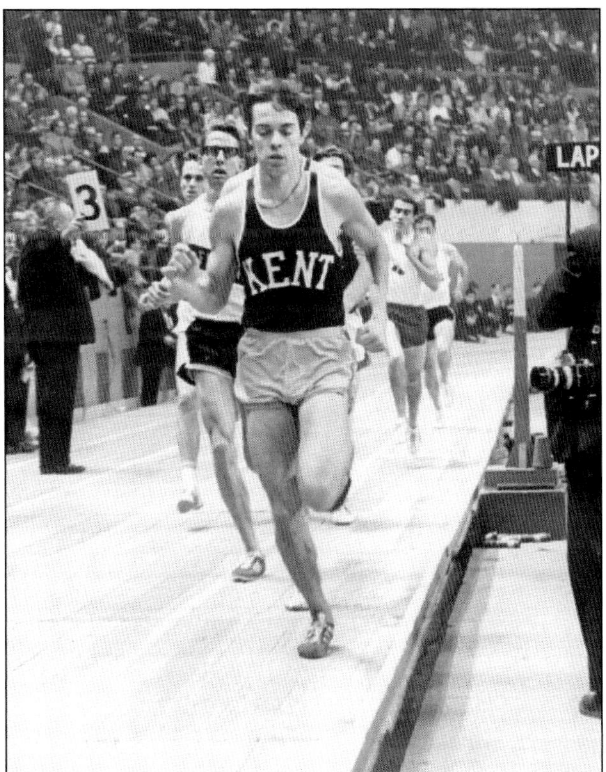

Sam Bair is pictured here winning the indoor mile at the Boston Garden in 1967. At Kent State University, he became a seven-time All-American. Bair, the 24th American to break the four-minute mile, has competed throughout the world. He coached three national championship teams at Community College of Allegheny County (CCAC) and was named National Junior College Cross Country Coach of the Year for five consecutive years. (Courtesy Sam and Martha Bair.)

Consistent with our mission to preserve history on a local level, this book was printed in South Carolina on American-made paper and manufactured entirely in the United States. Products carrying the accredited Forest Stewardship Council (FSC) label are printed on 100 percent FSC-certified paper.

MADE IN THE USA